DEVELOPING
the LEADER
WITHIN YOU

DEVELOPING
the LEADERS
AROUND YOU

JOHN C. MAXWELL

NEW YORK TIMES BEST-SELLING AUTHOR OF
THE 21 IRREFUTABLE LAWS OF LEADERSHIP

THOMAS NELSON
Since 1798

NASHVILLE   DALLAS   MEXICO CITY   RIO DE JANEIRO   BEIJING

Published in Nashville, Tennessee, by Thomas Nelson. Thomas Nelson is a registered trademark of Thomas Nelson, Inc.

Published in association with Yates & Yates, www.yates2.com.

Thomas Nelson, Inc., titles may be purchased in bulk for educational, business, fund-raising, or sales promotional use. For information, please e-mail SpecialMarkets@ThomasNelson.com.

Scripture quotations are from THE NEW KING JAMES VERSION. © 1982 by Thomas Nelson, Inc. Used by permission. All rights reserved.

ISBN 978-1-4002-8045-2

Printed in the United States of America
08 09 10 11 12 QW 6 5 4 3 2 1

DEVELOPING
the LEADER
WITHIN YOU

This book is dedicated to the man I most admire.
A friend whose touch warmed me;
A mentor whose wisdom guided me;
An encourager whose words lifted me;
A leader I love to follow . . .
My father,
Melvin Maxwell

CONTENTS

INTRODUCTION

It was a moment I will never forget. I was lecturing on the subject of leadership, and we had just taken a fifteen-minute break. A man named Bob rushed up to me and said, "You have saved my career! Thank you so much." As he turned to walk away, I stopped him and asked, "How have I 'saved' your career?" He replied, "I'm fifty-three years old and for the last seventeen years I have been in a position that demands leadership. Up until recently I have struggled, acutely aware of my lack of leadership skills and success. Last year I attended your leadership seminar and learned principles that I immediately began applying in my work situation. And it happened. People began to follow my direction—slowly at first, but now quite readily. I had plenty of experience but no expertise. Thanks for making me a leader!"

Testimonials like Bob's have encouraged me to devote much of my time to developing leaders. It is the reason why I hold leadership seminars in the United States and other countries about ten times a year. It is the reason for this book.

What you are about to read is a culmination of skills learned in twenty years of leading people. For more than twenty years I have taught these leadership principles and watched with great satisfaction as men and women have become more effective in leading others. Now I have the opportunity to share them with you.

THE KEY TO SUCCESS IN AN ENDEAVOR
IS THE ABILITY TO LEAD OTHERS SUCCESSFULLY

Everything rises and falls on leadership. Whenever I make that statement the listeners are tempted to change it to, "Almost everything rises and falls on leadership." Most people have a desire to look for the exception instead of the desire to become exceptional.

Right now you lead at a certain skill level. For the sake of teaching this principle, let's say that on a scale of 1 to 10, your leadership skills reach the level of 6. This is what I know: The effectiveness of your work will never rise above your ability to lead and influence others. You cannot produce consistently on a level higher than your leadership. In other words, your leadership skills determine the level of your success— and the success of those who work around you.

Recently I read these words in *Newsweek* magazine from the president of Hyatt Hotels: "If there is anything I have learned in my 27 years in the service industry, it is this: 99 percent of all employees want to do a good job. How they perform is simply a reflection of the one for whom they work."[1]

This humorous story underscores the importance of effective leadership: During a sales meeting, the manager was berating the sales staff for their dismally low sales figures. "I've had just about enough of poor performance and excuses," he said. "If you can't do the job, perhaps there are other salespeople out there who would jump at the chance to sell the worthy products that each of you has the privilege to represent." Then, pointing to a newly recruited, retired pro-football player, he said, "If a football team isn't winning, what happens? The players are replaced. Right?"

The question hung heavy for a few seconds; then the ex-football player answered, "Actually, sir, if the whole team was having trouble, we usually got a new coach."[2]

LEADERSHIP CAN BE TAUGHT

Leadership is not an exclusive club for those who were "born with it." The traits that are the raw materials of leadership can be acquired. Link them up with desire and nothing can keep you from becoming a leader. This book will supply the leadership principles. You must supply the desire.

Leonard Ravenhill in "The Last Days Newsletter" tells about a group of tourists who were visiting a picturesque village. As they walked by an old man sitting beside a fence, one tourist asked in a patronizing way, "Were any great men born in this village?"

The old man replied, "Nope, only babies."

Leadership is developed, not discovered. The truly "born leader" will always emerge; but, to stay on top, natural leadership characteristics must be developed. In working with thousands of people desirous of becoming leaders, I have discovered they all fit in one of four categories or levels of leadership:

THE LEADING LEADER:

- is born with leadership qualities.
- has seen leadership modeled throughout life.
- has learned added leadership through training.
- has self-discipline to become a great leader.

Note: Three out of four of these qualities are acquired.

THE LEARNED LEADER:

- has seen leadership modeled most of life.
- has learned leadership through training.
- has self-discipline to be a great leader.

Note: All three qualities are acquired.

THE LATENT LEADER:

- has just recently seen leadership modeled.
- is learning to be a leader through training.

- has self-discipline to become a good leader.

Note: All three qualities are acquired.

THE LIMITED LEADER:

- has little or no exposure to leaders.
- has little or no exposure to leadership training.
- has desire to become a leader.

Note: All three can be acquired.

THERE ARE VERY FEW LEADERSHIP BOOKS; MOST DEAL WITH MANAGEMENT

There seems to be a great deal of confusion over the difference between "leadership" and "management."

John W. Gardner, former Secretary of the U.S. Department of Health, Education, and Welfare, who directed a leadership study project in Washington, D.C., has pinpointed five characteristics that set "leader managers" apart from "run-of-the-mill managers":

1. Leader managers are long-term thinkers who see beyond the day's crisis and the quarterly report.

2. Leader managers' interests in their companies do not stop with the units they head. They want to know how all of the company's departments affect one another, and they are constantly reaching beyond their specific areas of influence.

3. Leader managers put heavy emphasis on vision, values, and motivation.

4. Leader managers have strong political skills to cope with conflicting requirements of multiple constituents.

5. Leader managers don't accept the status quo.[3]

Management is the process of assuring that the program and objectives of the organization are implemented. Leadership, on the other hand, has to do with casting vision and motivating people.

> People don't want to be managed. They want to be <u>lead</u>. Whoever heard of a world manager? World leader, yes. Education leader, yes. Political leader. Religious leader. Scout leader. Community leader. Labor leader. Business leader. Yes. They lead. They don't manage. The carrot always wins over the stick. Ask your horse. You can lead your horse to water, but you can't manage him to drink. If you want to manage somebody, manage yourself. Do that well and you'll be ready to stop managing and start leading.[4]

- Knowing how to do a job is the accomplishment of labor.
- Showing others is the accomplishment of a teacher.
- Making sure the work is done by others is the accomplishment of a manager.
- Inspiring others to do better work is the accomplishment of a leader.

My desire is that you be able to accomplish the work of a leader. This book is dedicated to that goal. While you read this book and begin applying these leadership principles, please be reminded of Bruce Larson. In his book *Wind and Fire*, Larson points out some interesting facts about Sandhill cranes: "These large birds, who fly great distances across continents, have three remarkable qualities. First, they rotate leadership. No one bird stays out in front all the time. Second, they choose leaders who can handle the turbulence. And then, all during the time one bird is leading, the rest are honking their affirmation."

Hopefully you will learn enough about leadership to take your place at the front of the pack. While you are making that attempt, I will be honking affirmation to you with great pride and inner satisfaction.

In every age there comes a time when leadership must come forth to meet the needs of the hour. Therefore, there is no potential leader who does not find his or her time. Read this book and be ready to seize your moment!

—John C. Maxwell

ONE

THE DEFINITION OF LEADERSHIP:
INFLUENCE

Everyone talks about it; few understand it. Most people want it; few achieve it. There are over fifty definitions and descriptions of it in my personal files. What is this intriguing subject we call "leadership"?

Perhaps because most of us want to be leaders, we become emotionally involved when trying to define leadership. Or, perhaps because we know one, we try to copy his or her behavior and describe leadership as a personality. Ask ten people to define leadership and you'll probably receive ten different answers. After more than five decades of observing leadership within my family and many years of developing my own leadership potential, I have come to this conclusion: *Leadership is influence.* That's it. Nothing more; nothing less. My favorite leadership proverb is: He who thinketh he leadeth and hath no one following him is only taking a walk.

James C. Georges, of the ParTraining Corporation, said it quite effectively in a recent interview with *Executive Communications*:

> What is leadership? Remove for a moment the moral issues behind it, and there is only one definition: *Leadership is the ability to obtain followers.*

Hitler was a leader and so was Jim Jones. Jesus of Nazareth, Martin Luther King, Jr., Winston Churchill, and John F. Kennedy all were leaders. While their value systems and management abilities were very different, each had followers.

Once you define leadership as the ability to get followers, you work backward from that point of reference to figure out how to lead.[1]

Therein lies the problem. Most people define leadership as the ability to achieve a position, not to get followers. Therefore, they go after a position, rank, or title and, upon their arrival, think they have become a leader. This type of thinking creates two common problems: those who possess the "status" of leader often experience the frustration of few followers, and those who lack the proper titles may not see themselves as leaders and therefore don't develop their leadership skills.

My goal with this book is to help you accept leadership as influence (that is, the ability to get followers), and then work backward from that point to help you learn how to lead. Each chapter is designed to place in your hand another principle that will assist your leadership development. This first chapter is designed to expand the level of your influence.

INSIGHTS ABOUT INFLUENCE

EVERYONE INFLUENCES SOMEONE

Sociologists tell us that even the most introverted individual will influence ten thousand other people during his or her lifetime! This amazing statistic was shared with me by my associate Tim Elmore. Tim and I concluded that each one of us is both influencing and being influenced by others. That means that all of us are leading in some areas, while in other areas we are being led. No one is excluded from being a leader or a follower. Realizing your potential as a leader is your responsibility. In any given situation with any given group, there is a prominent influencer. Let me illustrate. The mother may be the dominant influencer over a child in the morning before school begins. Mom may choose what to eat and what to wear. The child who is influenced before school may become the influencer of other children once school begins. Dad and Mom may meet at a restaurant for lunch and both be influenced by the waiter, who suggests the house specialty. The time dinner is served in the evening may be set because of either the husband's or wife's work schedule.

The prominent leader of any group is quite easily discovered. Just observe the people as they gather. If an issue is to be decided, who is the person whose opinion seems most valuable? Who is the one others watch the most when the issue is being discussed? Who is the one with whom people quickly agree? Most importantly, who is the one the others follow? Answers to these questions will help you discern who the real leader is in a particular group.

WE NEVER KNOW WHO OR HOW MUCH WE INFLUENCE

The most effective way to understand the power of influence is to think of the times you have been touched by the influence of a person or an event. Big events leave marks on all our lives and memories. For example, ask a couple of people born prior to 1930 what they were doing when they heard that Pearl Harbor had been bombed, and they will describe in detail their feelings and surroundings when they heard the terrible news. Ask someone born before 1955 to describe what he or she was doing when the news that John F. Kennedy had been shot was broadcast. Again, you will find no loss for words. A similar response occurs with the younger generation when asked about the day the *Challenger* blew up. These were big events that touched everyone.

Think also of the little things or people who influenced you in a powerful way. In reflecting on my own life, I think of the influence of a camp I attended as a youth and how it helped determine my career choice. I think of my seventh-grade teacher, Glen Leatherwood . . . the bubble lights on our Christmas tree that gave me the "Christmas feeling" every year . . . the affirming note I received from a professor in college . . . The list is endless. Life consists of influencers who daily find us vulnerable to their impressions and, therefore, have helped mold us into the persons we are. J. R. Miller said it well: "There have been meetings of only a moment which have left impressions for life, for eternity. No one can understand that mysterious thing we call influence . . . yet . . . everyone of us continually exerts influence, either to heal, to bless, to leave marks of beauty; or to wound, to hurt, to poison, to stain other lives."[2]

This truth also sobers me when I realize my influence as a father. A friend gave me a plaque with this poem on it. Now it sits on my desk:

The Little Chap Who Follows Me

A careful man I want to be,
A little fellow follows me;
I do not dare to go astray
For fear he'll go the self-same way.

I cannot once escape his eyes.
Whate'er he sees me do he tries.
Like ME he says he's going to be—
That little chap who follows me.

I must remember as I go
Through summer suns and winter snows,
I am building for the years to be—
That little chap who follows me.

THE BEST INVESTMENT IN THE FUTURE IS A PROPER INFLUENCE TODAY

The issue is not whether you influence someone. What needs to be settled is what kind of an influencer you will be. Will you grow into your leadership skills? In the book *Leaders*, Bennis and Nanus say, "The truth is that leadership opportunities are plentiful and within reach of most people."[3]

You must believe that! The rest of this chapter is committed to helping you make a difference tomorrow by becoming a better leader today.

INFLUENCE IS A SKILL THAT CAN BE DEVELOPED

Robert Dilenschneider, the CEO of Hill and Knowlton, a worldwide public relations agency, is one of the nation's major influence brokers. He skillfully weaves his persuasive magic in the global arena, where governments and megacorporations meet. He wrote a book entitled *Power and Influence*, in which he shares the idea of the "power triangle" to help leaders get ahead. He says, "The three components of this triangle are communication, recognition, and influence. You start to communicate effectively. This leads to recognition and recognition in turn leads to influence."[4]

We can increase our influence and our leadership potential. Out of this conviction I have developed a teaching tool to assist others in understanding their levels of leadership so they can increase their levels of influence (see chart on page 13).

THE FIVE LEVELS OF LEADERSHIP

LEVEL 1: POSITION

This is the basic entry level of leadership. The only influence you have is that which comes with a title. People who stay at this level get into territorial rights, protocol, tradition, and organizational charts. These things are not negative unless they become the basis for authority and influence, but they are poor substitutes for leadership skills.

A person may be "in control" because he has been appointed to a position. In that position he may have authority. But real leadership is more than having authority; it is more than having the technical training and following the proper procedures. Real leadership is being the person others will gladly and confidently follow. A real leader knows the difference between being the boss and being a leader, as illustrated by the following:

The boss drives his workers; the leader coaches them.

The boss depends on authority; the leader on goodwill.

The boss inspires fear; the leader inspires enthusiasm.

The boss says "I"; the leader, "we."

The boss fixes the blame for the breakdown; the leader fixes the breakdown.

The boss knows how it is done; the leader shows how.

The boss says, "Go"; the leader says, "Let's go!"

CHARACTERISTICS OF A "POSITIONAL LEADER"

Security is based on title, not talent. The story is told of a private in World War I who shouted on the battlefield, "Put out that match!" only to find to his chagrin that the offender was General "Black Jack" Pershing. When the private, who feared severe punishment, tried to stammer out his apology, General Pershing patted him on the back and said, "That's all right, son. Just be glad I'm not a second lieutenant." The point should be clear. The higher the person's level of true ability and the resulting influence, the more secure and confident he becomes.

This level is often gained by appointment. All other levels are gained by ability. Leo Durocher was coaching at first base in an exhibition game the Giants were playing at West Point. One noisy cadet kept shouting at Leo and doing his best to upset him.

"Hey, Durocher," he hollered. "How did a little squirt like you get into the major leagues?"

Leo shouted back, "My congressman appointed me!"[5]

People will not follow a positional leader beyond his stated authority. They will only do what they have to do when they are required to do it. Low morale is always present. When the leader lacks confidence, the followers lack commitment. They are like the little boy who was asked by Billy Graham how to find the nearest post office. When the lad told him, Dr. Graham thanked him and said, "If you'll come to the convention center this evening, you can hear me telling everyone how to get to heaven."

"I don't think I'll be there," the boy replied. "You don't even know your way to the post office."

Positional leaders have more difficulty working with volunteers, white-collar workers, and younger people. Volunteers don't have to work in the organization, so there is no monetary leverage that a positional leader can use to make them respond. White-collar workers are used to participating in decision-making and resent dictatorial leadership. Baby boomers in particular are unimpressed with symbols of authority.

Most of us have been taught that leadership is a position. Frustration rises within us when we get out into the real world and find that few people follow us because of our titles. Our joy and success in leading others depend on our abilities to keep climbing the levels of leadership.

LEVEL 2: PERMISSION

Fred Smith says, "Leadership is getting people to work for you when they are not obligated."[6] That will only happen when you climb to the second level of influence. People don't care how much you know until they know how much you care. Leadership begins with the heart, not the head. It flourishes with a meaningful relationship, not more regulation.

Leaders on the "position" level often lead by intimidation. They are like the chickens that Norwegian psychologist T. Schjelderup-Ebbe studied in developing the "pecking order" principle that today is used to describe all types of social gatherings.

Schjelderup-Ebbe found that in any flock one hen usually dominates all the others. She can peck any other without being pecked in return. Second comes a hen that pecks all but the top hen, and the rest are arranged in descending hierarchy, ending in one hapless hen that is pecked by all and can peck no one.

In contrast to this, a person on the "permission" level will lead by interrelationships. The agenda is not the pecking order but people development. On this level, time, energy, and focus are placed on the individual's needs and desires. A wonderful illustration of why it's so critical to put people and their needs first is found in the story of Henry Ford in Amitai Etzioni's book, *Modern Organizations*:

> He made a perfect car, the Model T, that ended the need for any other car. He was totally product-oriented. He wanted to fill the world with Model T cars. But when people started coming to him and saying, "Mr. Ford, we'd like a different color car," he remarked, "You can have any color you want as long as it's black." And that's when the decline started.

People who are unable to build solid, lasting relationships will soon discover that they are unable to sustain long, effective leadership. (Chapter 7 of this book, "Developing Your Most Appreciable Asset: People," will deal more extensively with this subject.) Needless to say, you can love people without leading them, but you cannot lead people without loving them.

One day one of my staff members, Dan Reiland, shared an insight with me that I have never forgotten: "If level 1, *Position*, is the door to leadership, then level 2, *Permission*, is the foundation."

Caution! Don't try to skip a level. The most often skipped level is 2, *Permission*. For example, a husband goes from level 1, *Position*, a wedding day title, to level 3, *Production*. He becomes a great provider for the family, but in the process he neglects the essential relationships that hold a family together. The family disintegrates, and so does the husband's business. Relationships involve a process that provides the glue and much of the staying power for long-term, consistent production.

LEVEL 3: PRODUCTION

On this level things begin to happen, good things. Profit increases. Morale is high. Turnover is low. Needs are being met. Goals are being realized. Accompanying this growth is the "big mo"—momentum. Leading and influencing others is fun. Problems are solved with minimum effort. Fresh statistics are shared on a regular basis with the people who undergird the growth of the organization. Everyone is results-oriented. In fact, results are the main reason for the activity.

This is a major difference between levels 2 and 3. On the "relationship" level, people get together just to get together. There is no other objective. On the "results" level, people come together to accomplish a purpose. They like to get together to get together, but they love to get together to accomplish something. In other words, they are results-oriented.

They are like a character played by Jack Nicholson, who, while in a restaurant in a famous scene from the movie *Five Easy Pieces*, is told he cannot get a side order of toast. He comes up with an imaginative solution. First, he orders a chicken salad sandwich on toast. Then he instructs the waitress: "No mayonnaise, but butter . . . and hold the chicken."

One of my favorite stories is about a newly hired traveling salesman who sent his first sales report to the home office. It stunned the brass in the sales department because it was obvious that the new salesman was ignorant! This is what he wrote: "I seen this outfit which they ain't never bot a dim's worth of nothin from us and I sole them some goods. I'm now goin to Chicawgo."

Before the man could be given the heave-ho by the sales manager, along came this letter from Chicago: "I cum hear and sole them haff a millyon."

Fearful if he did, and afraid if he didn't fire the ignorant salesman, the sales manager dumped the problem in the lap of the president. The following morning, the ivory-towered sales department members were amazed to see posted on the bulletin board above the two letters written by the ignorant salesman this memo from the president: "We ben spendin two much time trying to spel instead of trying to sel. Let's watch those sails. I want everybody should read these letters from Gooch who is on the rode doin a grate job for us and you should go out and do like he done."

Obviously, any sales manager would prefer to have a salesman who can both sell and spell. However, many people have produced great results who were not "qualified."

LEVEL 4: PEOPLE DEVELOPMENT

How do you spot a leader? According to Robert Townsend, they come in all sizes, ages, shapes, and conditions. Some are poor administrators, while some are not overly bright. There is a clue: Since some people are mediocre, the true leader can be recognized because somehow his people consistently demonstrate superior performances.

A leader is great, not because of his or her power, but because of his or her ability to empower others. Success without a successor is failure. A worker's main responsibility is developing others to do the work (see chapter 7).

Loyalty to the leader reaches its highest peak when the follower has personally grown through the mentorship of the leader. Note the progression: at level 2, the follower loves the leader; at level 3, the follower admires the leader; at level 4, the follower is loyal to the leader. Why? You win people's hearts by helping them grow personally.

One of the key players on my staff is Sheryl Fleisher. When she first joined the team, she was not a people person. I began to work closely with her until she truly became a people person. Today she successfully develops others. There is a bond of loyalty that Sheryl gives to my leadership, and we both know the reason. My time invested with her brought a positive change. She will never forget what I have done for her. Interestingly, her time invested in the lives of others has greatly helped me. I will never forget what she has done for me, either.

The core of leaders who surround you should all be people you have personally touched or helped to develop in some way. When that happens, love and loyalty will be exhibited by those closest to you and by those who are touched by your key leaders.

There is, however, a potential problem of moving up the levels of influence as a leader and becoming comfortable with the group of people you have developed around you. You may not realize that many new people view you as a "position" leader because you have had no contact with them. The following suggestions will help you become a people developer:

Walk slowly though the crowd. Have some way of keeping in touch with everyone. When I was a pastor, I did this in my congregation of five thousand by:

- learning names through the pictorial church directory.

- making communication cards available to the congregation and reading the cards as they were turned in (about 250 were received weekly).

- reading every interview form of a membership applicant.

- reading and replying to letters that were sent to me.

- visiting one social event of each Sunday school class each year.

Develop key leaders. I systematically meet with and teach those who are influencers within the organization. They, in turn, pass on to others what I have given them.

LEVEL 5: PERSONHOOD

Little time will be spent discussing this level, since most of us have not yet arrived at it. Only a lifetime of proven leadership will allow us to sit at level 5 and reap the rewards that are eternally satisfying. I do this—someday I want to sit atop this level. It's achievable.

CLIMBING THE STEPS OF LEADERSHIP

Here are some additional insights on the leadership-levels process:

THE HIGHER YOU GO, THE LONGER IT TAKES

Each time there is a change in your job or you join a new circle of friends, you start on the lowest level and begin to work yourself up the steps.

THE HIGHER YOU GO,
THE HIGHER THE LEVEL OF COMMITMENT

This increase in commitment is a two-way street. Greater commitment is demanded not only from you, but from the other individuals involved. When either the leader or the follower is unwilling to make the sacrifices a new level demands, influence will begin to decrease.

THE HIGHER YOU GO, THE EASIER IT IS TO LEAD

Notice the progression from level 2 through level 4. The focus goes from liking you, to liking what you do for the common interest of all concerned, to liking what you do for them personally. Each level climbed by the leader and the followers adds another reason why people will want to follow.

THE HIGHER YOU GO, THE GREATER THE GROWTH

Growth can only occur when effective change takes place. Change will become easier as you climb the levels of leadership. As you rise, other people will allow and even assist you in making needed changes.

YOU NEVER LEAVE THE BASE LEVEL

Each level stands upon the previous one and will crumble if the lower level is neglected. For example, if you move from a permission (relationships) level to a production (results) level and stop caring for the people who are following you and helping you produce, they might begin to develop a feeling of being used. As you move up in the levels, the deeper and more solid your leadership will be with a person or group of people.

THE FIVE LEVELS OF LEADERSHIP

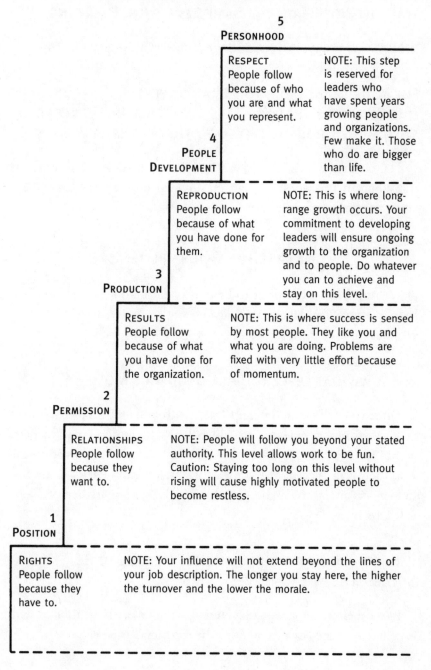

5
PERSONHOOD

RESPECT
People follow because of who you are and what you represent.

NOTE: This step is reserved for leaders who have spent years growing people and organizations. Few make it. Those who do are bigger than life.

4
PEOPLE DEVELOPMENT

REPRODUCTION
People follow because of what you have done for them.

NOTE: This is where long-range growth occurs. Your commitment to developing leaders will ensure ongoing growth to the organization and to people. Do whatever you can to achieve and stay on this level.

3
PRODUCTION

RESULTS
People follow because of what you have done for the organization.

NOTE: This is where success is sensed by most people. They like you and what you are doing. Problems are fixed with very little effort because of momentum.

2
PERMISSION

RELATIONSHIPS
People follow because they want to.

NOTE: People will follow you beyond your stated authority. This level allows work to be fun. Caution: Staying too long on this level without rising will cause highly motivated people to become restless.

1
POSITION

RIGHTS
People follow because they have to.

NOTE: Your influence will not extend beyond the lines of your job description. The longer you stay here, the higher the turnover and the lower the morale.

IF YOU ARE LEADING A GROUP OF PEOPLE, YOU WILL NOT BE ON THE SAME LEVEL WITH EVERYONE

Not every person will respond the same way to your leadership.

FOR YOUR LEADERSHIP TO REMAIN EFFECTIVE, IT IS ESSENTIAL THAT YOU TAKE THE OTHER INFLUENCERS WITHIN THE GROUP WITH YOU TO THE HIGHER LEVELS

The collective influence of you and the other leaders will bring the rest along. If this does not happen, divided interest and loyalty will occur within the group.

CONCLUSIONS OF INFLUENCE

We now have a blueprint to help us understand influence and how to increase it. The blueprint indicates that in order to get to the top, you must do two things:

1. KNOW WHAT LEVEL YOU ARE ON AT THIS MOMENT

Since you will be on different levels with different people, you need to know which people are on which level. If the biggest influencers within the organization are on the highest levels and are supportive of you, then your success in leading others will be attainable. If the best influencers are on the highest levels and not supportive, then problems will soon arise.

2. KNOW AND APPLY THE QUALITIES NEEDED TO BE SUCCESSFUL AT EACH LEVEL

Listed below are some characteristics that must be exhibited with excellence before advancement to the next level is possible.

Level 1: Position/Rights

- Know your job description thoroughly.

- Be aware of the history of the organization.

- Relate the organization's history to the people of the organization (in other words, be a team player).

- Accept responsibility.

- Do your job with consistent excellence.

- Do more than expected.

- Offer creative ideas for change and improvement.

Level 2: Permission/Relationship

- Possess a genuine love for people.

- Make those who work with you more successful.

- See through other people's eyes.

- Love people more than procedures.

- Do "win-win" or don't do it.

- Include others in your journey.

- Deal wisely with difficult people.

Level 3: Production/Results

- Initiate and accept responsibility for growth.

- Develop and follow a statement of purpose.

- Make your job description and energy an integral part of the statement of purpose.

- Develop accountability for results, beginning with yourself.

- Know and do the things that give a high return.
- Communicate the strategy and vision of the organization.
- Become a change agent, and understand timing.
- Make the difficult decisions that will make a difference.

Level 4: People Development/Reproduction

- Realize that people are your most valuable asset.
- Place a priority on developing people.
- Be a model for others to follow.
- Pour your leadership efforts into the top 20 percent of your people.
- Expose key leaders to growth opportunities.
- Be able to attract other winners/producers to the common goal.
- Surround yourself with an inner core that complements your leadership.

Level 5: Personhood/Respect

- Your followers are loyal and sacrificial.
- You have spent years mentoring and molding leaders.
- You have become a statesman/consultant, and are sought out by others.
- Your greatest joy comes from watching others grow and develop.
- You transcend the organization.

Everyone is a leader, because everyone influences someone. Not everyone will become a great leader, but everyone can become a better leader. Now, only two questions must be answered: "Will you unleash your leadership potential?" and "Will you use your leadership skills to better mankind?" This book was written to help you do both.

My Influence

My life shall touch a dozen lives
Before this day is done.
Leave countless marks of good or ill,
E'er sets the evening sun.

This, the wish I always wish,
The prayer I always pray;
Lord, may my life help others' lives
It touches by the way.[7]

ACTION STEPS TO UNLEASH
YOUR LEADERSHIP POTENTIAL

REVIEW:

1. Leadership is _INFLUENCE OR THE ABILITY TO OBTAIN FOLLOWERS._

2. The five levels of leadership are:
    (1) _POSITION_
    (2) _PERMISSION_
    (3) _PRODUCTION_
    (4) _PEOPLE DEVELOPMENT_
    (5) _PERSONHOOD_

3. What level am I currently on with most people?
    PERMISSION

4. What level am I currently on with other influencers?
    PERMISSION

RESPOND:

1.   List the five top influencers in your organization.

    (a) What level of influence are you on with them?

    (b) What level of influence are they on with others?

2. Spend one hour a month with the top five influencers, individually, building a relationship with them.

3. Spend two hours a month with the top influencers as a group, developing them. Spend one of the two hours reviewing a chapter in this book. Spend the other hour doing a project together that enhances the organization.

4. Review the characteristics of each of the five levels of leadership and pick out three that you are weak in and need to develop.
   (1)
   (2)
   (3)

THE KEY TO LEADERSHIP:
PRIORITIES

Recently, while attending a conference, I heard a speaker say, "There are two things that are most difficult to get people to do: to think, and to do things in order of importance." He went on to say that these two things are the difference between a professional and an amateur.

I also believe that thinking ahead and prioritizing responsibilities mark the major differences between a leader and a follower, because:

- practical people know how to get what they want.
- philosophers know what they ought to want.
- leaders know how to get what they ought to want.

Success can be defined as *the progressive realization of a predetermined goal*. This definition tells us that the discipline to prioritize and the ability to work toward a stated goal are essential to a leader's success. In fact, I believe they are the key to leadership.

> Success is the progressive realization of a predetermined goal.

Many years ago, while working toward a business degree, I learned about the Pareto Principle. It is commonly called the 20/80 principle. Although I received little information about this principle at the time, I began applying it to

The Pareto Principle

20 percent of your priorities will give you 80 percent
of your production
IF
you spend your time, energy, money, and personnel
on the top 20 percent of your priorities.

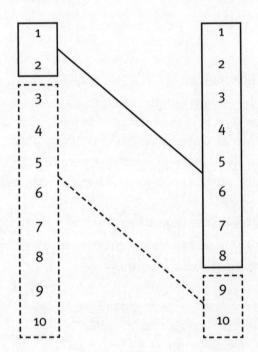

my life. Twenty years later I find it a most useful tool for determining priorities for any person's life or for any organization.

THE PARETO PRINCIPLE
THE 20/80 PRINCIPLE

The solid lines on the illustration of the 20/80 Principle on page 20 represent a person or organization that spends time, energy, money, and personnel on the most important priorities. The result is a fourfold return in productivity. The dotted lines represent a person or organization that spends time, energy, money, and personnel on the lesser priorities. The result is a very small return.

EXAMPLES OF THE PARETO PRINCIPLE:

TIME	20 percent of our time produces 80 percent of the results.
COUNSELING	20 percent of the people take up 80 percent of our time.
PRODUCTS	20 percent of the products bring in 80 percent of the profit.
READING	20 percent of the book contains 80 percent of the content.
JOB	20 percent of our work gives us 80 percent of our satisfaction.
SPEECH	20 percent of the presentation produces 80 percent of the impact.
DONATIONS	20 percent of the people will give 80 percent of the money.
LEADERSHIP	20 percent of the people will make 80 percent of the decisions.
PICNIC	20 percent of the people will eat 80 percent of the food!

Every leader needs to understand the Pareto Principle in the area of people oversight and leadership. For example, 20 percent of the people in an organization will be responsible for 80 percent of the company's success. The following strategy will enable a leader to increase the productivity of an organization.

1. Determine which people are the top 20 percent producers.

2. Spend 80 percent of your "people time" with the top 20 percent.

3. Spend 80 percent of your personal developmental dollars on the top 20 percent.

4. Determine what 20 percent of the work gives 80 percent of the return and train an assistant to do the 80 percent less effective work. This "frees up" the producer to do what he/she does best.

5. Ask the top 20 percent to do on-the-job training for the next 20 percent.

Remember, we teach what we know; we reproduce what we are. Like begets like.

I teach this principle at leadership conferences. I am often asked, "How do I identify the top 20 percent influencers/producers in my organization?" I suggest that you make a list of everyone in your company or department. Then ask yourself this question about each individual: "If this person takes a negative action against me or withdraws his or her support from me, what will the impact likely be?" If you won't be able to function, then put a check mark next to that name. If the person can help you or hurt you, but cannot make or break you in terms of your ability to get important things done, then don't put a check mark next to that name. When you get through making the check marks, you will have marked between 15 and 20 percent of the names. Those are the vital relationships that need to be developed and given the proper amount of resources needed to grow the organization.

> Efficiency is the foundation for survival. Effectiveness is the foundation for success.

It's Not How Hard You Work; It's How Smart You Work

] HEARD THIS A HUNDRED TIMES

A man was told that if he worked the very hardest he could he would become rich. The hardest work he knew was digging holes, so he set about digging great holes in his backyard. He didn't get rich; he only got a backache. He worked hard but he worked without any priorities.

Organize or Agonize

The ability to juggle three or four high-priority projects successfully is a must for every leader. A life in which anything goes will ultimately be a life in which nothing goes.

Prioritize Assignments

High Importance/High Urgency: Tackle these projects first.

High Importance/Low Urgency: Set deadlines for completion, and get these projects worked into your daily routine.

Low Importance/High Urgency: Find quick, efficient ways to get this work done without much personal involvement. If possible, delegate it to a "can do" assistant.

Low Importance/Low Urgency: This is busy or repetitious work, such as filing. Stack it up and do it in half-hour segments every week; get somebody else to do it; or don't do it at all. Before putting off until tomorrow something you can do today, study it clearly. Maybe you can postpone it indefinitely.

PARETO

DATE_____

PHONE CALLS TO MAKE	COMP	PERSONAL NOTES	COMP
1._____	n	1._____	n
2._____	n	2._____	n
3._____	n	3._____	n
4._____	n	4._____	n

20/80 TIME

ORDER OF
PRIORITY TIME ALLOWED DESCRIPTION—LIST OF THINGS TO DO <u>NOW</u> COMPLETED
(HIGH IMPORTANCE; HIGH URGENCY)

1._____ n

2._____ n

3._____ n

4._____ n

5._____ n

6._____ n

7._____ n

8._____ n

9._____ n

10._____ n

LIST OF THINGS TO DO		LIST OF THINGS TO DELEGATE	
(HIGH IMPORTANCE; LOW URGENCY)		(LOW IMPORTANCE; HIGH URGENCY)	
1._____	n	1._____	n
2._____	n	2._____	n
3._____	n	3._____	n
4._____	n	4._____	n
5._____	n	5._____	n
6._____	n	6._____	n
7._____	n	7._____	n
8._____	n	8._____	n

A few years ago I was teaching the 20/80 principle at a conference in Boston. A few weeks later my friend, John Bowen, sent me a tablet of paper that he designed from the lecture. I have used it for my own prioritizing ever since. Perhaps it will have value to you too (see page 24).

CHOOSE OR LOSE

Every person is either an initiator or a reactor when it comes to planning. An example is our calendar. The question is not, "Will my calendar be full?" but "Who will fill my calendar?" If we are leaders of others, the question is not, "Will I see people?" but "Who will I see?" My observation is that leaders tend to initiate, and followers tend to react. Note the difference.

LEADERS	FOLLOWERS
Initiate	React
Lead; pick up phone and make contact	Listen; wait for phone to ring
Spend time planning; anticipate problems	Spend time living day-to-day; react to problems
Invest time with people	Spend time with people
Fill the calendar by priorities	Fill the calendar by requests

EVALUATE OR STALEMATE

A veteran of many years of decision making gave me this short, simple advice: Decide what to do and do it. Decide what not to do and don't do it. Evaluation of priorities, however, is not quite that simple. Many times they are not black or white, but many tones of gray. I have found that the last thing one knows is what to put first.

The following questions will assist your prioritization process:

What is required of me? A leader can give up anything except final responsibility. The question that must always be answered before accepting a new job is, "What is required of me?" In other words, what do I have to do that no one but me can do? Whatever those things are, they must be put high on the priority list. Failure to do them will cause you to be among the unemployed. There will be many responsibilities of the levels under your position, but only a few that require you to be the one and only one who can do them. Distinguish between what you have to do and what can be delegated to someone else.

Take a minute and list what is required of you in your job (by priority, if possible).

1. MEET with CBU LEADERS AND ESTABLISH PROJECT PRIORITIES

2. UPDATE AND PUSH PROJECT STATUS

3. MEET WITH SUPPLIERS (INT + EXT.) FOR NEW PROJECT DETAILS

4. EVALUATE NEW TECHNOLOGY FOR MERIT AND FIT TO SEATING

What gives me the greatest return? The effort expended should approximate the results expected. A question I must continually ask myself is, "Am I doing what I do best and receiving a good return for the organization?" There are three common problems in many organizations.

- Abuse: too few employees are doing too much.
- Disuse: too many employees are doing too little.
- Misuse: too many employees are doing the wrong things.

Bo Jackson played defensive end for his high school football team. He was good, but he didn't lead his team to a championship. In fact, they finished the season with three wins and seven losses. At Auburn University, when all three running backs were injured, Bo's coach asked him to fill in "until the regulars are healthy again." Bo was apprehensive, but he did it. The rest is history. This is an excellent example of fulfilling the "return" questions.

Take a minute and list what gives you the greatest return on your job.

1. WORKING WITH SUPPLIERS TO PUSH FOR NEW TECHNOLOGY

2. CREATING PROJECT TIMELINES FOR SUCCESS
   ↳ WORK WITH TEAM TO EXECUTE

3.

4.

What is most rewarding? Life is too short not to be fun. Our best work takes place when we enjoy it. Some time ago I spoke at a leaders' conference where I attempted to teach this principle. The title of my lecture was "Take This Job and Love It." I encouraged the audience to find something they liked to do so much that they would gladly do it for nothing. Then I suggested they learn to do it so well that people would be happy to pay them for it. Andy Granatelli said that when you are making a success of something, it's not work. It's a way of life. You enjoy yourself because you are making your contribution to the world. I believe that! Take a minute and write down what is most satisfying in your job.

1. SUCCESSFUL TRIALS OF NEW TECHNOLOGY

2. WORKING WITH TEAM MEMBERS TO CREATE REALISTIC VISIONS OF FUTURE SEATING DEVELOPMENTS

3. RE WORK WITH INT. CUSTOMERS (CBU) TO PLUG IN NEW TECHNOLOGY

4.

Success in your work will be greatly increased if the 3 Rs (Requirements/Return/Reward) are similar. In other words, if the requirements of my job are the same as my strengths that give me the highest return, and doing those things brings me great pleasure, then I will be successful if I act on my priorities.

PRIORITY PRINCIPLES

PRIORITIES NEVER "STAY PUT"

Priorities continually shift and demand attention. H. Ross Perot said, "Anything that is excellent or praiseworthy moment-by-moment on the cutting edge must be constantly fought for." Well-placed priorities always sit on "the edge."

To keep priorities in place, do the following:

- Evaluate: Every month review the 3 Rs (Requirements/Return/ Reward).

- Eliminate: Ask yourself, "What am I doing that can be done by someone else?"

- Estimate: What are the top projects you are doing this month, and how long will they take?

YOU CANNOT OVERESTIMATE THE UNIMPORTANCE OF PRACTICALLY EVERYTHING

I love this principle. It's a little exaggerated but needs to be said. William James said that the art of being wise is the "art of knowing what to overlook." The petty and the mundane steal much of our time. Too many of us are living for the wrong things.

> You cannot overestimate the unimportance of practically everything.

Dr. Anthony Campolo tells about a sociological study in which fifty people over the age of ninety-five were asked one question: "If you could live your life over again, what would you do differently?" It was an open-ended question, and a multiplicity of answers constantly reemerged and dominated the results of the study. These were three answers:

- If I had it to do over again, I would reflect more.

- If I had it to do over again, I would risk more.

- If I had it to do over again, I would do more things that would live on after I am dead.

A young concert violinist was asked the secret of her success. She replied, "Planned neglect." Then she explained, "When I was in school, there were many things that demanded my time. When I went to my room after breakfast, I made my bed, straightened the room, dusted the floor, and did whatever else came to my attention. Then I hurried to my violin practice. I found I wasn't progressing as I thought I should, so I reversed things. Until my practice period was completed, I deliberately neglected everything else. That program of planned neglect, I believe, accounts for my success."[1]

THE GOOD IS THE ENEMY OF THE BEST

Most people can prioritize when faced with a right-or-wrong issue. The challenge arises when we are faced with two good choices. Now what should we do? What if both choices fall comfortably into the requirements, return, and reward of our work?

How to Break the Tie Between Two Good Options

- Ask your overseer or coworkers their preference.
- Can one of the options be handled by someone else? If so, pass it on and work on the one only you can do.
- Which option would be of more benefit to the customer? Too many times we are like the merchant who was so intent on trying to keep the store clean that he would never unlock the front door. The real reason for running the store is to have customers come in, not to clean it up!
- Make your decision based on the purpose of the organization.

A lighthouse keeper who worked on a rocky stretch of coastline received his new supply of oil once a month to keep the light burning.

Not being far from shore, he had frequent guests. One night a woman from the village begged some oil to keep her family warm. Another time a father asked for some to use in his lamp. Another needed some to lubricate a wheel. Since all the requests seemed legitimate, the light-house keeper tried to please everyone and grant the requests of all. Toward the end of the month he noticed the supply of oil was very low. Soon it was gone, and the beacon went out. That night several ships were wrecked and lives were lost. When the authorities investigated, the man was very repentant. To his excuses and pleading, their reply was, "You were given oil for one purpose—to keep that light burning!"

YOU CAN'T HAVE IT ALL

When my son, Joel Porter, was younger, every time we entered a store, I would say to him, "You can't have it all." Like many people, he had a hard time eliminating things in his life. Ninety-five percent of achieving anything is knowing what you want. Many years ago I read this poem by William H. Hinson:

> He who seeks one thing, and but one,
> May hope to achieve it before life is done.
> But he who seeks all things wherever he goes
> Must reap around him in whatever he sows
> A harvest of barren regret.

A group of people were preparing for an ascent to the top of Mont Blanc in the Alps in France. On the evening before the climb, a French guide outlined the main prerequisite for success. He said, "To reach the top, you must carry only equipment necessary for climbing. You must leave behind all unnecessary accessories. It's a difficult climb."

A young Englishman disagreed and the next morning showed up with a rather heavy, brightly colored blanket; some large pieces of cheese; a bottle of wine; a couple of cameras with several lenses hanging around his neck; and some bars of chocolate. The guide said, "You'll never make it with that. You can only take the bare necessities to make the climb."

But strong-willed as he was, the Englishman set off on his own in front of the group to prove to them he could do it. The group then followed under the direction of the guide, each one carrying just the bare necessities. On the way up to the summit of Mont Blanc, they began to notice certain things someone had left along the way. First, they encountered a brightly colored blanket, then some pieces of cheese, a bottle of wine, camera equipment, and some chocolate bars. Finally when they reached the top, they discovered the Englishman. Wisely, along the way he had jettisoned everything unnecessary.

Too Many Priorities Paralyze Us

Every one of us has looked at our desks filled with memos and papers, heard the phone ringing, and watched the door open all at the same time! Remember the "frozen feeling" that came over you?

William H. Hinson tells us why animal trainers carry a stool when they go into a cage of lions. They have their whips, of course, and their pistols are at their sides. But invariably they also carry a stool. Hinson says it is the most important tool of the trainer. He holds the stool by the back and thrusts the legs toward the face of the wild animal. Those who know maintain that the animal tries to focus on all four legs at once. In the attempt to focus on all four, a kind of paralysis overwhelms the animal, and it becomes tame, weak, and disabled because its attention is fragmented. (Now we will have more empathy for the lions.)

One day, Sheryl, one of our most productive staff members, came to see me. She looked exhausted. I learned that she was overloaded. Her "to do" list was getting too long. I asked her to list all her projects. We prioritized them together. I can still see the look of relief on her face as the load began to lift.

If you are overloaded with work, list the priorities on a separate sheet of paper before you take it to your boss and see what he will choose as the priorities.

The last of each month, I plan and lay out my priorities for the next month. I sit down with Barbara, my assistant, and have her place those projects on the calendar. She handles hundreds of things for me on a monthly basis. However, when something is of High Importance/High Urgency, I communicate that to her so it will be placed above other things. All true leaders have learned to say no to the good in order to say yes to the best.

WHEN LITTLE PRIORITIES DEMAND
TOO MUCH OF US, BIG PROBLEMS ARISE

Robert J. McKain said, "The reason most major goals are not achieved is that we spend our time doing second things first."

Some years ago a headline told of three hundred whales that suddenly died. The whales were pursuing sardines and found themselves marooned in a bay. Frederick Broan Harris commented, "The small fish lured the sea giants to their death . . . They came to their violent demise by chasing small ends, by prostituting vast powers for insignificant goals."[2]

Often the little things in life trip us up. A tragic example is an Eastern Airlines jumbo jet that crashed in the Everglades of Florida. The plane was the now-famous Flight 401, bound from New York to Miami with a heavy load of holiday passengers. As the plane approached the Miami airport for its landing, the light that indicates proper deployment of the landing gear failed to light. The plane flew in a large, looping circle over the swamps of the Everglades while the cockpit crew checked to see if the gear actually had not deployed, or if instead the bulb in the signal light was defective.

When the flight engineer tried to remove the lightbulb, it wouldn't budge, and the other members of the crew tried to help him. As they struggled with the bulb, no one noticed the aircraft was losing altitude, and the plane simply flew right into the swamp. Dozens of people were killed in the crash. While an experienced crew of high-priced pilots fiddled with a seventy-five-cent lightbulb, the plane with its passengers flew right into the ground.

Time Deadlines and Emergencies
Force Us to Prioritize

We find this in Parkinson's Law: If you have only one letter to write, it will take all day to do it. If you have twenty letters to write, you'll get them done in one day.

When is our most efficient time in our work? The week before vacation! Why can't we always run our lives the way we do the week before we leave the office: making decisions, cleaning off the desk, returning calls? Under normal conditions, we are efficient (doing things right). When time pressure mounts or emergencies arise, we become effective (doing the right things). Efficiency is the foundation for survival. Effectiveness is the foundation of success.

On the night of April 14, 1912, the great ocean liner, the *Titanic*, crashed into an iceberg in the Atlantic and sank, causing great loss of life. One of the most curious stories to come from the disaster was of a woman who had a place in one of the lifeboats.

She asked if she could return to her stateroom for something and was given just three minutes. As she hurried through the corridors, she stepped over money and precious gems littering the floor, where they had been dropped in haste. In her own stateroom she ignored her own jewelry, and instead grabbed three oranges. Then she quickly returned to her place in the boat.

Just hours earlier it would have been ludicrous to think she would have accepted a crate of oranges in exchange for even one small diamond, but circumstances had suddenly transformed all the values aboard the ship. The emergency had clarified her priorities.

Too Often We Learn Too Late What Is Really Important

We are like the family that had become fed up with the noise and traffic of the city and decided to move to the country and try life in the wide open spaces. Intending to raise cattle, they bought a Western ranch. Some friends came to visit a month later and asked them what they had named the ranch. The father said, "Well, I wanted to call it the Flying-W, and my wife wanted to call it the Suzy-Q. But one of our sons liked the Bar-J, and the other preferred the Lazy-Y. So we compromised and called it the Flying-W, Suzy-Q, Bar-J, Lazy-Y Ranch." Their friend asked, "Well, where are your cattle?" The man replied, "We don't have any. None of them survived the branding!"

The author is unknown who said, "An infant is born with a clenched fist; a man dies with an open hand. Life has a way of prying free the things we think are so important."

Gary Redding tells this story about Senator Paul Tsongas of Massachusetts. In January 1984, he announced that he would retire from the U.S. Senate and not seek reelection. Tsongas was a rising political star. He was a strong favorite to be reelected, and had even been mentioned as a potential future candidate for the presidency or vice presidency of the United States.

A few weeks before his announcement, Tsongas had learned he had a form of lymphatic cancer that could not be cured but could be treated. In all likelihood, it would not greatly affect his physical abilities or life expectancy. The illness did not force Tsongas out of the Senate, but it did force him to face the reality of his own mortality. He would not be able to do everything he might want to do. So what were the things he really wanted to do in the time he had?

He decided that what he wanted most out of his life, what he would not give up if he could not have everything, was being with his family and watching his children grow up. He would rather do that than shape the nation's laws or get his name in the history books.

Shortly after his decision was announced, a friend wrote a note to congratulate Tsongas on having his priorities straight. The note read: "Nobody on his death bed ever said, 'I wish I had spent more time on my business.'"

===

THREE

THE MOST IMPORTANT INGREDIENT OF LEADERSHIP:

INTEGRITY

The dictionary defines *integrity* as "the state of being complete, unified." When I have integrity, my words and my deeds match up. I am who I am, no matter where I am or who I am with.

Sadly, integrity is a vanishing commodity today. Personal standards are crumbling in a world that has taken to hot pursuit of personal pleasure and shortcuts to success.

On a job application one question read, "Have you ever been arrested?" The applicant printed the word *No* in the space. The next question was a follow-up to the first. It asked, "Why?" Not realizing he did not have to answer this part, the "honest" and rather naïve applicant wrote, "I guess it's because I never got caught."

A Jeff Danziger cartoon shows a company president announcing to his staff, "Gentlemen, this year the trick is honesty." From one side of the conference table, a vice president gasps, "Brilliant." Across the table, another VP mutters, "But so risky."

In a cartoon in the *New Yorker*, two clean-shaven middle-aged men are sitting together in a jail cell. One inmate turns to the other and says, "All along, I thought our level of corruption fell well within community standards."

The White House, the Pentagon, Capitol Hill, the church, the sports arena, the academy, even the day care center have all been hit hard by scandal. In every case, the lack of credibility can be traced back to the level of integrity of the individuals within those organizations and institutions.

A person with integrity does not have divided loyalties (that's duplicity), nor is he or she merely pretending (that's hypocrisy). People with integrity are "whole" people; they can be identified by their single-mindedness. People with integrity have nothing to hide and nothing to fear. Their lives are open books. V. Gilbert Beers says, "A person of integrity is one who has established a system of values against which all of life is judged."

Integrity is not what we do so much as who we are. And who we are, in turn, determines what we do. Our system of values is so much a part of us we cannot separate it from ourselves. It becomes the navigating system that guides us. It establishes priorities in our lives and judges what we will accept or reject.

We are all faced with conflicting desires. No one, no matter how "spiritual," can avoid this battle. Integrity is the factor that determines which one will prevail. We struggle daily with situations that demand decisions between what we want to do and what we ought to do. Integrity establishes the ground rules for resolving these tensions. It determines who we are and how we will respond before the conflict even appears. Integrity welds what we say, think, and do into a whole person so that permission is never granted for one of those to be out of sync.

Integrity binds our person together and fosters a spirit of contentment within us. It will not allow our lips to violate our hearts. When integrity is the referee, we will be consistent; our beliefs will be mirrored by our conduct. There will be no discrepancy between what we appear to be and what our family knows we are, whether in times of prosperity or adversity. Integrity allows us to predetermine what we will be regardless of circumstances, persons involved, or the places of our testing.

Integrity is not only the referee between two desires. It is the pivotal point between a happy person and a divided spirit. It frees us to be whole persons no matter what comes our way.

"The first key to greatness," Socrates reminds us, "is to be in reality what we appear to be." Too often we try to be a "human doing" before we have become a "human being." To earn trust a leader has to be authentic. For that to happen, one must come across as a good musical composition does—the words and the music must match.

If what I say and what I do are the same, the results are consistent. For example:

I say to the employees: "Be at work on time."	I arrive at work on time.	They will be on time.
I say to the employees: "Be positive."	I exhibit a positive attitude.	They will be positive.
I say to the employees: "Put the customer first."	I put the customer first.	They will put the customer first.

If what I say and do are not the same, the results are inconsistent. For example:

I say to the employees: "Be at work on time."	I arrive at work late.	Some will be on time; some won't.
I say to the employees: "Be positive."	I exhibit a negative attitude.	Some will be positive; some won't.
I say to the employees: "Put the customer first."	I put myself first.	Some will put customers first; some won't.

Eighty-nine percent of what people learn comes through visual stimulation, 10 percent through audible stimulation, and 1 percent through other senses. So it makes sense that the more followers see and hear their leader being consistent in action and word, the greater their consistency and loyalty. *What they hear, they understand. What they see, they believe!*

> Integrity is not what we do as much as who we are.

Too often we attempt to motivate our followers with gimmicks that are short-lived and shallow. What people need is not a motto to say, but a model to see.

THE CREDIBILITY ACID TEST

The more credible you are, the more confidence people place in you, thereby allowing you the privilege of influencing their lives. The less credible you are, the less confidence people place in you and the more quickly you lose your position of influence.

> Image is what people think we are. Integrity is what we really are.

Many leaders who have attended my conferences have said to me, "I hope you can give me some insights into how I can change my company." My response is always the same: "My goal is to inspire you to change; if that happens, the organization will also be changed." As I have said time and time again, everything rises and falls on leadership. The secret to rising and not falling is integrity. Let's look at some reasons why integrity is so important.

1. INTEGRITY BUILDS TRUST

Dwight Eisenhower said:

> In order to be a leader a man must have followers. And to have followers, a man must have their confidence. Hence, the supreme quality for a leader is unquestionably integrity. Without it, no real

success is possible, no matter whether it is on a section gang, a football field, in an army, or in an office. If a man's associates find him guilty of being phony, if they find that he lacks forthright integrity, he will fail. His teachings and actions must square with each other. The first great need, therefore, is integrity and high purpose.[1]

Pieter Bruyn, a Dutch specialist in administration, holds that authority is not the power a boss has over subordinates, but rather the boss's ability to influence subordinates to recognize and accept that power. He calls it a "bargain": Subordinates tacitly agree to accept the boss as boss in return for being offered the kind of leadership *they* can accept. What does Bruyn's theory boil down to? Quite simply, the manager must build—and maintain—credibility. Subordinates must be able to trust that their boss will act in good faith toward them.

Too often people who are responsible for leading look to the organization to make people responsible to follow. They ask for a new title, another position, an organization chart, and a new policy to curtail insubordination. Sadly they never get enough authority to become effective. Why? They are looking to the outside when their problem is on the inside. They lack authority because they lack integrity.

Only 45 percent of four hundred managers in a Carnegie-Mellon survey believed their top management; a third distrusted their immediate bosses.[2] With so much depending on credibility and trust, someone in every organization must provide the leadership to improve these numbers.

Cavett Roberts said: "If my people understand me, I'll get their attention. If my people trust me, I'll get their action." For a leader to have the authority to lead, he needs more than the title on his door. He has to have the trust of those who are following him.

2. INTEGRITY HAS HIGH INFLUENCE VALUE

Emerson said, "Every great institution is the lengthened shadow of a single man. His character determines the character of the organization."

That statement "lines up" with the words of Will Rogers, who said, "People's minds are changed through observation and not argument." People do what people see.

According to 1,300 senior executives who responded to a recent survey, integrity is the human quality most necessary to business success. Seventy-one percent put it at the top of a list of sixteen traits responsible for enhancing an executive's effectiveness.

Regrettably we tend to forget the high influence value of integrity in the home. R. C. Sproul, in his book *Objections Answered*, tells about a young Jewish boy who grew up in Germany many years ago. The lad had a profound sense of admiration for his father, who saw to it that the life of the family revolved around the religious practices of their faith. The father led them to the synagogue faithfully.

In his teen years, however, the boy's family was forced to move to another town in Germany. This town had no synagogue, only a Lutheran church. The life of the community revolved around the Lutheran church; all the best people belonged to it. Suddenly, the father announced to the family that they were all going to abandon their Jewish traditions and join the Lutheran church. When the stunned family asked why, the father explained that it would be good for his business. The youngster was bewildered and confused. His deep disappointment soon gave way to anger and a kind of intense bitterness that plagued him throughout his life.

Later he left Germany and went to England to study. Each day found him at the British Museum, formulating his ideas and composing a book. In that book he introduced a whole new worldview and conceived a movement that was designed to change the world. He described religion as the "opiate for the masses." He committed the people who followed him to life without God. His ideas became the norm for the governments for almost half the world's people. His name? Karl Marx, founder of the Communist movement. The history of the twentieth century, and perhaps beyond, was significantly affected because one father let his values become distorted.

3. INTEGRITY FACILITATES HIGH STANDARDS

Leaders must live by higher standards than their followers. This insight is exactly opposite of most people's thoughts concerning leadership. In a world of perks and privileges that accompany the climb to success, little thought is given to the responsibilities of the upward journey. Leaders can give up anything except responsibility, either for themselves or their organizations. John D. Rockefeller Jr. said, "I believe that every right implies a responsibility; every opportunity, an obligation; every possession, a duty." The diagram below illustrates this principle.

Too many people are ready to assert their rights, but not to assume their responsibilities. Richard L. Evans, in his book *An Open Road*, said:

> It is priceless to find a person who will take responsibility, who will finish and follow through to the final detail—to know when someone has accepted an assignment that it will be effectively, conscientiously completed. But when half-finished assignments keep coming back—to check on, to verify, to edit, to interrupt thought, and to take repeated attention—obviously someone has failed to follow the doctrine of completed work.

Tom Robbins said, "Don't let yourself be victimized by the age you live in. It's not the time that will bring us down, any more than it's society. There's a tendency today to absolve individuals of moral responsibility and treat them as victims of social circumstance. You buy that and you pay with your soul. What limits people is lack of character." When the character of leaders is low, so are their standards.

4. INTEGRITY RESULTS IN A SOLID REPUTATION, NOT JUST AN IMAGE

Image is what people think we are. Integrity is what we really are.

Two old ladies were walking around a somewhat overcrowded English country churchyard and came upon a tombstone. The inscription said: "Here lies John Smith, a politician and an honest man."

"Good heavens!" said one lady to the other. "Isn't it awful that they had to put two people in the same grave!"

All of us have known those who were not the same on the outside as they were inside. Sadly, many who have worked harder on their images than on their integrity don't understand when they suddenly "fall." Even friends who thought they knew them are surprised.

In ancient China the people wanted security against the barbaric hordes to the north, so they built the great wall. It was so high they believed no one could climb over it and so thick nothing could break it down. They settled back to enjoy their security. During the first hundred years of the wall's existence, China was invaded three times. Not once did the barbaric hordes break down the wall or climb over it. Each time they bribed a gatekeeper and then marched right through the gates. The Chinese were so busy relying on the walls of stone that they forgot to teach integrity to their children.

Your answers to the following questions will determine if you are into image-building instead of integrity-building:

Consistency:	Are you the same person no matter who you are with?
Choices:	Do you make decisions that are best for others when another choice would benefit you?
Credit:	Are you quick to recognize others for their efforts and contributions to your success?

Thomas Macauley said, "The measure of a man's real character is what he would do if he would never be found out." Life is like a vise; at times it will squeeze us. At those moments of pressure, whatever is inside will be found out. We cannot give what we do not have. Image promises much but produces little. Integrity never disappoints.

5. INTEGRITY MEANS LIVING IT MYSELF *BEFORE* LEADING OTHERS

We cannot lead anyone else farther than we have been ourselves. Too many times we are so concerned about the product that we try to shortcut the process. There are no shortcuts when integrity is involved. Eventually truth will always be exposed.

Recently I heard of a man who interviewed a consultant to some of the largest U.S. companies about their quality control. The consultant said, "In quality control, we are not concerned about the product. We are concerned about the process. If the process is right, the product is guaranteed." The same holds true for integrity; it guarantees credibility.

When the *Challenger* exploded, America was stunned to discover that Quality Control had warned NASA that the space shuttle was not fully prepared to go. But production said, "The show must go on!" *Crash*, just like many leaders.

HOLD IT! I CAN'T SWIM!

I remember hearing my basketball coach, Don Neff, repeatedly emphasize to our team, "You play like you practice; you play like you practice." When we fail to follow this principle, we fail to reach our personal potentials. When leaders fail to follow this principle, eventually they lose their credibility.

6. Integrity Helps a Leader Be Credible, Not Just Clever

I once had dinner with Fred Smith. This wise businessman shared with me the difference between being clever and being credible. He said that clever leaders never last. That statement reminded me of the words of Peter Drucker, given to pastors gathered to discuss important issues in the church:

> The final requirement of effective leadership is to earn trust. Otherwise there won't be any followers . . . A leader is someone who has followers. To trust a leader, it is not necessary to agree with him. Trust is the conviction that the leader means what he says. It is a belief in something very old-fashioned called "integrity." A leader's actions and a leader's professed beliefs must be congruent or at least compatible. Effective leadership—and again this is very old wisdom— is not based on being clever; it is primarily on being consistent.[3]

Leaders who are sincere don't have to advertise the fact. It's visible in everything they do and soon becomes common knowledge to everyone. Likewise, insincerity cannot be hidden, disguised, or covered up, no matter how competent a manager may otherwise be.

The only way to keep the goodwill and high esteem of the people you work with is to deserve it. No one can fool all of the people all of the time. Each of us, eventually, is recognized for exactly what we are—not what we try to appear to be.

Ann Landers said, "People of integrity expect to be believed. They also know time will prove them right and are willing to wait."

7. INTEGRITY IS A HARD-WON ACHIEVEMENT

Integrity is not a given factor in everyone's life. It is a result of self-discipline, inner trust, and a decision to be relentlessly honest in all situations in our lives. Unfortunately in today's world, strength of character is a rare commodity. As a result, we have few contemporary models of integrity. Our culture has produced few enduring heroes, few models of virtue. We have become a nation of imitators, but there are few leaders worth imitating.

The meaning of integrity has been eroded. Drop the word into conversations in Hollywood, on Wall Street, even on Main Street, and you'll get blank stares in return. For most Americans, the word conjures up ideas of prudishness or narrow-mindedness. In an age when the meanings of words are manipulated, foundational values such as integrity can be pulverized overnight.

Integrity is antithetical to the spirit of our age. The overarching philosophy of life that guides our culture revolves around a materialistic, consumer mentality. The craving need of the moment supersedes consideration of values that have eternal significance.

When we sell out to someone else, we also sell out ourselves. Hester H. Chomondelay underscores this truth in his short poem, "Judas":

> Still as of old
> Men by themselves are priced—
> For thirty pieces Judas sold
> Himself, not Christ.

Billy Graham said, "Integrity is the glue that holds our way of life together. We must constantly strive to keep our integrity intact.

"When wealth is lost, nothing is lost; when health is lost, something is lost; when character is lost, all is lost."[4]

To build your life on the foundation of integrity, use the following poem ("Am I True to Myself?" by Edgar Guest) as a "Mirror Test" to evaluate how you're doing.

I have to live with myself, and so
I want to be fit for myself to know,
I want to be able, as days go by,
Always to look myself straight in the eye;
I don't want to stand, with the setting sun,
And hate myself for things I have done.
I don't want to keep on a closet shelf
A lot of secrets about myself,
And fool myself, as I come and go,
Into thinking that nobody else will know
The kind of man I really am;
I don't want to dress up myself in sham.
I want to go out with my head erect,
I want to deserve all men's respect;
But here in the struggle for fame and pelf
I want to be able to like myself.
I don't want to look at myself and know
That I'm bluster and bluff and empty show.
I can never hide myself from me;
I see what others may never see;
I know what others may never know,
I never can fool myself, and so,
Whatever happens, I want to be
Self-respecting and conscience free.

Next, take the "Mentor Test." It asks, "Am I true to my leader?" Joseph Bailey interviewed more than thirty top executives. He found that all learned firsthand from a mentor.[5] Ralph Waldo Emerson said, "Our chief want in life is somebody who shall make us what we can be." When we find that person, we need to check our growth on a regular basis, asking, "Am I totally availing myself of the teaching I am receiving?" Taking shortcuts in this process will hurt both your mentor and you.

Finally, take the "Masses Test." It asks, "Am I true to my followers?" As leaders, we quickly understand that wrong decisions not only adversely affect us, but they affect those who follow us. However, making a bad decision because of wrong motives is totally different. Before reaching for the reins of leadership, we must realize that we teach what we know and reproduce what we are. Integrity is an inside job.

Advocates of modeling dependability before followers, James M. Kouzes and Barry Z. Posner report in their book, *The Leadership Challenge*, that followers expect four things from their leaders: honesty, competence, vision, and inspiration.[6]

Write out what you value in life. A conviction is a belief or principle that you regularly model, one for which you would be willing to die. What are your convictions?

Ask someone who knows you well what areas of your life he sees as consistent (you do what you say) and what areas he sees as inconsistent (you say but don't always live).

YOU WILL ONLY BECOME WHAT
YOU ARE BECOMING RIGHT NOW

> Though you cannot go back
> and make a brand-new start, my friend.
> Anyone can start from now
> and make a brand-new end.

FOUR

THE ULTIMATE TEST OF LEADERSHIP:
CREATING POSITIVE CHANGE

Change the leader, change the organization. Everything rises and falls on leadership! However, I have found that it's not easy to change leaders. In fact, I've discovered that leaders resist change as much as followers do. The result? Unchanged leaders equals unchanged organizations. People do what people see.

PROFILE OF A LEADER IN TROUBLE

Notice that of the twelve trouble spots for a leader listed below, five deal with an unwillingness to change. That spells trouble for the organization.

- Has a poor understanding of people
- Lacks imagination
- Has personal problems
- Passes the buck
- Feels secure and satisfied
- Is not organized
- Flies into rages

- Will not take a risk
- Is insecure and defensive
- Stays inflexible
- Has no team spirit
- Fights change

Niccolò Machiavelli said, "There is nothing more difficult to take in hand, more perilous to conduct or more uncertain in its success, than to take the lead in the introduction of a new order of things."

The first order of things to be changed is me, the leader. After I consider how hard it is to change myself, then I will understand the challenge of trying to change others. This is the ultimate test of leadership.

A Middle-Eastern mystic said:

> I was a revolutionary when I was young and all my prayer to God was: "Lord, give me the energy to change the world." As I approached middle age and realized that my life was half gone without my changing a single soul, I changed my prayer to: "Lord, give me the grace to change all those who come into contact with me, just my family and friends, and I shall be satisfied." Now that I am an old man and my days are numbered, I have begun to see how foolish I have been. My one prayer now is: "Lord, give me the grace to change myself." If I had prayed for this right from the start, I would not have wasted my life.[1]

Howard Hendricks, in his book *Teaching to Change Lives*, throws a challenge out to every potential leader:

> Write down somewhere in the margins on this page your answer to this question: How have you changed . . . lately? In the last week, let's say? Or in the last month? The last year? Can you be very specific? Or must your answer be incredibly vague? You say you're

growing. Okay . . . how? "Well," you say, "In all kinds of ways." Great! Name one. You see, effective teaching comes only through a changed person. The more you change, the more you become an instrument of change in the lives of others. If you want to become a change agent, you also must change.[2]

Hendricks could have also said, "If you want to continue leading, you must continue changing." Many leaders are no longer leading. They have become like Henry Ford, who is described in Robert Lacy's best-selling biography, *Ford: The Man and the Machine*.[3] Lacy says Ford was a man who loved his Model T so much that he didn't want to change a bolt on it. He even kicked out William Knudsen, his ace production man, because Knudsen thought he saw the sun setting on the Model T. That occurred in 1912, when the Model T was only four years old and at the crest of its popularity. Ford had just returned from a European jaunt, and he went to a Highland Park, Michigan, garage and saw the new design created by Knudsen.

> Change the leader—
> change the organization.

On-the-scene mechanics recorded how Ford momentarily went berserk. He spied the gleaming red lacquer sheen on a new, low-slung version of the Model T that he considered a monstrous perversion of his beloved Model T design. "Ford had his hands in his pockets, and he walked around that car three or four times," recounted an eyewitness. "It was a four-door job, and the top was down. Finally, he got to the left-hand side of the car, and he takes his hands out, gets hold of the door, and bang! He ripped the door right off! . . . How the man done it, I don't know! He jumped in there, and bang goes the other door. Bang goes the windshield. He jumps over the back seat and starts pounding on the top. He rips the top with the heel of his shoe. He wrecked the car as much as he could."

Knudsen left for General Motors. Henry Ford nursed along the Model T, but design changes in competitors' models made it more old-fashioned than he would admit. Competitive necessity finally backed him into making the Model A, though his heart was never in it. Even though General Motors was nipping at Ford's heels, the inventor wanted life to freeze where it was.

Underpinning this theme, William A. Hewitt, Chairman of Deere and Company, says, "To be a leader you must preserve all through your life the attitude of being receptive to new ideas. The quality of leadership you will give will depend upon your ability to evaluate new ideas, to separate change for the sake of change from change for the sake of me."

THE LEADER AS A CHANGE AGENT

Once the leader has personally changed and discerned the difference between novel change and needed change, then that leader must become a change agent. In this world of discontinuities and rapid change, the leader must be out in front to encourage change and growth and to show the way to bring it about. He must first understand the two important requisites to bringing about change: knowing the technical requirements of the change, and understanding the attitude and motivational demands for bringing it about.

> When you're through changing, you're through.

Both requisites are critically necessary. More often than not, though, when results fail to change, it is because of inadequate or inappropriate motivation, not a lack of technical smarts.

A manager usually will be more skilled in the technical requirements of change, whereas the leader will have a better understanding of the attitudinal and motivational demands that the followers need. Note the difference: In the beginning the skills of a leader are essential. No change will ever occur if the psychological needs are unmet. Once change has begun, the skills of a manager are needed to maintain needed change.

Bobb Biehl, in his book *Increasing Your Leadership Confidence*, states it this way: "A change can make sense logically, but still lead to anxiety in the psychological dimension. Everyone needs a niche, and when the niche starts to change after we've become comfortable in it, it causes stress and insecurities. So before introducing change, we have to consider the psychological dimension."[4]

A good exercise when you face change is to make a list of the logical advantages and disadvantages that should result from the change, and then make another list indicating the psychological impact. Just seeing this on a sheet of paper can be clarifying. You may find yourself saying, "I don't like to admit it, but I'm insecure at this point, even though the change makes sense logically."

Another possibility is that a change you're considering may not affect your psychological security, but it doesn't make sense logically when you examine the advantages and disadvantages. The key is to distinguish between the logical and the psychological aspects of any change.

A HISTORICAL ACCOUNT OF RESISTANCE TO CHANGE

There is nothing more difficult to undertake, more perilous to conduct, or more uncertain in its success than introducing change. Why? The leader has for enemies all those who have done well under the old conditions and only lukewarm defenders in those who may do well with the change.

Resistance to change is universal. It invades all classes and cultures. It seizes every generation by the throat and attempts to stop all forward movement toward progress. Many well-educated people, after being confronted with truth, have been unwilling to change their minds.

> Growth equals change.

For example, for centuries people believed that Aristotle was right when he said that the heavier an object, the faster it would fall to earth. Aristotle was regarded as the greatest thinker of all time, and surely he could not be wrong. All it would have taken was for one brave person to take two objects, one heavy and one light, and drop them from a great height to see whether or not the heavier object landed first. But no one stepped forward until nearly two thousand years after Aristotle's death. In 1589, Galileo summoned learned professors to the base of the Leaning Tower of Pisa. Then he went to the top and pushed off two weights, one weighing ten pounds and the other weighing one pound. Both landed at the same time. But the power of belief in the conventional wisdom was so strong that the professors denied what they had seen. They continued to say Aristotle was right.

With his telescope, Galileo proved the theory of Copernicus, that the earth is not the center of the universe; the earth and the planets revolve around the sun. Yet when he tried to change people's beliefs, he was thrown into prison and spent the rest of his life under house arrest.

Resisting change can unwittingly affect one's health and life, as the following account portrays. Hippocrates described scurvy in ancient times. The disease seemed to especially plague armies in the field and cities that were under siege for long periods of time. Later, following the discovery of America, when long sea voyages became common, scurvy became rampant among sailors. Little was known about what caused scurvy and less about its cure, although elaborate theories and remedies were prescribed. None of them was completely effective, and most were worthless.

In 1553, Cartier made his second voyage to Newfoundland. Of his 103-man crew, 100 developed agonizing scurvy and were in great anguish when the Iroquois Indians of Quebec came to their rescue with what was described as a "miraculous cure." The Iroquois Indians gave the sick sailors an infusion of bark and leaves of the pine tree.

In 1553, Admiral Sir Richard Hawkins noted that during his career on the high seas, ten thousand seamen under his command had died of scurvy. He also recorded that in his experience sour oranges and lemons had been most effective in curing the disease. Yet these observations had no sweeping effect in bringing about an awareness of what could prevent scurvy, and the observations of this admiral went unheeded.

James Lind, a British naval surgeon, who later became the chief physician of the Naval Hospital at Portsmouth, England, published a book in 1753 in which he stated explicitly that scurvy could be eliminated simply by supplying sailors with lemon juice. He cited many case histories from his experience as a naval surgeon at sea; he proved that such things as mustard cress, tamarinds, oranges, and lemons would prevent scurvy. In fact, anything that contains enough vitamin C, which is most abundant in citrus fruit, tomatoes, and to a lesser degree in most green vegetables and other fruits, will prevent scurvy.

You might rightfully expect that Dr. Lind would have been highly honored and praised for this great contribution, but the reverse is true. He was ridiculed. He became frustrated and remarked bitterly, "Some persons cannot be brought to believe that a disease so fatal and so dreaded can be cured or prevented by such easy means." They would have more faith in an elaborate composition dignified with the title of "an antiscorbutic golden elixir" or the like. The "some persons" to whom Dr. Lind referred were My Lords of the Admiralty and other physicians. In fact, they ignored Dr. Lind's advice for forty years. One sea captain did take his advice—the now-famous Captain James Cook, who stocked his ships with an ample supply of fresh fruits.

The Royal Society honored Captain Cook in 1776 for his success, but the officials of the navy ignored his report. Not until 1794, the year of Dr. Lind's death, was a British navy squadron supplied with lemon juice before a voyage. On that voyage, which lasted twenty-three weeks, there was not one case of scurvy, yet another decade passed before regulations were enacted requiring sailors to drink a daily ration of lemon juice to prevent scurvy. With this enactment, scurvy disappeared from the British Navy.[5]

The needless loss of life simply because masses of people were resistant to change was more than unfortunate. It was outrageous. Don't let your attitude toward change or your own predisposition to avoid it create detrimental hindrances to your own personal success as a leader.

How Do You Write the Word "Attitude"?

Directions:
1. Write the word *attitude* on the left line with your "writing" hand.
2. Write the word *attitude* on the right line with your other hand.

    ATTITUDE   ATTITUDE
    _____   _____

The word *attitude* written   The word *attitude* written
with your writing hand.   with your other hand.

Application:

When you look at the word *attitude* written by the hand you do not write with, you see a picture of the kind of attitude we usually have when we are trying to do something new. As one person said, "Nothing should ever be done for the first time."

WHY PEOPLE RESIST CHANGE

In a *Peanuts* cartoon, Charlie Brown says to Linus: "Perhaps you can give me an answer, Linus. What would you do if you felt that no one liked you?" Linus replies, "I'd try to look at myself objectively, and see what I could do to *improve*. That's *my* answer, Charlie Brown." To which Charlie replies, "I *hate* that answer!"

There are a number of reasons why many of us, like Charlie Brown, resist change.

THE CHANGE ISN'T SELF-INITIATED

When people lack ownership of an idea, they usually resist it, even when it is in their best interest! They simply don't like the idea of being manipulated or feeling like pawns of the system. Wise leaders allow followers to give input and be a part of the process of change. Most of the time the key to my attitude about change is whether I am initiating it (in which case I am all for it) or someone else is imposing the change on me (which tends to make me more resistant).

ROUTINE IS DISRUPTED

Habits allow us to do things without much thought, which is why most of us have so many of them. Habits are not instincts. They are acquired reactions. They don't just happen; they are caused. First we form habits, but then our habits form us. Change threatens our habit patterns and forces us to think, reevaluate, and sometimes unlearn past behavior.

When I was a teenager, I became interested in golf. Regrettably, I taught myself instead of taking lessons. After a few years and the innocent acquisition of many bad habits, I played a game of golf with an excellent player. At the close of the round, he jokingly said my main problem seemed to be that I was too close to the ball after I hit it! Then he seriously offered to help me. He shared honestly how I would need to make some changes if my golf game was to improve. When I asked him to specify what changes I needed to make, he said, "Everything!" For the next year I had to unlearn old habits. It was one of the most difficult experiences of my life. Many times I was tempted to return to my old habits for temporary relief from working so hard and still playing so badly.

Change Creates Fear of the Unknown

Change means traveling in uncharted waters, and this causes our insecurities to rise. Therefore, many people are more comfortable with old problems than with new solutions. They are like the congregation that desperately needed a new building but were afraid to venture out. During a service some plaster fell from the ceiling and hit the chairman of the board. Immediately a meeting was called and the following decisions were made:

One: We will build a new church.
Two: We will build a new church on the same site
       as the old one.
Three: We will use the materials of the old church
       to build the new one.
Four   We will worship in the old church until
       the new church is built.

Some people are open to change as long as it doesn't inconvenience them or cost anything.

The Purpose of the Change Is Unclear

Employees resist change when they hear about it from a secondhand source. When a decision has been made, the longer it takes for employees to hear and the further the desired change is from the decision maker, the more resistance it will receive. That's why decisions should be made at the lowest level possible. The decision maker, because of close proximity to the issue, will make a better decision, and those most affected by the decision will know it quickly by hearing it from a source close to them and to the problem.

Change Creates Fear of Failure

Elbert Hubbard said that the greatest mistake a person can make is to be afraid of making one. It is tragic when success has "gone to my head." It is even more tragic if failure goes to my head. When this happens, I begin to agree with Larry Anderson, the pitcher for the San Diego Padres. He said, "If at first you don't succeed, failure may be your thing." Too many people, fearing that failure is their thing, hold tenaciously to whatever they feel comfortable with and continually resist change.

The Rewards for Change Don't Match the Effort Change Requires

People will not change until they perceive that the advantages of changing outweigh the disadvantages of continuing with the way things are. What leaders sometimes fail to recognize is that the followers will always weigh the advantage/disadvantage issue in light of personal gain/loss, not organizational gain/loss.

People Are Too Satisfied with the Way Things Are

As the following story from *Parables* reveals, many organizations and people will choose to die before they will choose to change.

In the 1940s, the Swiss watch was the most prestigious and best quality watch in the world. Consequently, 80 percent of the watches sold in the world were made in Switzerland. In the late '50s, the digital watch was presented to the leaders of the Swiss watch company. They rejected this new idea because they knew they already had the best watch and the best watchmakers. The man who developed the digital watch subsequently sold the idea to Seiko.

In 1940, Swiss watch-making companies employed eighty thousand people. Today they employ eighteen thousand. In 1940, 80 percent of the watches sold in the world were made in Switzerland. Today 80 percent of the watches are digital. This story represents what happens to many organizations and people: We choose to die rather than choose to change.

CHANGE WON'T HAPPEN WHEN PEOPLE ENGAGE IN NEGATIVE THINKING

Regardless of his state in the present, the negative thinker finds disappointment in the future. The epitaph on a negative person's headstone should read, "I expected this." This type of thinking can best be described by a sign I read several years ago in an office building:

> Don't look—you might see.
> Don't listen—you might hear.
> Don't think—you might learn.
> Don't make a decision—you might be wrong.
> Don't walk—you might stumble.
> Don't run—you might fall.
> Don't live—you might die.

I would like to add one more thought to this depressing list:

> Don't change—you might grow.

THE FOLLOWERS LACK RESPECT FOR THE LEADER

When followers don't like the leader who oversees the change, their feelings won't allow them to look at the change objectively. In other words, people view the change according to the way they view the change agent.

One of the principles I share in leadership conferences is, "You've got to love 'em before you can lead 'em." When you love your followers genuinely and correctly, they'll respect and follow you through many changes.

THE LEADER IS SUSCEPTIBLE TO FEELINGS OF PERSONAL CRITICISM

Sometimes leaders resist change. For example, if a leader has developed a program that is now being phased out for something better, he or she may feel the change is a personal attack and will react defensively.

For growth and continual effectiveness, every organization must go through a continuous four-stage cycle of create, conserve, criticize, and change. The figure below illustrates the cycle.

Stages 1 and 4 are the offensive functions of an organization. Stages 2 and 3 are the defensive functions. Either the creators handle criticism positively and begin to make changes, or they will be replaced by those who will embrace change and, therefore, create.

CHANGE MAY MEAN PERSONAL LOSS

Whenever change is imminent, the question on everyone's mind is, "How will this affect me?" Usually there are three groups of people within the organization: (1) those who will lose; (2) those who are neutral; and (3) those who will benefit. Each group is different and must be handled with sensitivity, but also with straightforwardness.

CHANGE REQUIRES ADDITIONAL COMMITMENT

Time is the most precious commodity for many people. Whenever change is about to happen, we all look to see how it will affect our time. Usually we conclude that increased change will be fine *if* it does not increase our time commitment. Sidney Howard said that half of knowing what you want is knowing what you must give up before you get it. When the cost of change is time, many will resist the change.

When it comes to the commitment of time, the leader must determine if the person is *unwilling* or *unable* to change. Willingness deals with attitude, and there is little you can do if your followers resist change because of attitude. But ability to change deals with perspective. Many people are willing to change but, because of the way they perceive their present circumstances and responsibilities, they are unable to change. At this point, the leader can help by prioritizing tasks, eliminating nonessentials, and focusing on the consequential value of changing.

NARROW-MINDEDNESS THWARTS ACCEPTANCE OF NEW IDEAS

In 1993, approximately sixteen hundred people belonged to the International Flat Earth Research Society of America. Their president, Charles K. Johnson, said he's been a flat-earther all his life. "When I saw the globe in grade school I didn't accept it then and I don't accept it now."

That reminds me of the man who lived in Maine and turned one hundred years of age. A reporter drove up from New York City to interview the old man. Sitting on the front porch, the reporter said, "I'll bet you've seen a lot of changes in your lifetime." The old man replied, "Yes, and I've been agin' every one of them."

TRADITION RESISTS CHANGE

I love this joke: "How many people does it take to change a lightbulb?" Answer: "Four. One to change the bulb and three to reminisce about how good the old lightbulb was."

People like that remind me of the old army sergeant who was put in charge of a plot of grass in front of administrative headquarters in a camp in Michigan. The sergeant promptly delegated the job to a buck private and told him to water the grass every day at five o'clock. The private did this conscientiously. One day there was a terrific thunderstorm, and the sergeant walked into the barracks and saw the private doing bunk fatigue.

"What's the matter with you?" the sergeant bellowed. "It's five o'clock, and you're supposed to be out watering the grass!"

"But, Sergeant," the private said, looking confused, "it's raining; look at the thunderstorm."

"So what?" yelled the sergeant. "You've got a raincoat, haven't you?"

Cornfield's Law says that nothing is ever done until everyone is convinced that it ought to be done, and has been convinced for so long that it is now time to do something else.

A CHECKLIST FOR CHANGE

Below are the questions you should review *before* attempting changes within an organization. When the questions can be answered with a yes, change tends to be easier. Questions that can only be answered with no (or maybe) usually indicate that change will be difficult.

YES   NO

____   ____   Will this change benefit the followers?

____   ____   Is this change compatible with the purpose
of the organization?

____   ____   Is this change specific and clear?

____   ____   Are the top 20 percent (the influencers) in favor
of this change?

____   ____   Is it possible to test this change before making a
total commitment to it?

____   ____   Are physical, financial, and human resources
available to make this change?

____   ____   Is this change reversible?

____   ____   Is this change the next obvious step?

____   ____   Does this change have both short- and
long-range benefits?

____   ____   Is the leadership capable of bringing
about this change?

____   ____   Is the timing right?

At times every leader feels like Lucy, when she was leaning against a fence with Charlie Brown. "I would like to change the world," she said. Charlie Brown asked, "Where would you start?" She replied, "I would start with you!"

The last question, "Is the timing right?" is the ultimate consideration for implementing change. A leader's success in bringing about change in others will happen only if the timing is right. In my book *The Winning Attitude*, this subject is discussed in short order:

The wrong decision at the wrong time = disaster.

The wrong decision at the right time = mistake.

The right decision at the wrong time = unacceptance.

The right decision at the right time = success.

People change when they *hurt* enough that they *have* to change; *learn* enough that they *want* to change; *receive* enough that they are *able* to change. The leader must recognize when people are in one of these three stages. In fact, top leaders create an atmosphere that causes one of these three things to occur.[6]

THE EVOLUTIONARY PROCESS OF CHANGE

It is helpful to remember that change can be seen as either *revolutionary* (something totally different from what has been) or *evolutionary* (a refinement of what has been). It is usually easier to present change as a simple refinement of "the way we've been doing it" rather than something big, new, and completely different. When a proposal for change is introduced in the organization, people fall into five categories in terms of their response.

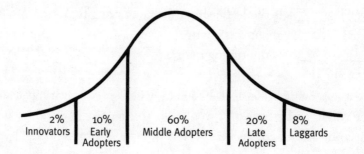

| 2% Innovators | 10% Early Adopters | 60% Middle Adopters | 20% Late Adopters | 8% Laggards |

Innovators Are the Dreamers

They are the originators of new ideas and generally are not acknowledged as leaders or policy makers.

Early Adopters Are Those Who Know a Good Idea When They See It

Their opinions are respected in the organization. Although they did not create the idea, they will try to convince others to accept it.

MIDDLE ADOPTERS ARE THE MAJORITY

They will respond to the opinions of others. Generally they are reasonable in their analysis of a new idea, but inclined to maintain the status quo. They can be influenced by the positive or negative influencers of the organization.

LATE ADOPTERS ARE THE LAST GROUP TO ENDORSE AN IDEA

They often speak against proposed changes and may never verbally acknowledge acceptance. Generally they will adopt it if the majority demonstrates support.

LAGGARDS ARE ALWAYS AGAINST CHANGE

Their commitment is to the status quo and the past. Often they try to create division within the organization.[7]

The evolutionary process of successful change within an organization can be summed up in the eight steps that must occur as the organization moves from ignorance about the desired change and the effects it will have to a mind-set of willingness and innovation.

Step 1: **Ignorance.** No unified direction or sense of priorities is felt among the followers. They are "in the dark."

Step 2: **Information.** General information is given to the people. Initially the ideas for change are not embraced.

Step 3: **Infusion.** The penetration of new ideas into the status quo may cause confrontations with apathy, prejudice, and tradition. The general tendency is to focus on problems.

Step 4: **Individual Change.** The "early adopters" begin to see the benefits of the proposed change and embrace them. Personal convictions replace complacency.

Step 5: **Organizational Change.** Two sides of the issue are being discussed. Less defensiveness and more openness concerning proposed changes can be observed. The momentum shifts from antichange to prochange.

Step 6: **Awkward Application.** Some failures and some successes are experienced as the change is implemented. The learning process is rapid.

Step 7: **Integration.** Awkwardness begins to decrease, and the acceptance level increases. A growing sense of accomplishment and a secondary wave of results and successes occur.

Step 8: **Innovation.** Significant results create confidence and a willingness to take risks. The result is a willingness to change more rapidly and boldly.

As Step 8 is taken, the organization as a whole is more willing to go through the process again. The major effect of the process develops as the majority of the organization is exposed repeatedly to the new idea.

1st Exposure: "I reject that thought because it conflicts with my preconceived ideas."

2nd Exposure: "Well, I understand it, but I can't accept it."

3rd Exposure: "I agree with the idea but have reservations as to its use."

4th Exposure: "You know, that idea pretty well expresses the way I feel about the subject."

5th Exposure: "I used that idea today. It's terrific!"

6th Exposure: "I gave that idea to someone yesterday. In the truest sense of the word, that idea now belongs to me."

CREATING A CLIMATE FOR CHANGE

Human behavior studies show that people do not basically resist change; they resist "being changed."[8] This section will emphasize how to create an atmosphere that will encourage others to be changed. Unless people are changed, change will not happen. The first statement of this chapter read, "Change the leader, change the organization." Now we will start with the leader and develop a strategy for the organization.

THE LEADER MUST DEVELOP TRUST WITH PEOPLE

It is wonderful when the people believe in the leader. It is more wonderful when the leader believes in the people. When both are a reality, trust is the result. The more people trust the leader, the more willing they will be to accept the leader's proposed changes. Warren Bennis and Bert Nanus say that "trust is the emotional glue that binds followers and leaders together."[9] Abraham Lincoln said, "If you would win a man to your cause, first convince him that you are his true friend. Next, probe to discover what he wants to accomplish."

My first question to a leader who wants to make changes within an organization is always, "What is your relationship with your people?" If the relationship is positive, then the leader is ready to take the next step.

THE LEADER MUST MAKE PERSONAL CHANGES BEFORE ASKING OTHERS TO CHANGE

Sadly, too many leaders are like my friend who made a list of New Year's resolutions: be nicer to people; eat nutritious food; be more giving to friends; cut down on sweets and fats; be less critical of others.

My friend showed me the list, and I was quite impressed. They were great goals. "But," I asked her, "do you think you'll be able to meet all of them?"

"Why should I?" she answered. "This list is for you!"

Andrew Carnegie said, "As I grow older, I pay less attention to what men say. I just watch what they do." Great leaders not only say what should be done, they show it!

Good Leaders Understand the History of the Organization

The longer an organization has gone without change, the more effort introducing it will require. Also, when change is implemented and the result is negative, people within the organization will be leery of embracing future changes. The opposite is also true. Successful changes in the past prepare people to readily accept more changes.

G. K. Chesterton suggests, "Don't take the fence down until you know the reason it was put up." It is important to know what happened in the past before making changes for the future.

Place Influencers in Leadership Positions

Leaders have two characteristics. First, they are going somewhere; and second, they are able to persuade other people to go with them. They are like the chairman of a large corporation, who was late for a meeting. Bolting into the room, he took the nearest available seat rather than moving to his accustomed spot. One of his young aides protested, "Please, sir, you should be at the head of the table." The executive, who had a healthy understanding of his place in the company, answered, "Son, wherever I sit is the head of the table."

Check the "Change in Your Pocket"

Every leader is given a certain amount of "change" (emotional support in the form of bargaining chips) at the beginning of a relationship. If the relationship weakens, the leader gives up "change" until it is possible for him to become bankrupt with the organization. If the relationship strengthens, the leader receives "change" until it is possible for him to become rich with the organization. Always remember: *it takes "change" to make change.* The more "change" in the pocket of the leader, the more changes that can be made in the lives of the people. Sadly, the opposite is also true.

GOOD LEADERS SOLICIT THE SUPPORT OF INFLUENCERS *BEFORE* THE CHANGE IS MADE PUBLIC

This ten-item checklist includes all the steps a good leader will go through in soliciting support for a change from the major influencers in his organization.

1. List the major influencer(s) of the major groups within your organization.

2. How many will be affected *directly* by this change? (These people are the most important group.)

3. How many will be affected *indirectly* by this change?

4. How many will probably be positive?

5. How many will probably be negative?

6. Which group is the majority?

7. Which group is the most influential?

8. If the positive group is stronger, bring the influencers together for discussion.

9. If the negative group is stronger, meet with the influencers individually.

10. Know the "key" to each influencer.

DEVELOP A MEETING AGENDA THAT WILL ASSIST CHANGE

Every new idea goes through three phases: it will not work; it will cost too much; and, I thought it was a good idea all along.

A wise leader, understanding that people change through a process, will develop a meeting agenda to enhance this process. One that I have used for fifteen years has proved quite effective.

Information Items: Items of interest to those attending the meeting; positive items that boost morale. (This starts the meeting off on a high level.)

Study Items: Issues to be discussed but not voted on. (This allows the sharing of ideas without the pressure to represent a particular point of view.)

Action Items: Issues to be voted on that have previously been study items. (This allows discussion to be made that has already been processed. If major change is required, keep the issue in the study category until it has been allowed time for acceptance.)

ENCOURAGE THE INFLUENCERS TO INFLUENCE OTHERS INFORMALLY

Major changes should not surprise people. A "leadership leak" done properly will prepare the people for the formal meeting.

Each year I explain to my key leaders that they carry two buckets around with them. One bucket is filled with gasoline and the other with water. Whenever there is a "little fire" of contention within the organization because the people fear a possible change, the influencers are the first to hear about it. When they arrive on the scene, they will either throw the bucket of gasoline on the situation and really cause a problem, or they will throw the bucket of water on the little fire and extinguish the problem. In other words, key influences are either the leader's greatest asset or his greatest liability.

Leadership leaks should be planned and positive, preparing the people for the meeting where the change will be formally presented.

SHOW THE PEOPLE HOW THE CHANGE WILL BENEFIT THEM

Assumption: The proposed change is what is best for the people, not the leader. The people must be first.

A sign on the door in a bus station read: "For the convenience of others, please close the door." Too often the door remained open until the sign was changed to read: "For your *own* personal comfort, please close the door." The door was always shut. Too often leaders of an organization tend to think and lead from the company's perspective, not the people's.

GIVE THE PEOPLE OWNERSHIP OF THE CHANGE

Openness by the leader paves the way for ownership by the people. Without ownership, changes will be short-term. Changing people's habits and ways of thinking is like writing instructions in the snow during a snowstorm. Every twenty minutes the instructions must be rewritten, unless ownership is given along with the instructions.

HOW TO OFFER OWNERSHIP OF CHANGE TO OTHERS

1. Inform people in advance so they'll have time to think about the implications of the change and how it will affect them.

2. Explain the overall objectives of the change—the reasons for it and how and when it will occur.

3. Show people how the change will benefit them. Be honest with the employees who may lose out as a result of the change. Alert them early and provide assistance to help them find another job if necessary.

4. Ask those who will be affected by the change to participate in all stages of the change process.

5. Keep communication channels open. Provide opportunities for employees to discuss the change. Encourage questions, comments, and other feedback.

6. Be flexible and adaptable throughout the change process. Admit mistakes and make changes where appropriate.

7. Constantly demonstrate your belief in and commitment to the change. Indicate your confidence in their ability to implement the change.

8. Provide enthusiasm, assistance, appreciation, and recognition to those implementing the change.[10]

CHANGE WILL HAPPEN

The question should not be "Will we ever change?" but "When and how much will we change?" Nothing stays the same except the fact that change is always present. Even in the beginning, Adam reportedly said to Eve, as they were led out of paradise, "My dear, we live in a time of transition."

Charles Exley, CEO of NCR Corporation, said, "I've been in business thirty-six years. I've learned a lot and most of it doesn't apply anymore."

Writer Lincoln Barnett once described the excitement he shared with a group of students emerging from a physics lecture at the Institute for Advanced Study at Princeton. "How did it go?" someone asked.

"Wonderful!" Mr. Barnett replied. "Everything we knew last week isn't true."

Keeping current with the changes and relating them to the organization is a constant challenge for the leader. Leaders should be aware, for example, of information such as the following, which was outlined in an article written by Dr. Richard Caldwell.[11] He contrasts some of the values of the 1950s with those of the 1990s.

1950s	1990s
Saving	Spending
Delayed gratification	Instant gratification
Ozzie and Harriet	Latchkey kids
Certainty	Ambivalence
Orthodoxy	Skepticism
Investing	Leveraging

Neighborhood	Lifestyle
Middle class	Under class
Export	Import
Public virtue	Personal well-being
Mom and Dad	Nanny and day care
Press conference	Photo opportunity
Achievement	Fame
Knowledge	Credentials
Manufacturing	Service
Duty	Divorce
"We"	"Me"

NOT ALL CHANGE IS IMPROVEMENT, BUT WITHOUT CHANGE THERE CAN BE NO IMPROVEMENT

Change = Growth

or

Change = Grief

Change represents both possible opportunity and potential loss. My observation is that change becomes grief when:

- the change proposed is a bad idea.

- the change proposed is not accepted by the influencers.

- the change proposed is not presented effectively.

- the change proposed is self-serving to the leaders.

- the change proposed is based solely on the past.

- the changes proposed are too many, happening too quickly.

In 1950, *Fortune* magazine asked eleven distinguished Americans to predict what life would be like in 1980. In those days, the United States enjoyed a trade surplus of $3 billion, so no one predicted a trade deficit thirty years later. David Sarnoff, chairman of RCA, was sure that by

1980, ships, airplanes, locomotives, and even individual automobiles would be atomically fueled. He said that homes would have atomic generators and that guided missiles would transport mail and other freight over great distances. Henry R. Luce, editor-in-chief of *Time* magazine, predicted the end of poverty by 1980. Mathematician John von Neumann expected energy to be free thirty years later.

IT'S NEVER TOO LATE TO CHANGE

Max Depree said, "In the end, it is important to remember that we cannot become what we need to be by remaining what we are."[12] It's a fact that when you're through changing, you're through.

When you hear the name Alfred Nobel, what do you think of? The Nobel Peace Prize might come to mind. However, that's only chapter 2 of his story. Alfred Nobel was the Swedish chemist who made his fortune by inventing dynamite and the other powerful explosives used for weapons. When his brother died, one newspaper accidentally printed Alfred's obituary instead. It described the dead man as one who became rich by enabling people to kill each other in unprecedented numbers. Shaken by this assessment, Nobel resolved to use his fortune from then on to award accomplishments that benefited humanity. Nobel had the rare opportunity to evaluate his life at its end and yet live long enough to change that assessment.[13]

Comedian Jerry Lewis says that the best wedding gift he received was a film of the entire wedding ceremony. He says that when things got really bad in his marriage, he would go into a room, close the door, run the film backward, and walk out a free man.

I doubt you will be able to run the film backward or read your obituary in the newspaper. You can, however, make a choice today to change. And when change is successful, you will look back at it and call it growth.

FIVE

THE QUICKEST WAY TO GAIN LEADERSHIP:
PROBLEM SOLVING

According to F. F. Fournies, writing in *Coaching for Improved Work Performance*,[1] there are four common reasons why people do not perform the way they should:

1. They do not know *what* they are supposed to do.

2. They do not know *how* to do it.

3. They do not know *why* they should.

4. There are obstacles beyond their control.

These four reasons why people fail to perform at their potential are all responsibilities of leadership. The first three reasons deal with starting a job correctly. A training program, job description, proper tools, and vision, along with good communication skills, will go a long way in effectively meeting the first three issues.

This chapter will deal with the fourth reason that causes many people to fail to reach their performance potential. Problems continually occur at work, at home, and in life in general. My observation is that people don't like problems, weary of them quickly, and will do almost anything to get away from them. This climate makes others place the reins of leadership into your hands—*if* you are willing and able to either tackle their problems or train them to solve them. Your problem-solving skills will always be needed, because people always have problems. And when problems occur, notice where people go to solve them (see chart below).

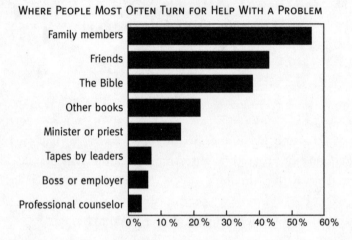

WHERE PEOPLE MOST OFTEN TURN FOR HELP WITH A PROBLEM

This chapter will deal with the two things needed to effectively solve problems: the right attitude and the right action plan.

Before these two areas are explored, I want to share with you some observations I have made about people and their problems.

WE ALL HAVE PROBLEMS

Sometimes our problems overwhelm us, as they did my friend Joe. Before Joe could get out of his house and head for work, he had four long-distance calls. Everyone seemed to have a problem. And they all wanted Joe to get on a plane that day and come help out. He finally told his wife to forget about his breakfast. He rushed out of the house as fast as he could. Then, when he stepped into the garage, he discovered his car would not start. So he called a taxi. While he was waiting for the taxi, he got another call about another problem. Finally, the taxi came and Joe rushed out, piled in the backseat, and yelled, "All right, let's get going."

"Where do you want me to take you?" the taxi driver asked.

> The size of the person is more important than the size of the problem.

"I don't care where we go," Joe shouted. "I've got problems everywhere."

Sometimes we think our generation has more problems than the last. I laughed at this idea after I reflected on the words of Dwight Bohmbach in *What's Right with America*:

America's elders lived through the great 1929 stock market crash that ruined many of their families; the Depression years; the Bonus March on Washington, when veterans were dispersed by Army troops; the New Deal years; Pearl Harbor; the loss of the Philippines; years of long days and nights in defense plants in the 1940s; fighting in Europe and the Pacific; D-Day; the Battle of the Bulge; V-E Day; the hope-filled beginning of the United Nations in America; the A-bomb; V-J Day; the Marshall Plan in Europe; the Berlin airlift; war in Korea; the U-2 incident; the Bay of Pigs invasion; the Cuban missile crisis; the killings of President Kennedy, Bobby Kennedy, and Martin Luther King Jr.; the civil rights struggle; the Vietnam War; Americans on the moon; Watergate and the resignation of a president and vice president; the energy crisis; Three-Mile Island; Iranian hostages; a new president shot in 1981; the bombing of our embassy and hundreds of Marines in Lebanon; becoming a debtor nation, with the highest budget deficit in history. What a lifetime!

We should remember the words of Paul Harvey, who said that in times like these it is always helpful to remember that there have always been times like these.

PROBLEMS GIVE MEANING TO LIFE

A wise philosopher once commented that an eagle's only obstacle to overcome for flying with greater speed and ease is the air. Yet, if the air were withdrawn and the proud bird were to fly in a vacuum, it would fall instantly to the ground, unable to fly at all. The very element that offers resistance to flying is at the same time the condition for flight.

People need to change their perspectives, not their problems.

The main obstacle that a powerboat has to overcome is the water against the propeller, yet, if it were not for this same resistance, the boat would not move at all.

The same law, that obstacles are conditions of success, holds true in human life. A life free of all obstacles and difficulties would reduce all possibilities and powers to zero. Eliminate problems, and life loses its creative tension. The problem of mass ignorance gives meaning to education. The problem of ill health gives meaning to medicine. The problem of social disorder gives meaning to government.

OPPORTUNITIES FOR CHANGE AND GROWTH

In the South, when cotton was "king," the boll weevil crossed over from Mexico to the United States and destroyed the cotton plants. Farmers were forced to grow a variety of crops, such as soybeans and peanuts. They learned to use their land to raise cattle, hogs, and chickens. As a result, many more farmers became prosperous than in the days when the only crop grown was cotton.

The people of Enterprise, Alabama, were so grateful for what had occurred that in 1910 they erected a monument to the boll weevil. When they turned from the single-crop system to diversified farming, they became wealthier. The inscription on the monument reads: "In profound appreciation of the boll weevil and what it has done to herald prosperity."

We all have a tendency all of our lives to want to get rid of problems and responsibilities. When that temptation arises, remember the youth who was questioning a lonely old man. "What is life's heaviest burden?" he asked. The old fellow answered sadly, "Having nothing to carry."

MANY OUTSTANDING PEOPLE HAVE OVERCOME PROBLEMS IN THEIR LIVES

Many of the Psalms were born in difficulty. "Most of the Epistles were written in prisons. Most of the greatest thoughts of the greatest thinkers of all time had to pass through the fire. Bunyan wrote *Pilgrim's Progress* from jail. Florence Nightingale, too ill to move from her bed, reorganized the hospitals of England. Semiparalyzed and under constant menace of apoplexy, Pasteur was tireless in his attack on disease. During the greater part of his life, American historian Francis Parkman suffered so acutely that he could not work for more than five minutes at a time. His eyesight was so wretched that he could scrawl only a few gigantic words on a manuscript, but he contrived to write twenty magnificent volumes of history."[2]

> Policies are many; principles are few. Policies will change; principles never do.

Bury a person in the snows of Valley Forge, and you have a George Washington. Raise him in abject poverty, and you have an Abraham Lincoln. Strike him down with infantile paralysis, and he becomes a Franklin D. Roosevelt. Burn him so severely that the doctors say he will never walk again, and you have a Glenn Cunningham, who set the world's one-mile record in 1934. Have him or her born black in a society filled with racial discrimination, and you have a Booker T. Washington, a Marian Anderson, a George Washington Carver, or a Martin Luther King Jr. Call him a slow learner and retarded—writing him off as uneducable—and you have an Albert Einstein.

Dolly Parton sums it all up with these words: "The way I see it, if you want the rainbow, you gotta put up with the rain."

MY PROBLEM IS *NOT* MY PROBLEM

There is a world of difference between a person who has a big problem and a person who makes a problem big. For several years I would do between twenty and thirty hours of counseling each week. I soon discovered that the people who came to see me were not necessarily the ones who had the most problems. They were the ones who were problem conscious and found their difficulties stressful. Naïve at first, I would try to fix their problems, only to discover that they would go out and find others. They were like Charlie Brown in a Christmas special—he just couldn't get the Christmas spirit. Linus finally said, "Charlie Brown, you're the only person I know who can take a wonderful season like Christmas and turn it into a problem."

Linus, I have news for you. There are many people like Charlie Brown! Their "problems" are not their real problems. The problem is that they react wrongly to "problems" and therefore make their "problems" real problems. What really counts is not what happens *to me* but what happens *in me*.

A study of three hundred highly successful people, people like Franklin Delano Roosevelt, Helen Keller, Winston Churchill, Albert Schweitzer, Mahatma Gandhi, and Albert Einstein, reveals that one-fourth had handicaps, such as blindness, deafness, or crippled limbs. Three-fourths had either been born in poverty, came from broken homes, or at least came from exceedingly tense or disturbed situations.

Always take the high road.

Why did the achievers overcome problems, while thousands are overwhelmed by theirs? They refused to hold on to the common excuses for failure. They turned their stumbling blocks into stepping-stones. They realized they could not determine every circumstance in life, but they could determine their choice of attitude toward every circumstance.

I read about a church choir that was raising money to attend a music competition and decided to have a car wash. To their dismay, after a busy morning, rain began to pour in midafternoon, and the customers stopped coming. Finally, one of the women printed this poster: "WE WASH; [and with an arrow pointed skyward] HE RINSES!"

The *Los Angeles Times* recently ran this quote: "If you can smile whenever anything goes wrong, you are either a nitwit or a repairman." I would add: or a leader in the making—one who realizes that the only problem you have is the one you allow to be a problem because of your wrong reaction to it. Problems can stop you temporarily. You are the only one who can do it permanently.

A Problem Is Something I Can Do Something About

My friend and mentor, Fred Smith, taught me this truth. If I can't do something about a problem, it's not my problem; it's a fact of life.

In 1925, an American company manufacturing and marketing shaving cream was concerned about the effectiveness of its roadside advertising. With the introduction of "high-speed" automobiles, they were concerned that nobody had time to read their billboards. So the company, Burma Shave, created a series of small signs spaced at sufficient intervals so they could be read even at high speeds. The unique approach to advertising made Burma Shave a household name for forty-six years.

As a child growing up in Ohio, I loved the Burma Shave advertisements. This was my favorite:

> A peach looks good
> With lots of fuzz . . .
> But man's no peach . . .
> And never was.

The Burma Shave company became creative with a changing society. If there had been no answer to the problem, then there would have been no problem—just a fact of life. Be careful in resigning yourself to the position that there is no answer to a problem. Someone else may come along with a solution.

A Test of a Leader is the Ability to Recognize a Problem Before It Becomes an Emergency

Under excellent leadership a problem seldom reaches gigantic proportions, because it is recognized and fixed in its early stages.

Great leaders usually recognize a problem in the following sequence:

1. They sense it before they see it (intuition).

2. They begin looking for it and ask questions (curiosity).

3. They gather data (processing).

4. They share their feelings and findings to a few trusted colleagues (communicating).

5. They define the problem (writing).

6. They check their resources (evaluating).

7. They make a decision (leading).

Great leaders are seldom blindsided. They realize that the punch that knocks them out is seldom the hard one—it's the one they didn't see coming. Therefore, they are always looking for signs and indicators that will give them insight into the problem ahead and their odds of fixing it. They treat problems like the potential trespasser of an Indiana farm who read this sign on a fence post, "If you cross this field, you better do it in 9.8 seconds. The bull can do it in 10 seconds."

YOU CAN JUDGE LEADERS BY THE SIZE OF THE PROBLEMS THEY TACKLE

Lots of Charlie Brown references

In one of the *Peanuts* comic strips, Charlie Brown says, "There's no problem so big that I can't run from it." We all have felt exactly like the lion tamer who put this advertisement in the paper: "Lion tamer wants tamer lion."

Yet, in my observations of people and their problems, I have noticed that the size of the person is more important than the size of the problem. Problems look larger or smaller according to whether the person is large or small.

Recently, I spoke with Marcia, a lady who was diagnosed with cancer two years ago and had a mastectomy. She is doing very well. But she shared with me a concern for others who had the problem and were not doing well. There seemed to be a big difference between Marcia and others who had the same problem. I could have predicted physical recovery for Marcia. She was positive from the beginning of her problem. Our focus as a leader should be to build big people. Big people will handle big issues effectively.

SOLVE TASK PROBLEMS QUICKLY; PEOPLE PROBLEMS WILL TAKE LONGER

Solving problems may be the immediate agenda, but that should never be where we spend most of our time. If all we do is focus on solving the next problem at hand, we will soon feel like the farmer who said, "The hardest thing about milking cows is that they never stay milked." Problems never stop, but people can stop problems. My suggestion for producing problem solvers are:

1. *Make a time commitment to people.* Those who never take time to develop people are forced to take time to solve their problems.

2. *Never solve a problem for a person; solve it with that person.* Take that individual through the sequence that has already been given for recognizing a problem. In fact, spend time with that person and study this entire chapter together.

Problems should be solved at the lowest level possible. President John F. Kennedy said that President Eisenhower gave him this advice the day before his inauguration: "You'll find no easy problems ever come to the president of the United States. If they are easy to solve, somebody else has solved them." That statement should be true of every leader. Climbing the ladder of leadership means that fewer but more important decisions will be made. The problem-solving skills of a leader must be sharpened, because every decision becomes a major decision. John E. Hunter said, "A situation only becomes a problem when one does not have sufficient resources to meet it." The rest of the chapter will deal with what is needed to effectively solve problems.

THE RIGHT ATTITUDE

The subject of our attitude is so important for potential leaders that the next chapter will be given to it totally. Therefore, a few thoughts will be sufficient at this time. Norman Vincent Peale was right when he said that positive thinking is how you *think* about a problem. Enthusiasm is how you *feel* about a problem. The two together determine what you *do* about a problem. If I could do anything for people, I would help them change their perspectives, not their problems. Positive thinking does not always change our circumstances, but it will always change us. When we are able to think right about tough situations, then our journeys through life become better.

G. W. Target, in his essay "The Window," tells the story of two men confined to hospital beds in the same room. Both men were seriously ill, and though they were not allowed much diversion—no television, radio, or books—their friendship developed over months of conversation. They discussed every possible subject in which they both had interest or experience, from family to jobs to vacations, as well as much of their own personal histories.

Neither man left his bed, but one was fortunate enough to be next to the window. As part of his treatment, he could sit up in bed for just an hour a day. At this time he would describe the world outside to his roommate. In very descriptive terms he would bring the outside world inside to his friend, describing to him the beautiful park he could see, with its lake, and the many interesting people he saw spending their time there. His friend began to live for those descriptions.

After a particularly fascinating report, the one man began to think it was not fair that his friend got to see everything, while he could see nothing. He was ashamed of his thoughts, but he had quite a bit of time to think, and he couldn't get this out of his mind. Eventually his thoughts began to take their effect on his health, and he became even more ill, with a disposition to match.

One evening his friend, who sometimes had difficulty with congestion and breathing, awoke with a fit of coughing and choking and was unable to push the button for the nurse to come to his aid. The frustrated, sour man lay there looking at the ceiling, listening to this struggle for life next to him, and doing nothing.

The next morning the day nurse came in to find the man by the window dead.

After a proper interval, the man who was so eager to see out that window asked if he could be moved, and it was quickly done. As soon as the room was empty, the man struggled up on his elbow to look out the window and fill his spirit with the sights of the outside world.

It was then he discovered the window faced a blank wall.[3]

THE RIGHT ACTION PLAN

Is it not true that too many times we have a surplus of simple answers and a shortage of simple problems? Occasionally we all feel like the guy in a cartoon who said, "I try to take just one day at a time, but lately several days have attacked me at once." One thing is certain, life is not problem-free!

The story is told that when the Apollo series of space vehicles was being designed, a rift developed between the scientists and the engineers. The scientists insisted that every available ounce of weight be reserved for scientific equipment that could be used to explore and report on outer space. They wanted the engineers to design a space vehicle that would be free from all defects. (That was the era when "zero defects" was a popular expression in industry.) That would mean a large proportion of the space and weight would be available for scientific equipment.

The engineers argued that this was an impossible goal. They contended that the only safe assumption was that something would go wrong, but they could not predict with certainty where the malfunctions would occur. Therefore, they would need to build in a series of backup systems to compensate for every possible malfunction. That would mean far less weight and cargo space would be available for scientific equipment.

Allegedly this conflict was resolved by asking the astronauts in training which assumption they supported. They all voted in favor of lots of backup systems! This story illustrates the importance of assumptions. Some people assume that a defect-free system can be developed for their lives. Others assume that something will go wrong, and they need a backup system. Too many times when a problem arises, we want to blame someone else and take the easy way out. Recently I studied a humorous problem-solving chart (see opposite page) that underscores our desire to duck responsibility.

THE PROBLEM-SOLVING PROCESS

Now, even if we don't wish to duck responsibilities and we have the right attitude and a solid action plan, it is still important to follow a process when we're looking for a solution. I suggest following these steps to problem solving.

IDENTIFY THE PROBLEM

Too many times we attack the symptoms, not the cause. Ordering your staff to stay at their desks until quitting time is a Band-Aid solution that does not answer the question, "Why does the staff leave early?" Your job is to identify the real issues that lie beneath the symptoms. Failing to do this places you in the same situation as a young soldier who was learning to parachute. He was given the following instructions:

1. Jump when you are told;

2. Count to ten and pull the ripcord;

3. In the very unlikely event that it doesn't open, pull the second chute open; and

4. When you get down, a truck will take you back to the base.

PROBLEM-SOLVING FLOW CHART

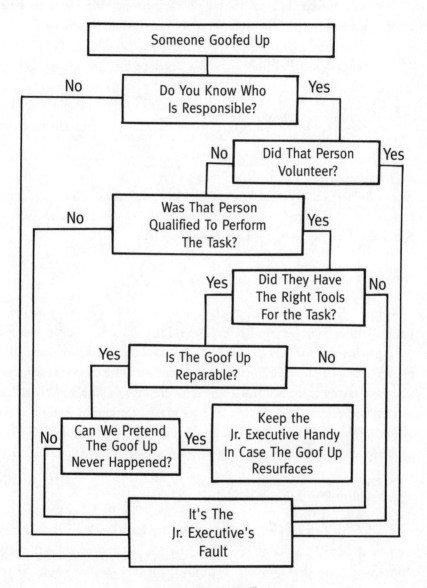

Created by David B. McGinnis

The plane got up to the proper altitude and the men started peeling out; the soldier jumped when it was his turn. He counted to ten, pulled the cord, but the chute failed to open. He proceeded to the backup plan and pulled the cord of the second chute. It, too, failed to open. "And I suppose," he complained to himself, "the truck won't be there when I get down."

PRIORITIZE THE PROBLEM

Richard Sloma says never to try to solve all the problems all at once—make them line up for you one by one. Whether you face three problems, thirty, or three hundred, "make them stand in single file so you face only one at a time." Approach these problems, not with a view of finding what you hope will be there, but to get the truth and the realities that must be grappled with. You may not like what you find. In that case, you are entitled to try to change it. But do not deceive yourself. What you do find may or may not be the real problem.

DEFINE THE PROBLEM

In a single sentence, answer the question, "What is the problem?" Bobb Biehl encourages us to keep in mind the difference between solving a problem and making a decision. A "decision is a choice you make between two or more alternatives, such as 'Should I fly to Phoenix or Chicago?' A problem is a situation that's counter to your intentions or expectations: 'I meant to fly to Chicago, but I ended up in Detroit,' or 'I meant to have $50,000 in the bank, but I'm $50,000 in the hole.'"[4]

Defining the problem in a single sentence is a *four-step process.*

1. Ask the Right Questions

If you have a vague idea, don't ask a general question, such as "What is happening here?" and don't speculate. Instead, ask process-related questions. Two words that always govern my questions are *trends* and *timing.* Most problem trails can be sniffed out if specific questions are asked in these two areas.

2. Talk to the Right People

Beware of authorities with a we-know-better attitude. These people have blind spots and are resistant to change. Creativity is essential for problem solving. In leadership conferences I often illustrate the principle by using the nine-dot problem.

Connect the nine points below with four straight lines without lifting your pen or pencil from the paper.

If you haven't encountered this problem before, try it. You were stymied if you made certain assumptions about the problem that limited your range of answers. Did you assume the lines could not extend beyond the imaginary square formed by the dots? Break that assumption and you can solve the puzzle more easily.

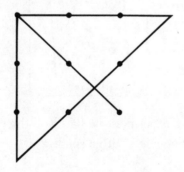

This creative solution is fairly commonplace. Less well-known are alternate solutions that stem from breaking other assumptions, such as these suggested by astronomer Tom Wujec. Assumption: The lines must pass through the center of the dots. If you draw lines that just touch the dots, you can solve the puzzle in just three strokes.

Assumption: The lines must be thin. Connect the lines with one fat line to solve this problem.

Assumption: You may not crease the paper. Fold the paper twice, so the dots all are together on the surface, and you need only one wide line.

Assumption: The paper must be flat. Roll the paper into a tube. It's possible to connect the dots with a spiral.

Assumption: You cannot rip the paper. Tear the paper into nine pieces with one dot on each, and connect all the dots by poking a hole through all the dots with your pencil.

These alternate solutions make the classic nine-dot problem even more effective in conveying the message that we can find more ways to solve more problems if we break stultifying assumptions.[5]

3. Get the Hard Facts

Remember Peter Drucker's words, "Once the facts are clear, the decisions jump out at you." For example, don't let someone say to you, "That person is a good worker." Get concrete examples of that individual's performance. Listen to what is *not* being said and gather the important data.

4. Get Involved in the Process

Most problems are not what they seem. Don't just ask the right questions and gather hard facts. Get involved in the process by doing the actual jobs of the people concerned and see what problems arise. Problems should be solved at the lowest level possible, because that is where they appear. That is also the level where they are most clearly defined.

SELECT PEOPLE TO HELP YOU IN THE PROBLEM-SOLVING PROCESS

Socrates developed this method 2,400 years ago: After defining the problem at hand, he would gather others around him and ask for their opinions and logical support to back their opinions up. As self-appointed gadfly, Socrates spent most of his life causing trouble in complacent, conservative Athens. By debating, cajoling, and prodding, he forced Athenians to question beliefs they took for granted.

This finally got him into trouble. The Athenians charged him with impiety toward the gods and corrupting Athens' youth. He was thrown into prison, tried, and sentenced to death. After a month, during which he refused friends' offers to help him escape, Socrates drank a cup of hemlock and died.

Nobody expects you to go that far. But practicing the Socratic method will help you to be a better leader.[6]

Before inviting people to attend a problem-solving meeting, ask these questions:

- Is it a real problem?
- Is it urgent?
- Is the true nature of the problem known?
- Is it specific? (If people talk about everything, they will eventually talk about nothing.)
- Has the group most competent to discuss the problem been invited, and is each participant concerned about solving this issue?

COLLECT PROBLEM CAUSES

List all the possible causes of the problem by asking what caused the problem and how the problem can be avoided in the future.

COLLECT PROBLEM-SOLVING SOLUTIONS

List as many solutions to a problem as possible. The more, the better. Seldom is there just one way to solve a problem. Options are essential because a problem continually shifts and changes. The leader without a backup solution for the primary answer will soon be in trouble.

PRIORITIZE AND SELECT THE "BEST" SOLUTIONS

Weigh all the possible solutions before deciding. The following questions should always be asked by the leader:

- Which solution has the greatest potential to be right?
- Which solution is in the best interests of the organization?
- Which solution has momentum and timing on its side?
- Which solution has the greatest chance for success?

IMPLEMENT THE BEST SOLUTION

Norman Bushnell, founder of Atari, said, "Everyone who's ever taken a shower has an idea. It's the person who gets out of the shower, dries off, and does something about it who makes a difference."

EVALUATE THE SOLUTION

Let others test it out and punch holes in it. If they punch intellectual holes (such as, "I don't think it will continue working because . . ."), ignore them. If they point out real operative problems you can observe, then you must make the adjustment. Ask these questions to evaluate the responses:

- Were we able to identify the real causes of the problem?
- Did we make the right decision?
- Has the problem been resolved?
- Have the key people accepted this solution?

- Did I help people to develop problem-solving skills to manage conflict in the future?

SET UP PRINCIPLES OR POLICIES TO KEEP PROBLEMS FROM RECURRING

Whereas policies are set up for a particular function in a specific area, principles are guidelines for everyone and are more general. Policies change when their use is no longer essential. Principles do not change.

> Policies are many,
> Principles are few,
> Policies will change,
> Principles never do.

Policies work well for lower management and operational matters. A policy should never be held on to and defended when it impedes the program and delays the change needed to make progress. A policy's intent is to give clear direction and allow a better flow in the organization. Many operational problems will stay solved with the implementation of solid policy.

A principle within my organization is: "Always take the high road." This principle means that whenever there is debate, question, tension, or confrontation between staff and people, I always expect my staff to give the benefit of the doubt to others. This principle is for everyone in my organization at all times. It may have nothing to do with an operational procedure that concerns machines and paper, but it has everything to do with people. To teach principles effectively to my staff, I must:

- model them;

- relate them by answering the question, "How can I use this in my life?"; and

- applaud when I see the principles being applied in their lives.
Later on in this book I will spend an entire chapter on the impor-

tance of having the right people around you. In regard to problem solv-ing, if you are always the problem solver and never teach the people around you to think and decide for themselves, you will have a depen-dent group of followers. Many years ago I decided to focus on helping people solve problems rather than helping solve people's problems. These suggestions are some approaches you should find effective:

- Never allow others to think you always have the best answers. This will only make them dependent on you.

- Ask questions. Help people to think through the entire process of their problem.

- Become a coach, not a king. A coach brings out the best in others, helping them to reach deep down inside and discover their potential. A king only gives commands.

- List their solutions on paper. Integrate your ideas with theirs until they have ownership of them.

- Ask them to decide on the best solution to their problem.

- Develop a game plan.

- Ask them to take ownership and responsibility for the game plan. Let them set up a time frame and an accountability process.

Your goal should be that when the meeting is over, the other person has processed the problem, selected a solution, developed a game plan, and taken ownership of it. His or her relationship with you will not be a dependent one, but a deepening one.

SIX

THE EXTRA PLUS IN LEADERSHIP:
ATTITUDE

When I speak at a leadership conference, I often ask everyone to do this exercise:

Write the name of a friend whom you greatly admire:

KEITH

Write one thing that you admire most about that friend:

PASSION

I'd like you to take a moment and complete this exercise before you continue reading. I think you'll gain an interesting and important insight. The odds are high that the thing you most admire about your friend has to do with attitude. After all the conference participants have completed this exercise, I ask them to tell me their answers. I list the first twenty-five responses on an overhead projector for everyone to see. I put an A beside the characteristics that describe attitudes, an S beside those describing skills, and an L if the words deal with looks. Every time I conduct this exercise, 95 percent of the descriptive words represent attitudes for which the friends are admired.

TRUE

Charles Swindoll said:

> The longer I live, the more I realize the impact of attitude on life. Attitude, to me, is more important than facts. It is more important than the past, than education, than money, than circumstances, than failures, than successes, than what other people think or say or do. It is more important than appearance, giftedness, or skill. It will make or break a company, a church, or a home. The remarkable thing is that we have a choice every day regarding the attitude we will embrace for that day. We cannot change our past. Nor can we change the fact that people will act in a certain way. We also cannot change the inevitable. The only thing that we can do is play on the one string we have, and that is our attitude. I am convinced that life is 10 percent what happens to me and 90 percent how I react to it. And so it is with you—we are in charge of our attitudes.[1]

Just as our attitudes are the extra pluses in life, they also make the difference in leading others. Leadership has less to do with position than it does with disposition. The disposition of a leader is important because it will influence the way the followers think and feel. Great leaders understand that the right attitude will set the right atmosphere, which enables the right responses from others.

OUR ATTITUDES ARE OUR MOST IMPORTANT ASSETS

Our attitude may not be the asset that makes us great leaders, but without good ones we will never reach our full potential. Our attitudes are the "and then some" that allows us the little extra edge over those whose thinking is wrong. Walt Emerson said, "What lies behind us and what lies before us are tiny matters compared to what lies within us."

The 1983 Cos Report on American Business said that 94 percent of all Fortune 500 executives attributed their success more to attitude than to any other basic ingredient.

Robert Half International, a San Francisco consulting firm, recently asked vice presidents and personnel directors at one hundred of America's largest companies to name the single greatest reason for firing an employee. The responses are very interesting and underscore the importance of attitude in the business world:

- Incompetence: 30 percent

- Inability to get along with other workers: 17 percent

- Dishonesty or lying: 12 percent

- Negative attitude: 10 percent

- Lack of motivation: 7 percent

- Failure or refusal to follow instructions: 7 percent

- All other reasons: 8 percent

Notice that although incompetence ranked first on the list, the next five were all attitude problems.

The Carnegie Institute not long ago analyzed the records of ten thousand persons and concluded that 15 percent of success is due to technical training. The other 85 percent is due to personality, and the primary personality trait identified by the research is attitude.

Our attitudes determine what we see and how we handle our feelings. These two factors greatly determine our success

What we see: Psychology 101 taught me that we see what we are prepared to see. A suburbanite, unable to find his best saw, suspected that his neighbor's son—who was always tinkering around with woodworking—had stolen it. During the next week everything the teenager did looked suspicious—the way he walked, the tone of his voice, his gestures. But when the older man found the saw behind his own workbench, where he had accidentally knocked it, he could no longer see anything at all suspicious in his neighbor's son.

Nell Mohney, in her book *Beliefs Can Influence Attitudes*, pointedly illustrates this truth. Mohney tells of a double-blind experiment conducted in the San Francisco Bay area. The principal of a school called three professors together and said, "Because you three teachers are the finest in the system and you have the greatest expertise, we're going to give you ninety high-IQ students. We're going to let you move these students through this next year at their own pace and see how much they can learn."

Everyone was delighted—faculty and students alike.

> Life is 10 percent what happens to me and 90 percent how I react to it.

Over the next year the professors and the students thoroughly enjoyed themselves. The professors were teaching the brightest students; the students were benefiting from the close attention and instruction of highly skilled teachers. By the end of the experiment, the students had achieved from 20 to 30 percent more than the other students in the whole area.

The principal called the teachers in and told them, "I have a confession to make. You did not have ninety of the most intellectually prominent students. They were run-of-the-mill students. We took ninety students at random from the system and gave them to you."

> Leadership has less to do with position than it does disposition.

The teachers said, "This means that we are exceptional teachers."

The principal continued, "I have another confession. You're not the brightest of the teachers. Your names were the first three names drawn out of a hat."

The teachers asked, "What made the difference? Why did ninety students perform at such an exceptional level for a whole year?"[2]

The difference, of course, was the teachers' expectations. Our expectations have a great deal to do with our attitudes. And these expectations may be totally false, but they will determine our attitudes.

How we handle our feelings: Notice I did not say our attitudes determine how we feel. There is a great difference between how we feel and how we handle our feelings. Everyone has times when they feel bad. Our attitudes cannot stop our feelings, but they can keep our feelings from stopping us. Unfortunately too many allow their feelings to control them until they end up like poor Ziggy in the comic strip.

> We cannot continue to function in a manner that we do not truly believe about ourselves.

He is sitting beneath a tree, gazing at the moon, and says, "I've been here and I've been there. I've been up and I've been down. I've been in and I've been out. I've been around and I've been about. But not once, not even once, have I ever been 'where it's at'!"

Every day I see people who are feeling controlled. A recent survey indicates that people with emotional problems are 144 percent more likely to have automobile accidents than those who are emotionally stable. An alarming factor revealed by this study is that one out of every five victims of fatal accidents had a quarrel within six hours before his or her accident.

IT IS IMPROBABLE THAT A PERSON WITH A BAD ATTITUDE CAN CONTINUOUSLY BE A SUCCESS

Norman Vincent Peale relates this story in his book, *Power of the Plus Factor*:

> Once walking through the twisted little streets of Kowloon in Hong Kong, I came upon a tattoo studio. In the window were displayed samples of the tattoos available. On the chest or arms you could have tattooed an anchor or flag or mermaid or whatever. But what struck me with force were three words that could be tattooed on one's flesh, *Born to lose*.
>
> I entered the shop in astonishment and, pointing to those words, asked the Chinese tattoo artist, "Does anyone really have that terrible phrase, *Born to lose*, tattooed on his body?"

> A leader's attitude is caught by his or her followers more quickly than his or her actions.

He replied, "Yes sometimes." "But," I said, "I just can't believe that anyone in his right mind would do that."

The Chinese man simply tapped his forehead and in broken English said, "Before tattoo on body, tattoo on mind."[3]

Once our minds are "tattooed" with negative thinking, our chances for long-term success diminish. We cannot continue to function in a manner that we do not truly believe about ourselves. Often I see people sabotage themselves because of wrong thinking.

The sports world has always appreciated Arnold Palmer. The members of "Arnie's army" can still be counted among young and old. This great golfer never flaunted his success. Although he has won hundreds of trophies and awards, the only trophy in his office is a battered cup that he got for his first professional win at the Canadian Open in 1955. In addition to the cup, he has a lone framed plaque on the wall. The plaque tells you why he has been so successful on and off the golf course. It reads:

> If you think you are beaten, you are.
> If you think you dare not, you don't.
> If you'd like to win but think you can't,
> It's almost certain you won't.
> Life's battles don't always go
> To the stronger or faster man,
> But sooner or later, the man who wins
> Is the man who thinks he can.

What is the difference between a golfer who wins one golf tournament and an Arnold Palmer? Is it ability? Lucky breaks? Absolutely not! When an average of less than two strokes per tournament separates the top twenty-five golfers in the world, the difference has to be something more than ability.

It's the attitude that makes the difference. People with negative thinking may start well, have a few good days, and win a match. But sooner or later (it's usually sooner), their attitude will pull them down.

WE ARE RESPONSIBLE FOR OUR ATTITUDES

Our destinies in life will never be determined by our complaining spirits or high expectations. Life is full of surprises, and the adjustment of our attitudes is a lifelong project.

> The pessimist complains about the wind.
> The optimist expects it to change.
> The leader adjusts the sails.

My father, Melvin Maxwell, has always been my hero. He is a leader's leader. One of his strengths is his positive attitude. Recently Dad and Mom spent some time with my family. As he opened his briefcase, I noticed a couple of motivational attitude books.

I said, "Dad, you're seventy years old. You've always had a great attitude. Are you still reading that stuff?"

He looked me in the eye and said, "Son, I have to keep working on my thought life. I am responsible to have a great attitude and to maintain it. My attitude does not run on automatic."

Wow! That's a lesson for all of us. We choose what attitudes we have right now. And it's a continuing choice. I am amazed at the large number of adults who fail to take responsibility for their attitudes. If they're grumpy and someone asks why, they'll say, "I got up on the wrong side of the bed." When failure begins to plague their lives, they'll say, "I was born on the wrong side of the tracks." When life begins to flatten out and others in the family are still climbing, they'll say, "Well, I was in the wrong birth order in my family." When their marriages fail, they believe they married the wrong person. When someone else gets a promotion they wanted, it's because they were in the wrong place at the wrong time.

Do you notice something? They are blaming everyone else for their problems.

The greatest day in your life and mine is when we take total responsibility for our attitudes. That's the day we truly grow up.

An advisor to President Lincoln suggested a certain candidate for the Lincoln cabinet. But Lincoln refused, saying, "I don't like the man's face."

"But, sir, he can't be responsible for his face," insisted the advisor.

"Every man over forty is responsible for his face," replied Lincoln, and the subject was dropped. No matter what you think about your attitude, it shows on your face!

The other day I saw a bumper sticker that read, "Misery is an option." I believe it! So does the daughter of a woman I heard about. The woman and her daughter went Christmas shopping together. The crowds were awful. The woman had to skip lunch because she was on a tight schedule. She became tired and hungry, and her feet were hurting. She was more than a little irritable.

As they left the last store, she asked her daughter, "Did you see the nasty look that salesman gave me?

The daughter answered, "He didn't give it to you, Mom. You had it when you went in."

> We cannot choose how many years we will live, but we can
>   choose how much life those years will have.
> We cannot control the beauty of our face, but we can
>   control the expression on it.
> We cannot control life's difficult moments, but we can
>   choose to make life less difficult.
> We cannot control the negative atmosphere of the world,
>   but we can control the atmosphere of our minds.
> Too often, we try to choose to control things we cannot.
> Too seldom, we choose to control what we can . . . our attitude.[4]

IT'S NOT WHAT HAPPENS *TO* ME THAT MATTERS BUT WHAT HAPPENS *IN* ME

Hugh Downs says that a happy person is not a person with a certain set of circumstances, but rather a person with a certain set of attitudes.

Too many people believe that happiness is a condition. When things are going great, they're happy. When things are going bad, they're sad. Some people have what I call "destination disease." They think that happiness can be found in a position or a place. Others have what I call "someone sickness." They think happiness results from knowing or being with a particular person.

I am impressed with the philosophy of the following statement: "God chooses what we go through. We choose how we go through it." It describes Viktor Frankl's attitude as he was terribly mistreated in a Nazi concentration camp. His words to his persecutors have been an inspiration to millions of people. He said, "The one thing you cannot take away from me is the way I choose to respond to what you do to me. The last of one's freedoms is to choose one's attitude in any given circumstance."[5]

Clara Barton, the founder of the American Red Cross, understood the importance of choosing a right attitude even in wrong situations. She was never known to hold a grudge against anyone. One time a friend recalled to her a cruel thing that had happened to her some years previously, but Clara seemed not to remember the incident.

"Don't you remember the wrong that was done to you?" the friend asked.

"No," Clara answered calmly. "I distinctly remember forgetting that."

Many times people who have suffered adverse situations in their lives become bitter and angry. Over time, their lives will be negative and hardened toward others. The tendency for them is to point back to a difficult time and say, "That incident ruined my life." What they do not realize is that the incident called for an attitude decision—a response. Their wrong attitude choice, not the condition, ruined their lives.

C. S. Lewis said, "Every time you make a choice you are turning the control part of you, the part that chooses, into something a little different from what it was before. And taking your life as a whole, with all your innumerable choices, you are slowly turning this control thing either into a heavenly creature or into a hellish one."[6]

THE LEADER'S ATTITUDE HELPS DETERMINE
THE ATTITUDES OF THE FOLLOWERS

Leadership is influence. People catch our attitudes just like they catch our colds—by getting close to us. One of the most gripping thoughts to ever enter my mind centers on my influence as a leader. It is important that I possess a great attitude, not only for my own success, but also for the benefit of others. My responsibilities as a leader must always be viewed in light of the many, not just myself.

Dr. Frank Crane reminds us that a ball rebounds from the wall with precisely the force with which it was thrown against the wall. There is a law in physics to the effect that action is equal to reaction. The law is also true in the realm of influence. In fact, its effects multiply with a leader's influence. The action of a leader multiplies in reaction because there are several followers. To a smile given, many smiles return. Anger unleashed toward others results in much anger returned from many. There are few actual victims of fate. The generous are helped and the stingy are shunned.

Remember the four-minute mile? People had been trying to achieve it since the days of the ancient Greeks. In fact, folklore has it that the Greeks had lions chase the runners, thinking that would make them run faster. They also tried drinking tiger's milk—not the stuff you get down at the health food store, but the real thing. Nothing they tried worked. So they decided it was impossible for a person to run a mile in four minutes or less. And for over a thousand years everyone believed it. Our bone structure is all wrong. Wind resistance is too great. We have inadequate lung power. There were a million reasons.

Then one man, one single human being, proved that the doctors, the trainers, the athletes, and the millions of runners before him who tried and failed, were all wrong. And, miracle of miracles, the year after Roger Bannister broke the four-minute mile, thirty-seven other runners broke the four-minute mile. The year after that, three hundred runners broke the four-minute mile. And a few years ago in a single race in New York, thirteen out of thirteen runners broke the four-minute mile. In other words, a few decades ago the runner who finished dead last in the New York race would have been regarded as having accomplished the impossible.

What happened? There were no great breakthroughs in training. No one discovered how to control wind resistance. Human bone structure and physiology didn't suddenly improve. But human attitudes did.

You can accomplish your goals, if you set them. Who says you're not tougher, smarter, better, harder working, more able than your competition? It does not matter if they say you can't do it. What matters, the *only* thing that matters, is if *you* say it.

Until Roger Bannister came along, we all believed the experts. And "the experts" continue to keep others from reaching their potential. Why? Because experts have influence. I believe that a leader's attitude is caught by his followers more quickly than his actions. An attitude is reflected by others even when they don't follow the action. An attitude can be expressed without a word being spoken.

The effect of a leader's attitude on others is the main reason for the importance of considering a candidate's attitude when hiring executives. Practicing psychologists list areas needing significant appraisal when employees are being considered for executive promotion: ambition; attitudes toward policy; attitudes toward colleagues; supervisory skills; and attitudes toward excessive demands on time and energy. A candidate who is out of balance in one or more of these areas would be likely to project a negative attitude and, therefore, prove to be a poor leader.

Take a moment and list the negative attitudes you possess that are influencing others right now.

1. I DON'T LIKE THE WAY MGMT TREATS EMPLOYEES TIME
2. I DON'T LIKE HOW OUR CUSTOMER BEHAVES
3. I THINK OUR PLANT MAILS TEAM IS INCOMPETENT
4. I DON'T LIKE HOW I FEEL ABOUT MY PHYSICAL SELF

HOW TO CHANGE YOUR ATTITUDE

Many people seem to suffer from what Ashley Montagu, the great Rutgers anthropologist, called *psychosclerosis*. Psychosclerosis is like arteriosclerosis, which is hardening of the arteries. Psychosclerosis is *hardening of the attitude.*

David Neiswanger of the Menninger Foundation says that if each of us can be helped by science to live a hundred years, "what will it profit us if our hates and fears, our loneliness and our remorse, will not permit us to enjoy them?"

The following sections will help you to help yourself in changing your attitude.

REVIEW

Many years ago my wife, Margaret, and I bought our first house. Our limited finances forced us to find some ways of getting what we wanted without spending a great deal of money. We agreed we would work on the front yard ourselves to save labor expenses and still create a proper setting for our home. It looked great.

One day, while I was standing in our backyard, I began to realize that we had spent no time or money making the back look good. Why? Because it couldn't be seen by others as they passed our house. We were careless about the area that was hidden.

That is exactly what people do in their personal lives. Their appearances, which can be seen outwardly, are spared no expense or energy. Yet their attitudes are neglected and underdeveloped. Remember the opening part of this chapter? Go back and read it again, and then put the necessary energy and effort into changing the inner areas of your life.

THE SIX STAGES OF ATTITUDE CHANGE

1. Identify Problem Feelings

This is the earliest stage of awareness and the easiest to declare.

2. Identify Problem Behavior

Now we go beneath the surface. What triggers wrong feelings? Write down actions that result in negative feelings.

3. Identify Problem Thinking

William James said, "That which holds our attention determines our action."

4. Identify Right Thinking

Write on paper the thinking that is right and what you desire. Because your feelings come from your thoughts, you can control your feelings by changing one thing—your thoughts!

↳ ONLY WITH THE HOLY SPIRIT'S HELP

5. Make a Public Commitment to Right Thinking

Public commitment becomes powerful commitment.

- YOU MUST FIRST WANT TO CHANGE

6. Develop a Plan for Right Thinking

MY ISSUE IS COMPLACENCY

This plan should include:

- a written definition of desired right thinking

- a way to measure progress

- a daily measuring of progress

- a person to whom you are accountable

- a daily diet of self-help materials

- associating with right-thinking people

This is a general plan for attitude self-improvement. The following steps will increase the probability of your success.

RESOLVE

Whenever a leader needs to ask others to make a commitment of time, two questions must always be answered: "Can they?" (this deals with ability) and "Will they?" (this deals with attitude). The more important question of the two is "Will they?" Two other questions usually answer the "Will they?" issue. The first is, "Is the timing right?" In other words, are the conditions right to enable positive change? The second question is, "Is their temperature hot?" Are right conditions accompanied with a red-hot desire to pay the price necessary for needed change? When both questions can be answered with a resounding Yes!, then the resolve is strong and success is possible.

Reframe

Denis Waitley says that the winners in life think constantly in terms of I can, I will, and I am. Losers, on the other hand, concentrate their waking thoughts on what they should have done or what they didn't do. If we don't like our performances, then we must first change the picture.

Cancer researchers at King's College in London did a long-term study of fifty-seven breast cancer victims who'd had mastectomies. They found that seven out of ten women "with a fighting spirit" were alive ten years later, while four out of five women "who felt hopeless" at the diagnosis had died.

The study of hope as it affects health even has a fancy name—*psychoneuroimmunology*. Harborview Medical Center in Seattle is researching in this field, and their findings support the conclusions of the King's College researchers. In a two-year study of burn victims, the Harborview research team discovered that patients with positive attitudes recovered more quickly than those with negative ones.[7]

Reframing your attitude means: *proven*

I may not be able to change the world I see around me,
but I can change the way I see the world within me.

Reenter

As you begin changing your thinking, start immediately to change your behavior. Begin to act the part of the person you would like to become. Take action on the behavior you admire by making it your behavior. Too many people want to feel, then take action. This never works.

One day while visiting a doctor's office, I read this in a med magazine:

> We hear it almost every day . . . sigh . . . sigh . . . sigh. "I just can't get myself motivated to lose weight, test my blood sugar, etc." And we hear an equal number of sighs from diabetes educators who can't get their patients motivated to do the right things for their diabetes and health.
>
> We have news for you. Motivation is not going to strike you like lightning. And motivation is not something that someone else— nurse, doctor, family member—can bestow or force on you. The whole idea of motivation is a trap. Forget motivation. Just do it. Exercise, lose weight, test your blood sugar, or whatever. Do it without motivation. And then, guess what? After you start doing the thing, that's when the motivation comes and makes it easy for you to keep on doing it.

THE FEELING OF LOVE — NOT JOY

"Motivation," says John Bruner, "is like love and happiness. It's a by-product. When you're actively engaged in doing something, the motivation to keep on doing it sneaks up and zaps you when you least expect it."

As Harvard psychologist Jerome Bruner says, you're more likely to act yourself into feeling than feel yourself into action. So act! Whatever it is you know you should do, do it.

The attitude development of our children, Elizabeth and Joel Porter, is very important to my wife, Margaret, and me. We learned a long time ago that the most effective way to change our children's attitudes is to work on their behaviors. But when we tell one of our children, "Change your attitude," the message is too general and the change we want is unclear. A more effective approach is explaining behaviors that signify bad attitudes. If we help them change their behaviors, the attitudes will change on their own. Instead of saying to our kids, "Get a grateful attitude," we ask them to give one compliment to every member of the family each day. As this becomes a habit in their lives, the attitude of gratitude follows.

REPEAT

Paul Meier said, "Attitudes are nothing more than habits of thought, and can be acquired. An action repeated becomes an attitude realized." Once, while leading a conference, I was asked for a simple plan to help a person change some wrong attitudes. I recommended two things to help her change her attitude. First:

> Say the right words,
> Read the right books,
> Listen to the right tapes,
> Be with the right people,
> Do the right things,
> Pray the right prayer.

The second was to do number one every day, not just once or only when you feel like it, and watch your life change for the better.

RENEWAL

Fortunately, over a period of time a positive attitude can replace a negative one. Again, let me emphasize that the battle is never over, but it is well worth our efforts. The more that negative thoughts are weeded out and replaced by positive ones, the more personal renewal will be experienced. My friend Lena Walker wrote a tribute about her grandfather and a practice in his life that he passed on to her. These words effectively describe the ongoing process of attitude development and the worthiness of overcoming negative thinking.

Each year as spring approaches, my thoughts turn to a whitehaired old man who went forth at this time of year to do battle. The enemy was not flesh and blood, but a small yellow flower called "mustard." As one gazes out over the fields and meadows, this yellow touch seems harmless enough, but year by year it continues its march, and can eventually take over entire fields.

Each spring my grandfather would walk through his fields, pulling these yellow flowers out by the roots.

Eventually I was married and lived on a farm in Ohio. Each spring I, too, would look out and see these same yellow flowers. The first few years on the farm I did nothing about them, but as maturity came upon me, I could see the wisdom of my grandfather's efforts. I, too, decided to go forth as he had done and do battle with the enemy.

Now, each year I walk through the fields, pulling an occasional mustard plant, I feel I am doing it in tribute to my grandfather.

To me this weed represents our bad habits and negative thoughts. We need to constantly prune out these things so our lives can be lush and green in our quest for a happy and productive life.

SEVEN

DEVELOPING YOUR MOST APPRECIABLE ASSET:
PEOPLE

The one who influences others to follow only is a leader with certain limitations. The one who influences others to lead others is a leader without limitations. As Andrew Carnegie said, no man will make a great leader who wants to do it all himself or to get all the credit for doing it. Guy Ferguson puts it this way:

> To know how to do a job is the accomplishment of labor;
> To be available to tell others is the accomplishment of the teacher;
> To inspire others to do better work is the accomplishment of management;
> To be able to do all three is the accomplishment of true leaders.

This chapter will focus on the importance of developing people to share in and assist you with the implementation of your dreams as a leader. The thesis is: *The more people you develop, the greater the extent of your dreams.*

People who are placed in leadership positions, but attempt to do it all alone, will someday come to the same conclusion as the bricklayer who tried to move five hundred pounds of bricks from the top of a four-story building to the sidewalk below. His problem was that he tried to do it alone. On an insurance claim form, he explained what happened: "It would have taken too long to carry the bricks down by hand, so I decided to put them in a barrel and lower them by a pulley that I had fastened to the top of the building. After tying the rope securely at the ground level, I then went up to the top of the building. I fastened the rope around the barrel, loaded it with bricks, and swung it out over the sidewalk for the descent.

"Then I went down to the sidewalk and untied the rope, holding it securely to guide the barrel down slowly. But, since I weigh only one hundred and forty pounds, the five-hundred-pound load jerked me from the ground so fast I didn't have time to think of letting go of the rope. And as I passed between the second and third floors, I met the barrel coming down. This accounts for the bruises and lacerations on my upper body.

"I held tightly to the rope until I reached the top, where my hand became jammed in the pulley. This accounts for my broken thumb. At the same time, however, the barrel hit the sidewalk with a bang, and the bottom fell out. With the weight of the bricks gone, the barrel weighed only about forty pounds. Thus, my one-hundred-forty-pound body began a swift descent, and I met the empty barrel coming up. This accounts for my broken ankle.

"Slowed only slightly, I continued the descent and landed on the pile of bricks. This accounts for my sprained back and broken collarbone.

"At this point, I lost my presence of mind completely and let go of the rope. And the empty barrel came crashing down on me. This accounts for my head injuries.

"As for the last question on the form, 'What would you do if the same situation arose again?' please be advised that I am finished trying to do the job alone."

I have observed that there are three levels of people/work skills:

Level 1: The person who works better with people is a follower.
Level 2: The person who helps people work better is a manager.
Level 3: The person who develops better people to work is a leader.

PRINCIPLES FOR PEOPLE DEVELOPMENT

My success in developing others will depend on how well I accomplish each of the following:

- **Value of people.** This is an issue of my attitude.

- **Commitment to people.** This is an issue of my time.

- **Integrity with people.** This is an issue of my character.

- **Standard for people.** This is an issue of my vision.

- **Influence over people.** This is an issue of my leadership.

From my own experience and through observation of other leaders who excel in this vital area, I have discovered that there are three areas in which successful people developers are different from those who are not successful in developing others. Successful people developers:

1. make the right assumptions about people;

2. ask the right questions about people; and

3. give the right assistance to people.

SUCCESSFUL PEOPLE DEVELOPERS
MAKE THE RIGHT ASSUMPTIONS ABOUT PEOPLE

Motivating others has always been relatively easy for me. For years I was asked, "John, how do you motivate people?" My pat answers were things like, "Stay enthusiastic"; "encourage others"; "lead the way"; "believe in people." I would watch others follow my advice and be successful for a short time, only to fall back into the old habit patterns and the resulting low morale.

Observing this downward cycle, I would ask myself why the people who took my advice couldn't continually motivate others. Then one day it hit me! I was giving them the *fruit* of my motivational gifts, but not the *root*. They were writing down my outward answers without the benefit of my inward assumptions about people. My assumptions about others are what allow me to continually motivate and develop them. In fact, a leader's having the right assumptions about people is the key factor in their continual development.

> The one who influences others to lead is a leader without limitations.

An assumption is an opinion that something is true. My assumptions about people largely determine how I treat them. Why? What I assume about people is what I look for. What I look for is what I find. What I find influences my response. Therefore, negative assumptions about others will stimulate negative leadership of them. Positive assumptions about others will stimulate positive leadership of them. Here are several such assumptions about people that I have found to be extremely valuable.

ASSUMPTION: EVERYONE WANTS TO FEEL WORTHWHILE

The most successful teachers, writers, managers, politicians, philosophers, and leaders who deal with people instinctively know this simple fact: Every person in the world is hungry. Yes, every person in this world is hungry for something, be it recognition, companionship, understanding, love—the list is endless. One thing I always find on a list of people's needs is the desire to feel worthwhile. People want to feel important! Donald Laird says to always help people increase their own self-esteem. Develop your skills in making other people feel important. There is hardly a higher compliment you can pay an individual than to help that person be useful and find satisfaction and significance. I believe that!

My travel schedule is heavy, and often I stop in the terminal in San Diego to get my shoes shined. Melvin, the man who shines my shoes, has become a friend. As we talk, I always try to bring two things into the conversation. I inquire about the Little League team he coaches, because that is the love of his life. And then I tell him, and anyone else who might be listening, that Melvin can polish shoes better than anyone I've ever known.

Napoleon Bonaparte, a leader's leader, knew every officer of his army by name. He liked to wander through his camp, meet an officer, greet him by name, and talk about a battle or maneuver he knew this officer had been involved in. He never missed an opportunity to inquire about a soldier's hometown, wife, and family; the men were always amazed to see how much detailed personal information about each one the emperor was able to store in his memory.

Since every officer felt Napoleon's personal interest in him—proved by his statements and questions—it is easy to understand the devotion they all felt for him.

ASSUMPTION: EVERYONE NEEDS AND RESPONDS TO ENCOURAGEMENT

For twenty-three years I have been responsible for developing people. I have yet to find a person who did not do better work and put forth greater effort under a spirit of approval than under a spirit of criticism. Encouragement is oxygen to the soul.

Researchers are turning up new evidence to support the old truth that encouragement brings out the best in people. In one experiment, adults were given ten puzzles to solve. All ten were exactly the same for all the adults. They worked on them and turned them in and were given results at the end. However, the results were fictitious. Half of the exam takers were told they had done well, getting seven of ten correct. The other half were told they had done poorly, getting seven of ten wrong. Then all were given another ten puzzles. Again, the puzzles were the same for each person. The half who had been told they had done well with the first puzzles did better with the second set. The other half did worse.[1] Criticism, even though it was given falsely, ruined them.

Viktor Frankl said:

> If you treat people to a vision of themselves, if you apparently overrate them, you make them become what they are capable of becoming. You know, if we take people as they are, we make them worse. If we take them as they should be, we help them become what they can be. . . . If you say this is idealism—overrating man— then I must answer, "Idealism is the real realism, because you help people actualize themselves."[2]

Take a moment and link the definition of leadership (influence) with the responsibility of leadership (people development). How do we who influence others truly motivate and develop them? We do it through encouragement and belief in them. People tend to become what the most important people in their lives think they will become. I try to model and then encourage my staff to say something uplifting to others in the first sixty seconds of a conversation. That sets a positive tone for everything else.

> People tend to become what the most important people in their lives think they will become.

In describing what makes a great baseball manager, Reggie Jackson said that a great manager has a knack for making ballplayers think they are better than they are. He forces you to have a good opinion of yourself. He lets you know he believes in you. He makes you get more out of yourself. And once you learn how good you really are, you never settle for playing anything less than your best.

Henry Ford said, "My best friend is the one who brings out the best in me." How true. Every leader wants to bring out the best that is in people. And every successful leader knows that encouragement is the way to do it.

ASSUMPTION: PEOPLE "BUY INTO" THE LEADER BEFORE THEY "BUY INTO" HIS OR HER LEADERSHIP

Too often we expect people to be loyal to the position of a leader instead of the person who occupies that position. But people are not motivated by organizational charts; they respond to people. The first thing a leader must declare is not authority because of rights, but authority because of relationships. People do not care how much you know until they know how much you care. You've got to give loyalty down before you receive loyalty up. If people do not believe in their leader, anything will hinder them from following. If people believe in their leader, nothing will stop them.

> People do not care how much you know until they know how much you care.

Most of us think of Christopher Columbus as a great discoverer, but he was also a great leader and salesman. Before he could begin his voyage of discovery that changed the world, he had to sell what, to his contemporaries, was an utterly ridiculous idea! And that was no "one call" sale! Consider the circumstances and conditions that were stacked against him.

First, there was absolutely no market for a transatlantic voyage. And hundreds of years of tradition and superstition practically guaranteed there never would be.

Second, although Columbus had made sea voyages as a passenger, he had never been the captain of a ship.

Third, Columbus was a foreigner (an Italian) living in Portugal and then in Spain.

Fourth, Columbus did not have sufficient money to fund such an adventure. In fact, the only one who could legally fund a voyage of discovery was a head of state—a king or a queen. So his prospect list of benefactors was rather short.

Fifth, his price was not cheap. In addition to needing ships and support, Columbus had a long list of personal demands, including: (a) a 10 percent commission on all commerce between his discoveries and the mother country; (b) a title—Admiral of the Ocean Sea; (c) the permanent position of governor of all new territories; and (d) all of his honors and rights passed on to his heirs.

Remarkably, Columbus made the sale and did it on his own terms! Modern salespeople could learn a lot from Columbus's sales techniques.

He was propelled by a single-minded passion. He wholeheartedly believed he could reach Asia by crossing the Atlantic. Even though his belief was wrong, it gave him the stamina, conviction, and confidence to convince others. And he never stopped selling.

He didn't mind asking for the order again and again and again! He spent seven years asking King John of Portugal to fund the voyage. Then he went to Spain and worked on Ferdinand and Isabella for seven years before he finally got his Yes.

Columbus had to see before he could sail. Any successful leader knows this truth. People must buy into you before they buy into your dreams. High morale in an organization comes from having faith in the person at the top.

ASSUMPTION: MOST PEOPLE DO NOT KNOW HOW TO BE SUCCESSFUL

Most people think success is luck, and they keep trying to win the lottery of life. But success is really the result of planning. It happens where preparation and opportunity meet.

Most people think success is instantaneous. They look at it as a moment, an event, or a place in time. It's not. Success is really a process. It is growth and development. It is achieving one thing and using that as a stepping-stone to achieve something else. It is a journey.

> Failure is the opportunity to begin again more intelligently.

Most people think that success is learning how to never fail. But that's not true. Success is learning from failure. Failure is the opportunity to begin again more intelligently. Failure only truly becomes failure when we do not learn from it.

Once people realize that you, as a leader, can help them become successful, they're yours! Someone said, "Success is relative. Once you have it, all the relatives come." This is also true in an organization. Once the leader has proven to be successful and shown an interest in helping others achieve success through the company, that leader will have loyal followers who are willing to develop and grow.

ASSUMPTION: MOST PEOPLE ARE NATURALLY MOTIVATED

Just watch a one-year-old try to explore and find out what is in a house. That is natural motivation. My observation is that people begin an endeavor with a desire to participate, but are often de-motivated and then must be re-motivated to participate.

Little children want to go to school. Three- and four-year-old children "play" school. They can't wait to begin. They start off in first grade with shiny new lunch boxes and a high degree of motivation. However, by the time they are in school for two or three years, some kids hate it. They make excuses not to go, complaining, "I have a sore tummy." What happened? The schools effectively de-motivated the original high degree of enthusiasm and excitement.

The true secret of motivation is creating an environment in which people are free from the influences that demotivate.

What Motivates People?

Significant contributions. People want to join in a group or pursue a cause that will have lasting impact. They need to see that what they are doing is not wasted effort, but is making a contribution. People must see value in what they are doing. Motivation comes not by activity alone, but by the desire to reach the end result.

Goal participation. People support what they create. Being part of the goal-setting process is motivating, and it allows people to feel needed. They like to feel they are making a difference. When people have given input, they have a stake in the issue. They own it and support it. Seeing goals become reality and helping to shape the future is fulfilling. Goal participation builds team spirit, enhances morale, and helps everyone feel important.

Positive dissatisfaction. Someone said that *dissatisfaction* is the one-word definition for *motivation*. Dissatisfied people are highly motivated people, for they see the need for immediate change. They know something is wrong and often know what needs to be done. Dissatisfaction can inspire change or it can lead to a critical spirit. It can lead to apathy or stir one to action. The key is harnessing this energy toward effective change.

Recognition. People want to be noticed. They want credit for personal achievements and appreciation for their contributions. Often, giving recognition is another way of saying thanks. Personal accomplishment is motivating, but it is much more so when someone notices the accomplishment and gives worth to it. Recognition is one way to give meaning to a person's existence.

Clear expectations. People are motivated when they know exactly what they are to do and have the confidence that they can do it successfully. No one wants to jump into a task that is vague or a job whose description is uncertain. Motivation rises in a job when the goals, expectations, and responsibilities are clearly understood. When delegating responsibility, be sure to give the necessary authority to carry out the task. People perform better when they have some control over their work and their time.

What Demotivates People?

Certain behavior patterns can be demotivating. We sometimes behave in these ways without realizing the negative influences they have on others. Here's how we can avoid demotivating behavior.

Don't belittle anyone. Public criticism and cutting conversations, even in jest, can hurt. We must be alert and sensitive. Taken to the extreme, belittling can destroy a person's self-esteem and self-confidence. If you have to give criticism, remember that it takes nine positive comments to balance one negative correction. REALLY?

Don't manipulate anyone. No one likes to feel maneuvered or used. Manipulation, no matter how slight, tears down the walls of trust in a relationship. We gain more by being honest and transparent than we do by being cunning and crafty. Build people up through affirmation and praise, and they'll be motivated and loyal. Remember, give and it shall be given to you.

Don't be insensitive. Make people your priority. People are our greatest resources; therefore, take time to know and care about them. This means being responsive in conversation, never appearing preoccupied with self or in a hurry. Stop talking and develop the art of really listening. Quit thinking of what you will say next, and begin to hear, not only what they say, but how they feel. Your interest in even insignificant matters will demonstrate your sensitivity.

Don't discourage personal growth. Growth is motivating, so encourage your staff to stretch. Give them opportunities to try new things and acquire new skills. We should not feel threatened by the achievements of others, but should be very supportive of their successes. Allow your staff to succeed and fail. Build the team spirit approach that says, "If you grow, we all benefit."

SUCCESSFUL PEOPLE DEVELOPERS ASK THE RIGHT QUESTIONS ABOUT PEOPLE

Now we have completed the discussion of how making the right assumptions about people must be our first principle to follow as a successful people developer. Next we need to become familiar with the right questions to ask people. There are six.

AM I BUILDING PEOPLE, OR AM I BUILDING MY DREAM AND USING PEOPLE TO DO IT?

People must come first. Fred Smith says that Federal Express, from its inception, has put its people first because it is right to do so and because it is good business as well. "Our corporate philosophy is succinctly stated: People-Service-Profits."

This question deals with the leader's motives. There is a slight but significant difference between manipulation and motivation.

Manipulation is moving together for *my* advantage.

Motivation is moving together for *mutual* advantage.

DO I CARE ENOUGH TO CONFRONT PEOPLE WHEN IT WILL MAKE A DIFFERENCE?

Confrontation is very difficult for most people. If you feel uneasy just reading the word *confront*, I'd like to suggest that you substitute the word *clarify*. Clarify the issue instead of confronting the person. Then follow these ten commandments.

The Ten Commandments of Confrontation

1. Do it privately, not publicly.

2. Do it as soon as possible. That is more natural than waiting a long time.

3. Speak to one issue at a time. Don't overload the person with a long list of issues.

4. Once you've made a point, don't keep repeating it.

5. Deal only with actions the person can change. If you ask the person to do something he or she is unable to do, frustration builds in your relationship.

6. Avoid sarcasm. Sarcasm signals that you are angry at people, not at their actions, and may cause them to resent you.

7. Avoid words like *always* and *never*. They usually detract from accuracy and make people defensive.

8. Present criticisms as suggestions or questions if possible.

9. Don't apologize for the confrontational meeting. Doing so detracts from it and may indicate you are not sure you had the right to say what you did.

10. Don't forget the compliments. Use what I call the "sandwich" in these types of meetings: Compliment—Confront—Compliment.

AM I LISTENING TO PEOPLE WITH MORE THAN MY EARS, THAT IS, AM I HEARING MORE THAN WORDS?

The following test is one I have found useful and have given to my own staff.

Am I a Good Listener?

Give yourself four points if the answer to the following questions is *Always*: three points for *Usually*; two points for *Rarely*; and one point for *Never*.

_3_ Do I allow the speaker to finish without interrupting?

_2_ Do I listen "between the lines," that is, for the subtext?

_3_ When writing a message, do I listen for and write down the key facts and phrases?

_2_ Do I repeat what the person just said to clarify the meaning?

_3_ Do I avoid getting hostile and/or agitated when I disagree with the speaker?

_2_ Do I tune out distractions when listening?

_3_ Do I make an effort to seem interested in what the other person is saying?

Scoring:

26 or higher: You are an excellent listener.

22–25: Better than average score.

18–21: Room for improvement.

17 or lower: Get out there right away and practice your listening.[3]

David Burns, a medical doctor and professor of psychiatry at the University of Pennsylvania, says: "The biggest mistake you can make in trying to talk convincingly is to put your highest priority on expressing your ideas and feelings. What most people really want is to be listened to, respected, and understood. The moment people see that they are being understood, they become more motivated to understand your point of view."

What Are the Major Strengths of This Individual?

Anyone who continually has to work in areas of personal weakness instead of personal strengths will not stay motivated. If individuals have been grinding away at tasks assigned in their weak areas and you reassign them to work in areas of strength, you'll see a dramatic increase in natural motivation.

Have I Placed a High Priority on the Job?

People tend to stay motivated when they see the importance of the things they are asked to do. The five most encouraging words in an organization are: "It will make a difference." The five most discouraging words in an organization are: "It won't make any difference."

I can still remember the day Linda was hired to oversee the computer system in our offices. She came into my office for an initial meeting. My goal was to give her the big picture to help her see that her work was more than computers. I conveyed that doing her job with excellence would encourage every worker to do a better job. I can still see her eyes moisten as she realized that her work would positively contribute to everyone's success.

HAVE I SHOWN THE VALUE THE PERSON WILL RECEIVE FROM THIS RELATIONSHIP?

People tend to stay motivated when they see the value to them of the things they are asked to do. The simple fact is when we hear an announcement, see a commercial, or are asked to make a commitment, a small voice in the back of our minds asks, "What's in it for me?" The reason people skip the meeting you worked so hard to plan is simple: they haven't seen the value (benefits and rewards) they will receive by being there.

Think about an important relationship you have with a subordinate or perhaps with your boss. On the left-hand side of a page, draw up a list of all the contributions you are making to this relationship, that is, what you are giving. With a subordinate, your list might include pay, job security, time, and professional development. Title this list "What I Give."

On the right-hand side of the page, make a second list, entitled "What I Get." Write all the benefits you are receiving. Then sit back and compare your two lists. Don't count the number of items on each one. (Some things are more important than others, and you probably left some items off both lists.) Instead, answer this simple question: *Considering all that you give to your relationship versus all that you're getting from it, who is getting the better deal?* Choose your answer from the following options:

1. *I am getting a better deal.* This can produce complacency and ingratitude.

2. *The other person is getting a better deal.* This can produce resentment.

3. *We are getting an equally good deal.* This usually produces mutual respect and motivation.

Analyze your answer by looking at the three axioms of the Equity Factor (found in Huseman and Hatfield's *Managing the Equity Factor*):

1. People evaluate relationships by comparing what they give to a relationship with what they get from it.

2. When what people give does not equal what they get, they feel distress.

3. People who feel distress because they give more than they get will restore equity. This becomes a negative. Do you commit here?[4]

SUCCESSFUL PEOPLE DEVELOPERS GIVE THE RIGHT ASSISTANCE TO PEOPLE

I need to work out their strengths and work on their weaknesses. The question that as a leader I must continually ask is not, "How hard does this person work?" (Is he or she faithful?) but "How much does this person accomplish?" (Is he or she fruitful?).

Some of the most capable people in an organization never utilize their greatest strengths. They may be locked into what management considers important jobs, and they may do them well. But they may never get an opportunity to do what they can do best. When this happens, everybody loses. The person loses because of lack of opportunity and lack of job satisfaction; the organization loses because it wastes some of its most valuable assets. The whole venture operates at less than capacity.

I must give them myself. You can *impress* people at a distance, but you can only *impact* them up close.

- List all the people you spent thirty minutes with this week.

- Did you initiate the time or did they?

- Did you have an agenda before the meeting?

- Was the meeting for the purpose of relationships, counseling, communication, or development?

- Was it a win-win meeting?

- Was it with the influential top 20 or the lower 80 percent?

Love everyone, but give yourself to the top 20 percent in your organization. Encourage the many; mentor the few. Be transparent with them. Develop a plan for their growth. Become a team.

I must give them ownership. As Sidney J. Harris believes:

> People want to be appreciated, not impressed.
> They want to be regarded as human beings,
> Not as sounding boards for other people's egos.
> They want to be treated as an end in themselves,
> Not as a means toward the gratification of another's vanity.

I must give them every chance for success. My responsibility as a leader is to provide assistance for those who work with me by giving them:

- An excellent atmosphere to work in. It should be positive, warm, open, creative, and encouraging.

- The right tools to work with. Do not hire excellent people to do excellent work with average tools.

- A continual training program to work under. Growing employees make growing companies.

- Excellent people to work for. Develop a team. Coming together is the beginning. Working together is success.

- A compelling vision to work toward. Allow your people to work for something larger than themselves.

Great leaders always give their people a head start over those who work under an average leader. Excellent leaders add value to their people and help them become better than they would be if they worked alone. The first question a leader should ask is: "How can I help make those around me more successful?" When that answer is found and implemented, everyone wins!

PEOPLE-DEVELOPMENT PRINCIPLES

PEOPLE DEVELOPMENT TAKES TIME

At one time Andrew Carnegie was the wealthiest man in America. He came to America from his native Scotland when he was a small boy, did a variety of odd jobs, and eventually ended up as the largest steel manufacturer in the United States. At one time he had forty-three millionaires working for him. In those days, a millionaire was a rare person; conservatively speaking, a million dollars in his day would be equivalent to at least twenty million dollars today.

A reporter asked Carnegie how he hired forty-three millionaires. Carnegie responded that those men were not millionaires when they started working for him but had become millionaires as a result.

The reporter then asked how he had developed these men to become so valuable that he would pay them so much money.

Carnegie replied that men are developed the same way gold is mined. When gold is mined, several tons of dirt must be moved to get an ounce of gold, but one doesn't go into the mine looking for dirt. One goes in looking for gold.

Robert Half said, "There is something that is much more scarce, something rarer than ability. It is the ability to recognize ability." There is still another step that must be taken beyond the ability to discover the gold that is in the leader's mine. It must also be developed. It is better to train ten people to work than to do the work of ten people, but it is harder. "The man who goes alone can start the day. But he who travels with another must wait until the other is ready."[5]

PEOPLE SKILLS ARE ESSENTIAL FOR SUCCESS

Companies that go along successfully have leaders who get along with people. Dave E. Smalley records in his book, *Floorcraft*, that Andrew Carnegie once paid Charles Schwab a salary of one million dollars a year simply because Schwab got along with the people. Carnegie had men who understood the job better and who were better fitted by experience and training to execute it, but they lacked the essential human quality of being able to get others to help them—to get the best out of the workers.

Most chief executives of major companies, when asked what one single characteristic is most needed by those in leadership positions, replied, "The ability to work with people."

Teddy Roosevelt said, "The most important single ingredient to the formula of success is knowing how to get along with people."

John Rockefeller, who built giant corporations, stated that he would pay more for the ability to deal with people than any other ability under the sun.

The Center for Creative Leadership in Greensboro, North Carolina, studied 105 successful executives and discovered the following:

- They admitted their mistakes and accepted the consequences, rather than trying to blame others.

- They were able to get along with a wide variety of people.

- They had strong interpersonal skills, sensitivity to others, and tact.

- They were calm and confident, rather than moody and volatile.

Unsuccessful executives tended to be too tough, abusive, sarcastic, aloof, or unpredictable. Their worst fault was being insensitive to others.

Lack of people skills can result in the kind of situation former Denver Bronco coach John Ralston experienced when he left the team. "I left because of illness and fatigue—the fans were sick and tired of me."

Be a Model That Others Can Follow

The number one motivational principle in the world is: *People do what people see.* The speed of the leader determines the speed of the followers. And followers will never go any further than their leader. For years I have followed and taught this process for developing others:

ACTION	RESULT
I do it:	I model.
I do it, and you are with me:	I mentor.
You do it, and I am with you:	I monitor.
You do it:	You move forward.
You do it, and someone is with you:	We multiply.

People's minds are changed more through observation than through arguments.

Benjamin Franklin learned that plaster scattered in the fields would make things grow. He told his neighbors, but they did not believe him. They argued with him, trying to prove that plaster could be of no use at all to grass or grain. After a little while he allowed the matter to drop and said no more about it.

Early the next spring Franklin went into the field and sowed some grain. Close by the path, where men would walk, he traced some letters with his finger, put plaster into them, and then sowed seed in the plaster. After a week or two the seed sprang up.

As they passed that way, the neighbors were very surprised to see, in brighter green than all the rest of the field, large letters saying, "This has been plastered." Benjamin Franklin did not need to argue with his neighbors anymore about the benefits of plaster for the field.

LEAD OTHERS BY LOOKING THROUGH THEIR EYES

Henry Wadsworth Longfellow said, "We judge ourselves by what we feel capable of doing; while others judge us by what we have already done."

Any leader who successfully deals with a group of people realizes that they each have their own agenda and perception of how things are. Long ago I learned that people think their:

> problems are the biggest,
> children are the smartest,

jokes are the funniest, and
faults ought to be overlooked.

An amusing story beautifully illustrates how each of us views life.

After World War II, a general and his young lieutenant boarded a train in England. The only seats left were across from a beautiful young lady and her grandmother. The general and the lieutenant sat facing the women. As the train pulled out, it went through a long tunnel. For about ten seconds there was total darkness. In the silence of the moment, those on the train heard two things—a kiss and a slap. Everyone on the train had his or her own perception of what happened.

The young lady thought to herself, *I'm flattered that the lieutenant kissed me, but I'm terribly embarrassed that Grandmother hit him!*

The Grandmother thought, *I'm aggravated that the young man kissed my granddaughter, but I'm proud she had the courage to retaliate!*

The general sat there, thinking to himself, *My lieutenant showed a lot of guts in kissing that girl, but why did she slap me by mistake?*

The lieutenant was the only one on the train who really knew what happened. In that brief moment of darkness, he had the opportunity to kiss a pretty girl *and* slap his general.[6]

These questions will help you discover another person's agenda in a variety of situations:

- Background question: What is this person's history with this organization or another?

- Temperament question: What is this person's primary and secondary temperament?

- Security question: Is this, in any way, affecting the individual's job?

- Relationship question: How is he or she related to me, or someone else, organizationally?

- Motive question: What is the real reason this is on his or her agenda?

- Potential question: Does this person or issue merit the leader's time and energy?

I have discovered that the development of people is more successful when I:

> listen well enough to lead through their eyes;
> relate well enough to communicate with their hearts:
> work well enough to place tools in their hands;
> think well enough to challenge and expand their minds.

LEADERS MUST CARE FOR PEOPLE BEFORE THEY CAN DEVELOP THEM

Too often I see leaders who request commitment from people without showing them proper care. They are like Narvaez, the Spanish patriot who, while dying, was asked by his father-confessor whether he had forgiven all his enemies. Narvaez looked astonished and said, "Father, I have no enemies. I shot them all."

Narvaez didn't know that "nice guys" get the best results from subordinates. Teleometrics International studied the perception high-achieving executives have of the people in their organizations, compared to low-achieving executives. Their results were reported in the *Wall Street Journal*.

Of the sixteen thousand executives studied, the 13 percent identified as "high achievers" tended to care about people as well as profits. Average achievers concentrated on production, while low achievers were preoccupied with their own security. High achievers viewed subordinates optimistically, while low achievers showed a basic distrust of subordinates' abilities. High achievers sought advice from their subordinates; low achievers didn't. High achievers were listeners; moderate achievers listened only to superiors; low achievers avoided communication and relied on policy manuals.

PEOPLE DEVELOPERS LOOK FOR OPPORTUNITIES TO BUILD UP PEOPLE

Most people in leadership positions daily steal someone's ego food—the satisfaction of their needs for esteem. In fact, they steal it and don't even know it. For example, someone says, "I've really had a busy day," and the leader replies, "You've been busy! You should see all the work piled on my desk, and I can't even get to it." Or someone says, "I finally finished that project I've been working on for eight months," and the leader replies, "Yeah, Jim finally finished that big project he's been working on too."

What is the leader doing? Well, he's taking away the food that people need for their ego. In effect, he's saying, "You may think you're pretty good, but let me tell you about someone else who is probably better."

Just for fun, check yourself tomorrow and see how many times you catch yourself satisfying your own esteem needs by stealing away someone else's ego food.

J. C. Staehle, after analyzing many surveys, found that the principal causes of unrest among workers are actions good leaders can avoid. They are listed in the order of their importance.

1. Failure to give credit for suggestions

2. Failure to correct grievances

3. Failure to encourage

4. Criticizing employees in front of other people

5. Failure to ask employees their opinions

6. Failure to inform employees of their progress

7. Favoritism

Note: Every issue is an example of the leader stealing or keeping ego food from the workers.

THE GREATEST POTENTIAL FOR GROWTH OF A COMPANY IS GROWTH OF ITS PEOPLE

In a survey of workers across the United States, nearly 85 percent said they could work harder on the job. More than half claimed they could double their effectiveness "if [they] wanted to."[7]

People are the principal asset of any company, whether it makes things to sell, sells things made by other people, or supplies intangible services. Nothing moves until your people can make it move. In actual studies of leadership in American business, the average executive spends three-fourths of his working time dealing with *people*. The largest single cost in most business is *people*. The largest, most valuable asset any company has is its *people*. All executive plans are carried out, or fail to be carried out, by *people*.

According to William J. H. Boetcker, people divide themselves into four classes:

1. Those who always do less than they are told

2. Those who will do what they are told, but no more

3. Those who will do things without being told

4. Those who will inspire others to do things

It's up to you.

As Ralph Waldo Emerson said, "Trust men and they will be true to you: treat them greatly and they will show themselves great."

Some of the best advice you can find about being a good leader is found in this old Chinese poem:

> Go to the people,
> Live among them.
> Learn from them.
> Love them.
> Start with what they know,
> Build on what they have.
> But of the best leaders,
> When their task is accomplished,
> Their work is done,
> The people will remark,
> "We have done it ourselves."

EIGHT

THE INDISPENSABLE QUALITY OF LEADERSHIP:
VISION

Robert K. Greenleaf, in his book, *The Servant as Leader*, says, "Foresight is the 'lead' that the leader has. Once he loses this lead and events start to force his hand, he is leader in name only. He is not leading; he is reacting to immediate events, and he probably will not long be a leader. There are abundant current examples of loss of leadership which stem from a failure to foresee what reasonably could have been foreseen, and from failure to act on that knowledge while the leader has freedom to act."[1]

My observation over the last twenty years has been that all effective leaders have a vision of what they must accomplish. That vision becomes the energy behind every effort and the force that pushes through all the problems. With vision, the leader is on a mission and a contagious spirit is felt among the crowd until others begin to rise alongside the leader. Unity is essential for the dream to be realized. Long hours of labor are given gladly to accomplish the goal. Individual rights are set aside because the whole is much more important than the part. Time flies, morale soars upward, heroic stories are told, and commitment is the watchword. Why? Because the leader has a vision!

All that is necessary to remove the excitement from the preceding paragraph is one word—*vision*. Without it, energy ebbs low, deadlines are missed, personal agendas begin to surface, production falls, and people scatter.

Helen Keller was asked, "What would be worse than being born blind?" She replied, "To have sight without vision." Sadly, too many people are placed into leadership positions without a vision for the organization that they will lead. All great leaders possess two things: They know where they are going, and they are able to persuade others to follow. They are like the sign in an optometrist's office: "If you don't see what you want, you've come to the right place." This chapter will deal with the leader's foresight and the ability to gather people around it.

The word *vision* has perhaps been overused in the last few years. The first goal of many a management workshop is to develop a statement of purpose for the organization. Others will look at you oddly if you cannot recite your organization's purpose by memory and produce a card with the statement of purpose printed on it.

Why all the pressure to develop a purpose for your organization? There are two reasons. First, vision becomes the distinctive, rallying cry of the organization. It is a clear statement in a competitive market that you have an important niche among all the voices clamoring for customers. It is your real reason for existence. Second, vision becomes the new control tool, replacing the 1,000-page manual that is boxy and constrains initiative. In an age when decentralization all the way to the front line is required to survive, the vision is the key that keeps everyone focused.

VISION STATEMENTS

What you see is what you can be. This deals with your potential. I have often asked myself, does the vision make the leader? Or, does the leader make the vision?

I believe the vision comes first. I have known many leaders who lost the vision and, therefore, lost their power to lead. People do what people see. That is the greatest motivational principle in the world. Stanford Research says that 89 percent of what we learn is visual, 10 percent of what we learn is auditory, and 1 percent of what we learn is through other senses.

In other words, people depend on visual stimulation for growth.

Couple a vision with a leader willing to implement that dream, and a movement begins. People do not follow a dream in itself. They follow the leader who has that dream and the ability to communicate it effectively. Therefore, vision in the beginning will make a leader, but for that vision to grow and demand a following, the leader must take responsibility for it.

FOUR VISION LEVELS OF PEOPLE

1. Some people never see it. (They are wanderers.)

2. Some people see it but never pursue it on their own. (They are followers.)

3. Some people see it and pursue it. (They are achievers.)

4. Some people see it and pursue it and help others see it. (They are leaders.)

Hubert H. Humphrey is an example of "what you see is what you can be." During a trip to Washington, D.C., in 1935, he wrote this in a letter to his wife: "Honey, I see how someday, if you and I just apply ourselves and make up our minds to work for bigger and better things, we can someday live here in Washington and probably be in government, politics, or service . . . Oh, gosh, I hope my dream comes true—I'm going to try anyhow."

> All great leaders possess two things: one, they know where they are going, and two, they are able to persuade others to follow.

YOU SEE WHAT YOU ARE PREPARED TO SEE

This deals with perception. Konrad Adenauer was correct when he said, "We all live under the same sky, but we don't all have the same horizon."

Automobile genius Henry Ford once came up with a revolutionary plan for a new kind of engine. We know it today as the V-8. Ford was eager to get his great new idea into production. He had some men draw up the plans and presented them to the engineers.

As the engineers studied the drawings, one by one they came to the same conclusion. Their visionary boss just didn't know much about the fundamental principles of engineering. He'd have to be told gently—his dream was impossible.

Ford said, "Produce it anyway."

They replied, "But it's impossible."

"Go ahead," Ford commanded, "and stay on the job until you succeed, no matter how much time is required."

> Leaders can never take their people farther than they have traveled. Like leader, like people.

For six months they struggled with drawing after drawing, design after design. Nothing. Another six months. Nothing. At the end of the year, Ford checked with his engineers, and once again they told him that what he wanted was impossible. Ford told them to keep going. They did. And they discovered how to build a V-8 engine.

Henry Ford and his engineers both lived under the same sky, but they didn't all have the same horizon.

In *A Savior for All Seasons*, William Barker related the story of a bishop from the East Coast who many years ago paid a visit to a small, Midwestern religious college. He stayed at the home of the college president, who also served as professor of physics and chemistry. After dinner the bishop declared that the millennium couldn't be far off, because just about everything about nature had been discovered and all inventions conceived.

The young college president politely disagreed and said he felt there would be many more discoveries. When the angered bishop challenged the president to name just one such invention, the president replied he was certain that within fifty years men would be able to fly.

"Nonsense!" sputtered the outraged bishop. "Only angels are intended to fly."

The bishop's name was Wright, and he had two boys at home who would prove to have greater vision than their father. Their names were Orville and Wilbur. The father and his sons both lived under the same sky, but they didn't all have the same horizon.

How can this be? Why is it that two people can be in the same place at the same time and both see entirely different things? It's simple. We see what we are prepared to see, not what is. Every successful leader understands this about people and asks three questions: What do others see; why do they see it that way; and how can I change their perception?

What You See Is What You Get

The following illustration originated in Luis Palau's book *Dream Great Dreams* (Multnomah Press, 1984).

Think about how nice and refreshing it is to taste a cold Coke. Hundreds of millions of people around the world have enjoyed this experience, thanks to the vision of Robert Woodruff. During his tenure as president of Coca-Cola (1923–1955), Woodruff boldly declared, "We will see that every man in uniform gets a bottle of Coca-Cola for five cents wherever he is and whatever the costs." When World War II had ended, Woodruff stated that before he died he wanted every person in the world to have tasted Coca-Cola. Robert Woodruff was a man of vision!

With careful planning and a lot of persistence, Woodruff and his colleagues reached their generation around the globe for Coke.

> God's gift to me is my potential. My gift back to God is what I do with that potential.

When Disney World first opened, Mrs. Walt Disney was asked to speak at the Grand Opening, since Walt had died. She was introduced by a man who said, "Mrs. Disney, I just wish Walt could have seen this." She stood up and said, "He did," and sat down. Walt Disney knew it. Robert Woodruff knew it. Even Flip Wilson knew it! What you see is what you get.

At this point, I feel compelled to ask a question before we go on to the subject of personal ownership of a vision: "Is my dream going to make a difference in the world in which I live?"

Bobb Biehl, in his book *Increasing Your Leadership Confidence*, says, "Keep in mind the difference between a winner's and a loser's mentality. Winners focus on winning big—not just how to win, but how to win big. Losers, however, don't focus on losing; they just focus on getting by!"[2]

Keep asking yourself, "Survival, success, or significance?" Are you striving to simply survive, are you dreaming about success, or are you really out to make a truly significant difference?

Moishe Rosen teaches a one-sentence mental exercise that's an effective tool in dreaming. It is simply this:

If I had _____,

I would _____.

If you had anything you wanted—unlimited time, unlimited money, unlimited information, unlimited staff—all the resources you could ask for, what would you do? Your answer to that question is your dream. Make it worthwhile.

One day Lucy and Linus had a chicken wishbone and were going to pull it to make a wish. Lucy explained to Linus that if he got the bigger half of the wishbone, his wish would come true. Linus said, "Do I have to say the wish out loud?" Lucy said, "Of course. If you don't say it out loud, it won't come true." So Lucy went ahead and made her wish first. She said, "I wish for four new sweaters, a new bike, a new pair of skates, a new dress, and one hundred dollars." Then it was time for Linus to make his wish. He said, "I wish for a long life for all my friends, I wish for world peace, I wish for great advancements in medical research." About that time, Lucy took the wishbone and threw it away. She said, "Linus, that's the trouble with you. You're always spoiling everything."

PERSONAL OWNERSHIP OF A VISION

My friend Rick Warren says, "If you want to know the temperature of your organization, put a thermometer in the leader's mouth." Leaders can never take their people farther than they have traveled. Therefore, the focus of vision must be on the leader—like leader, like people. Followers find the leader and then the vision. Leaders find the vision and then the people.

I am asked many questions when I speak at leadership conferences throughout the country. One of the most common questions asked by those in leadership positions is: "How do I get a vision for my organization?" This question is crucial. Until it is answered, a person will be a leader in name only. Although I cannot give you a vision, I can share the process of receiving one for you and those around you.

LOOK WITHIN YOU: WHAT DO YOU FEEL?

Theodore Hesburgh said, "The very essence of leadership is that you have a vision. It's got to be a vision you can articulate clearly and forcefully on every occasion. You can't blow an uncertain trumpet." An "uncertain trumpet" is usually the result of an individual who either lacks a vision or is trying to lead with someone else's dream. Certain trumpet sounds come forth from a leader who has birthed a vision from within. There is a vast difference between a person with a vision and a visionary person.

- A person with a vision talks little but does much.

- A visionary person does little but talks much.

- A person with a vision finds strength from inner convictions.

- A visionary person finds strength from outward conditions.

- A person with vision continues when problems arise.

- A visionary person quits when the road becomes difficult.

Many great people began life in the poorest and most humble of homes, with little education and no advantages. Thomas Edison was a newsboy on trains. Andrew Carnegie started work at $4 a month, John D. Rockefeller at $6 a week. The remarkable thing about Abraham Lincoln was not that he was born in a log cabin, but that he got out of the log cabin.

Demosthenes, the greatest orator of the ancient world, stuttered! The first time he tried to make a public speech, he was laughed off the rostrum. Julius Caesar was an epileptic. Napoleon was of humble parentage and far from being a born genius (he stood forty-sixth in his class at the military academy in a class of sixty-five). Beethoven was deaf, as was Thomas Edison. Charles Dickens was lame; so was Handel. Homer was blind; Plato was a hunchback; Sir Walter Scott was paralyzed.

What gave these great individuals the stamina to overcome severe setbacks and become successful? Each person had an inner dream that lit a fire that could not be extinguished. Great visions begin as an "inside job." Napoleon Hill said, "Cherish your visions and dreams as they are the children of your soul: the blueprints of your ultimate achievements."

LOOK BEHIND YOU: WHAT HAVE YOU LEARNED?

A person without experience sees a vision idealistically. To this individual the vision alone is enough. Naively this person casts the vision to others, expecting the dream to do the work and failing to realize that a vision needs support. A person with experience learns that people buy into the leader *before* they buy into the vision. Experienced leaders realize that people are fickle and dreams are fragile. Experience has taught me these principles about vision:

- The credibility of a vision is determined by the leader.
- The acceptance of a vision is determined by the timing of its presentation.
- The value of a vision is determined by the energy and direction it gives.
- The evaluation of a vision is determined by the commitment level of people.

- The success of a vision is determined by its ownership by both the leader and the people.

Leonard Lauder, president of Estee Lauder, said, "When a person with experience meets a person with money, the person with experience will get the money. And the person with the money will get the experience."

LOOK AROUND YOU: WHAT IS HAPPENING TO OTHERS?

A little boy attended his first symphonic concert. He was excited by the splendid hall, the beautiful people in their formal finery, and the sound of the large, enthusiastic orchestra. Of all the instruments in the orchestra, however, his favorite was the cymbals. The first loud, dramatic crash of those brass disks won him over without reservation. He noticed, though, that most of the evening the cymbal player stood motionless while the other musicians played. Only occasionally was the cymbal player called upon to make his contribution, and even then his time of glory was quite brief.

After the concert, the little boy's parents took him backstage to meet some of the musicians. The little fellow immediately sought out the cymbalist. "Say, mister," he said sincerely, "how much do you need to know to play the cymbals?" The musician laughed and answered, "You don't have to know much at all. You only have to know when."

A good idea becomes great when the people are ready. The individual who is impatient with people will be defective in leadership. The evidence of strength lies not in streaking ahead, but in adapting your stride to the slower pace of others while not forfeiting your lead. If we run too far ahead, we lose our power to influence.

LOOK AHEAD OF YOU: WHAT IS THE BIG PICTURE?

This question often separates leaders from managers. Leaders are concerned with the organization's basic purpose—why it exists and what it should achieve. They are not preoccupied with the "how to" or nuts-and-bolts aspect of the operation.

LOOK ABOVE YOU: WHAT DOES GOD EXPECT OF YOU?

Richard E. Day said, "Every golden era in human history proceeds from the devotion and righteous passion of some single individual. There are no bona fide mass movements; it just looks that way. There is always one man who knows his God and knows where he is going."

God's gift to me is my potential. My gift back to God is what I do with that potential. I believe great leaders sense a "higher calling"—one that lifts them above themselves. What a terrible waste of life to be climbing the ladder of success only to find when you reach the top that you were leaning against the wrong building. Great visions are bigger than the person. My definition of success is:

knowing God and His desires for me;
growing to my maximum potential; and
sowing seeds that benefit others.

LOOK BESIDE YOU: WHAT RESOURCES ARE AVAILABLE TO YOU?

A vision should be greater than the person who has it. Its accomplishment must be the result of many people bringing many resources to the job. Many times I have read the speech of President John F. Kennedy that cast the vision of America landing on the moon during the decade of the '60s. That dream captured the people and resources of our country and became a reality.

The experienced leader is always looking for others to make the dream come true. My top priority in the vision for the twenty-five-million-dollar relocation of the congregation I pastor is to develop and find winners to help make the vision a reality. I continually evaluate the progress of this relocation project by the commitment of the people.

Too often leaders hesitate to test the commitment levels of those around them. What is the result? They are never sure where the project stands, or where their people stand. I remember well the conclusions I felt when we finished our first four-million-dollar fund-raising effort. We worked hard, and I knew where the people stood.

The leader continually passes on the vision to those who come around, knowing that dreams, if presented right, are contagious.

In the movie *Tucker: The Man and His Dream,* Abe, the bottom-line businessman and beleaguered bookkeeper for Preston Tucker, who conceived a radical new automobile—a low-cost car with fuel injector, rear-mounted engine, disc brakes, pop-out windows, seat belts, and aerodynamic design—caught Tucker's dream.

Despite a misremembered warning from his mother, he bought a share of Tucker's idealism.

Abe thought his mother said, "Don't get too close to people; you'll catch their dreams."

Years later he realized she had said *germs,* not *dreams.*[3]

CORPORATE OWNERSHIP OF A VISION

A vision is a clear picture of what the leader sees his or her group being or doing. According to a survey reported by *Leadership* magazine, communicating a vision is one of the most frustrating areas of leading an organization.

Recently I was a guest on a radio talk show. The host poured out his frustration to me during the break concerning this very issue. He said, "I have a vision for my people but find it difficult to transfer that vision to others." One fact is true: leaders who effectively communicate goals to their followers achieve far more than those who don't.

Successful leaders see on three levels:

Level 1. Perception: seeing what is now with the eyes of reality
Level 2. Probability: seeing what will be with the eyes of discernment
Level 3. Possibility: seeing what can be with the eyes of vision

A *futurist* lives only on Level 3. A *forecaster* lives only on Level 2. A *follower* lives only on Level 1. A *leader* lives on Level 3, leads on Level 2, and listens on Level 1.

For example, an organization sets changing its name as a goal. The great leader, through eyes of vision, already sees a new name for the company (Level 3). That leader, through the eyes of discernment, sees the trend of the organization (Level 2). The leader knows the direction of the company by looking through the eyes of reality (Level 1).

Surprisingly, vision casting does not begin with Level 3 (the big picture). It begins with Level 1 (the small picture) and will only be successful if the leader can influence Level 2 (the next picture).

UNDERSTANDING WHAT HINDERS A VISION — LEVEL 1

We see things, not as they are, but as we are. Therefore, when a vision is hindered, it is usually a people problem. There are ten types of people who usually hinder the vision of the organization.

1. LIMITED LEADERS

Everything rises and falls on leadership. That statement is certainly true with vision casting. A limited leader will either lack the vision or the ability to successfully pass it on.

The prime minister of France once said, "If you are doing big things, you attract big men. If you are doing little things, you attract little men. Little men usually cause trouble." Then he paused, shook his head sadly, and added, "We are having an awful lot of trouble.

2. CONCRETE THINKERS

George Bernard Shaw said, "Some men see things as they are and say, 'Why?' [concrete thinker] I dream of things that never were and say 'Why not?' [creative thinker]"

Charlie Brown holds up his hands before his friend Lucy and says,

"These are hands which may someday accomplish great things. These are hands which may someday do marvelous works! They may build mighty bridges, or heal the sick, or hit home runs, or write soul-stirring novels! These are hands which may someday change the course of destiny!"

Lucy, who always sees things as they are, replies, "They've got jelly on them."

3. DOGMATIC TALKERS

Many visions aren't realized because of strong, dogmatic people. To be absolutely certain about something, one must either know everything or nothing about it. Most of the time, the dogmatist knows nothing but conventionally says something. For example, "Everything that can be invented has been invented." That was Charles H. Duell, director of the U.S. Patent Office, speaking in 1899! Of course, Duell was not alone. President Grover Cleveland once commented (in 1905) that "sensible and responsible women do not want to vote." Then there was Robert Miliken, Nobel Prize winner in physics, who said in 1923, "There is no likelihood man can ever tap the power of the atom." Lord Kelvin, president of England's Royal Society (a scientific organization), noted in 1885, "Heavier-than-air flying machines are impossible."

My favorite is a statement of baseball great Tris Speaker. He was quoted in 1921 as saying, "[Babe] Ruth made a big mistake when he gave up pitching."

4. CONTINUAL LOSERS

Many people look at their past failures and fear the risk of pursuing a vision. Their motto is, "If at first you don't succeed, destroy all evidence that you've tried." They also destroy everyone's attempt to ever try again.

5. SATISFIED SITTERS

People strive for comfort, predictability, and security in life. On the heels of comfort comes complacency; of predictability, boredom; and of security, a lack of vision. A nest is good for a robin while it is an egg. But it is bad for a robin when it has wings. It's a good place to be hatched in, but it's a poor place to fly in. It's always sad when people don't want to leave the nests of their lives.

In a *Leadership* magazine article, Lynn Anderson described what happens when people lose their vision. A group of pilgrims landed on the shores of America nearly four hundred years ago. With great vision and courage they had come to settle in the new land. In the first year, they established a town. In the second, they elected town council. In the third, the government proposed building a road five miles westward into the wilderness. But in the fourth year, the people tried to impeach the town council because the people thought such a road into the forest was a waste of public funds. Somehow these forward-looking people had lost their vision. Once able to see across oceans, they now could not look five miles into the wilderness.

6. Tradition Lovers

The British have always been good with the patronage system. John F. Barker in *Roll Call* tells the story that for more than twenty years, for no apparent reason, an attendant stood at the foot of the stairway leading to the House of Commons. At last someone checked and discovered that the job had been held in the attendant's family for three generations. It seems it originated when the stairs were painted and the current attendant's grandfather was assigned the task of warning people not to step on the wet paint.

One British newsman, told of the situation, commented, "The paint dried up but not the job."

7. Census Takers

Some people never feel comfortable stepping out of the crowd. They desire to be a part of, not apart from, the group. These people will only embrace the vision when the majority does. They are never in front.

True leaders are always in the minority because they are thinking ahead of the present majority. Even when the majority catches up, these leaders will have moved ahead and so, again, will be in the minority.[4]

8. PROBLEM PERCEIVERS

Some people can see a problem in every solution. Usually obstacles are the things you see when you take your eyes off the goal. Interestingly, some people think the ability to see problems is a mark of maturity. Not so. It's the mark of a person without a vision. These people abort great visions by presenting problems without any solutions.

Cardinal John Henry Newman said that nothing would get done at all if a man waited until he could do something so well that no one could find fault with it.

9. SELF-SEEKERS

People who live for themselves are in a mighty small business. They also never accomplish much. Great goals are only reached by the united effort of many. Selfish people are vision busters.

10. FAILURE FORECASTERS

Some people have a faculty for touching the wrong keys. From the finest instrument, they extract only discord. All their songs are in a minor key. They send the note of pessimism everywhere. The shadows dominate all their pictures. Their outlook is always gloomy, times are always bad, and money is tight. Everything in them seems to be contracting; nothing in their lives expands or grows.

These people are like the man who gathered with many others at the Hudson River to see the first steamship launched. He kept saying, "They'll never get her going. They'll never get her going." But they did. The steamship belched and moved out fast. Immediately the same man said, "They'll never get her stopped. They'll never get her stopped."

I love the Chinese proverb that states, "Man who says, 'It cannot be done' should not interrupt man who is doing it."

SETTING THE PROPER ENVIRONMENT—LEVEL 2

Knowing people and the keys to their lives will allow the leader to go to the "next picture" in Level 2. It is essential that the leader begin to influence what will be seen by the people. Remember, if the leader and a few others see Level 3, then only they will know if Level 2 is set correctly to take others into the vision area. The following steps will set Level 2 correctly.

COME ALONGSIDE OF THEM

Let them see your heart before they see your hope. People don't care how much you see until they see how much you care. I emphasize again: people buy into the leader before they buy into that leader's vision. Cultivate trust. Be transparent and patient. Start where they are by seeing through their eyes. Seek to find their hopes and dreams. Begin building a bridge between the vision of the organization and their personal goals. Done correctly, both can be accomplished. Go for the win-win. Remember, when you help people get what they want, they will help you get what you want. This can only be accomplished by building strong relationships with people.

PAINT THE PICTURE FOR THEM

One time I read that a great teacher never strives to explain his vision; he simply invites you to stand beside him and see for yourself. I agree with the relationship part of this statement, but I believe great leaders explain their vision by painting a picture for the people. John W. Patterson, founder of National Cash Register, said, "I have been trying all my life, first to see for myself, and then to get other people to see with me. To succeed in business it is necessary to make the other man see things as you see them. Seeing . . . was the objective. In the broadest sense, I am a visualizer."

Every great vision has certain ingredients, and the great leader makes the people understand, appreciate, and "see" them:

Horizon: A leader's vision of the horizon allows people to see the heights of their possibilities. Each individual will determine how high he or she wants to go. Your responsibility is to put plenty of sky into the picture. Paul Harvey said that a blind man's world is bounded by the limits of his touch; an ignorant man's world by the limits of his knowledge; a great man's world by the limits of his vision.

Sun: This element represents warmth and hope. Light brings out the optimism in people. A prime function of a leader is to keep hope alive. Napoleon said, "Leaders are dealers in hope."

Mountains: Every vision has its challenges. Edwin Land, founder of Polaroid, said, "The first thing you do is teach the person to feel that the vision is very important and nearly impossible. That draws out the drive in the winner."

Birds: This element represents freedom and the spirit of man. Watching an eagle rise causes you to feel your own spirit soar. "Wars may be fought with weapons, but it is the spirit of the men who fight and of the man who leads that gains victory."[5]

Flowers: The journey toward the realization of any great vision takes time. Make sure the scenery includes rest stops—places to smell flowers and become refreshed mentally and physically. Success is the progressive realization of a predetermined, worthwhile goal.

Path: People need direction, a place to begin, and a path to follow. A traveler through a rugged country asked his Indian guide, "How are you able to pick your way over these jagged peaks, by treacherous trails, without ever losing your direction?"

The guide answered, "I have the near look and the far vision. With the one I see what is directly ahead of me; with the other I guide my course by the stars."[6]

Yourself: Never paint the vision without placing yourself in the picture. This will show your commitment to the vision and your desire to walk with the people through the process. They need a model to follow. As Warren R. Austin said in *UN World*, "If you would lift me, you must be on higher ground."

Why should a leader paint the picture and place these essentials in it? Roger von Oech, in his book, *A Kick in the Seat of the Pants*, gives an excellent answer:

> Take a look around where you're sitting and find five things that have blue in them. Go ahead and do it.
>
> With a "blue" mind-set, you'll find that blue jumps out at you: a blue book on the table, a blue pillow on the couch, blue in the painting on the wall, and so on.
>
> In like fashion, you've probably noticed that after you buy a new car, you promptly see that make of car everywhere. That's because people find what they are looking for.[7]

The leader helps the people develop this sensitivity and an eye for knowing what to look for. If the picture is painted clearly and shown continually, soon others will begin to see how to see how it fits into everything they do. They will have a vision mind-set. Then there will be only one thing left to bring the vision into the ownership of others.

PUT THE THINGS THEY LOVE IN THE PICTURE

People carry pictures of other people and things they love. Put what is important to the people within the frame of the vision and you will have transferred the vision to the people.

During World War II, parachutes were being constructed by the thousands. From the workers' point of view, the job was tedious. It involved crouching over a sewing machine eight to ten hours a day and stitching endless lengths of colorless fabric. The result was a formless heap of cloth. But every morning the workers were told that each stitch was part of a life-saving operation. They were asked to think as they sewed that each parachute might be the one worn by their husbands, their brothers, their sons.

Although the work was hard and the hours long, the women and the men on the home front understood their contribution to the larger picture.[8]

Opening Eyes to Possibilities — Level 3

On this level we need to ask ourselves how to grow people to the size of the vision. This represents the one thing the leader must continually do . . . grow people to the vision once they see it.

There are several steps a Level 3 leader must take. First, the leader must seek and find winners to add to the team. These qualities of winners will guide the search:

- Winners are less sensitive to disapproval and rejection—they brush it off.
- Winners think "bottom line."
- Winners focus on the task at hand.
- Winners are not superstitious—they say, "That's life."
- Winners refuse to equate failure with self-worth.
- Winners don't restrict thinking to established, rigid patterns.
- Winners see the big picture.
- Winners welcome challenge with optimism.
- Winners don't waste time in unproductive thought.

Once the winners are added to the team, they join others as the major influencers in the organization. At this point, it is extremely important for the leader to spend time with the influencers to discover the "keys" to their lives. What is most valued by these influencers should help them through tough personal issues; provide a time and place for them to grow; add value to their family and job; assist them in finding their strengths; and plug them into the organization.

Also, it is very important for the leader to mentor these winners. They should be exposed to great books (past and present), great places, great events, and great people. They should find great ideas in you, the leader, and they should develop a desire to pursue your interests and vision in an attempt to build a mutually beneficial relationship. When this occurs, you will find that the winners naturally pass on the vision that you hold dear for your organization and for them.

The successful Level 3 leader will see on three levels:

1. **The Perceptible Level:** What is now seen—the eyes of reality. A leader listens on this level.

2. **The Probable Level:** What will be seen—the eyes of discernment. A leader leads on this level.

3. **The Possible Level:** What can be seen—the eyes of vision. A leader lives on this level.

Vision is empowering to the leader who has it. The leader with vision believes not only that what he envisions can be done, but that it must be done. There was a study done of concentration camp survivors regarding the common characteristics of those who did not succumb in the concentration camps. Viktor Frankl was a living answer to that question. He was a successful Viennese psychiatrist before the Nazis threw him into such a camp. Years later, when giving lectures, he would say:

> There is only one reason why I am here today. What kept me alive was you. Others gave up hope. I dreamed that some day I would be here telling you how I, Viktor Frankl, had survived Nazi

concentration camps. I've never been here before, I've never seen any of you before, I've never given this speech before. But in my dreams I have stood before you and said these words a thousand times.

It was the vision that made the difference. As a young man I learned this poem. It is an appropriate way to end this chapter.

> Ah, great it is to believe the dream,
> As we stand in youth by the starry stream.
> But a greater thing is to live life through,
> And say at the end, the dream came true.

Leaders do that for themselves, and others.

NINE

THE PRICE TAG OF LEADERSHIP:
SELF-DISCIPLINE

I n reading the lives of great men, I found that the first victory they won was over themselves . . . Self-discipline with all of them came first."[1]

The Greek word for *self-control* comes from a root word meaning "to grip" or "take hold of." This word describes people who are willing to get a grip on their lives and take control of areas that will bring them success or failure.

Aristotle used this same word to describe "the ability to test desire by reason . . . to be resolute and ever in readiness to end natural vent and pain." He explained that people who are not controlled have strong desires which try to seduce them from the way of reason; but to succeed they must keep those desires under control.

Once, while conducting a leadership seminar, I defined discipline in the beginning of life as the choice of achieving what you really want by doing things you don't really want to do. After successfully doing this for some time, discipline becomes the choice of achieving what you really want by doing things you now want to do! I truly believe we can become disciplined and enjoy it—after years of practicing it.

All great leaders have understood that their number one responsibility was for their own discipline and personal growth. If they could not lead themselves, they could not lead others. Leaders can never take others farther than they have gone themselves, for no one can travel without until he or she has first traveled within. A great person will lead a great organization, but growth is only possible when the leader is willing to "pay the price" for it. Many potentially gifted leaders have stopped short of the payment line and found out that shortcuts don't pay off in the long run.

This is what Edwin Markham has to say about human worth:

> We are blind until we see
> That in the human plan
> Nothing is worth the making
> If it does not make the man.
> Why build these cities glorious
> If man unbuilded goes?
> In vain we build the world
> Unless the builder also grows.[2]

THE PROCESS FOR DEVELOPING PERSONAL DISCIPLINE

Frederick the Great of Prussia was walking on the outskirts of Berlin when he encountered a very old man proceeding in the opposite direction.

"Who are you?" asked Frederick.

"I am a king," replied the old man.

"A king!" laughed Frederick. "Over what kingdom do you reign?"

"Over myself," was the proud reply.

"Reigning" over yourself requires personal discipline.

START WITH YOURSELF

A reporter once asked the great evangelist D. L. Moody which people gave him the most trouble. He answered immediately, "I've had more trouble with D. L. Moody than any man alive." The late Samuel

Hoffenstein said, "Wherever I go, I go too, and spoil everything." And there is the classic Jack Paar line, "Looking back, my life seems to be one long obstacle course, with me as the chief obstacle."

My observation is that more potential leaders fail because of inner issues than outer ones.

Each month I teach a leadership lesson to my staff, which is recorded live and sent to other leaders across the United States. Recently I spoke on the subject "How to Get out of Your Own Way." A tremendous response was received from many listeners, who said, "The lesson was needed in my life. I am my worst problem!" Most of us can relate to the sign I saw in an office: "If you could kick the person responsible for most of your troubles, you wouldn't be able to sit down for weeks."

> We cannot travel without until we first travel within.

> When we are foolish, we want to conquer the world. When we are wise, we want to conquer ourselves.

Your Competitor

An enemy I had, whose face I stoutly strove to know,
For hard he dogged my steps unseen, wherever I did go.
My plans he balked, my aims he foiled, he blocked my onward way.
When for some lofty goal I toiled, he grimly said to me, Nay.
One night I seized him and held him fast, from him the veil did draw,
I looked upon his face at last and lo . . . myself I saw.

When we are foolish, we want to conquer the world. When we are wise, we want to conquer ourselves.

START EARLY

Perhaps the most valuable result of all education is the ability to make yourself do the thing you have to do, when it ought to be done, whether you like it or not; it is the first lesson that ought to be learned and, however early a man's training begins, it is probably the last lesson that he learns thoroughly.

> Hard work is the accumulation of easy things you didn't do when you should have.

My parents modeled discipline and insisted that their three children develop that lifestyle. Time management, hard work, persistence, honesty, responsibility, and a positive attitude, regardless of the situation, were always expected of us. However, I didn't appreciate this training until I went to college. There I saw many students who couldn't get a grip on their lives or their studies. I began to realize that I had a decided advantage over others because of the disciplines already "under my belt." It is true—when you do the things you ought to do when you ought to do them, the day will come when you will do the things you want to do when you want to do them. Hard work is the accumulation of the easy things you didn't do when you should have.

> What you are going to be tomorrow, you are becoming today.

START SMALL

What you are going to be tomorrow, you are becoming today. It is essential to begin developing self-discipline in a small way today in order to be disciplined in a big way tomorrow.

A Small Plan That Will Make a Big Difference

1. List five areas in your life that lack discipline.

2. Place them in order of your priority for conquering them.

3. Take them on, one at a time.

4. Secure resources, such as books and tapes, that will give you instruction and motivation to conquer each area.

5. Ask a person who models the trait you want to possess to hold you accountable for it.

6. Spend fifteen minutes each morning getting focused in order to get control of this weak area in your life.

7. Do a five-minute checkup on yourself at midday.

8. Take five minutes in the evening to evaluate your progress.

9. Allow sixty days to work on one area before you go to the next.

10. Celebrate with the one who holds you accountable as you show continued success.

Remember, having it all doesn't mean having it all at once. It takes time. Start small and concentrate on today. The slow accumulation of disciplines will one day make a big difference. Ben Franklin said, "It is easier to suppress the first desire than to satisfy all that follow it."

START NOW

As John Hancock Field says, "All worthwhile men have good thoughts, good ideas, and good intentions, but precious few of them ever translate those into action."

In 1976, Indiana University's basketball team was undefeated throughout the regular season and captured the NCAA National Championship. Controversial and colorful coach Bobby Knight led them to that championship. Shortly afterward, Coach Knight was interviewed on the

> Great leaders never set themselves above their followers except in carrying out responsibilities.

television show *60 Minutes*. The commentators asked him, "Why is it, Bobby, that your basketball teams at Indiana are always so successful? Is it the will to succeed?"

"The will to succeed is important," Knight replied, "but I'll tell you what's more important: It's the will to prepare. It's the will to go out there every day training and building those muscles and sharpening those skills!"

I'm PREPARING FOR RAIN

> Success depends not merely on how well you do the things you enjoy, but how conscientiously you perform those duties you don't.

Abraham Lincoln said, "I will get ready, and then perhaps my chance will come." Too often the disciplines have not been developed and an opportunity is missed. Charlie Brown of the *Peanuts* comic strip once said that his life was mixed up because he missed all of the rehearsals. Before you can become a "star," you have to start. Now is the best time.

ORGANIZE YOUR LIFE

"One of the advantages of being disorderly is that one is constantly making exciting discoveries." That statement by A. A. Milne is true, but the discoveries are usually too late and consequently an opportunity is missed. Then you as a leader are perceived as being "out of control." This leads to uncertainty and insecurity among followers.

When you are organized, you have a special power. You walk with a sure sense of purpose. Your priorities are clear in your mind. You orchestrate complex events with a masterful touch. Things fall into place when you reveal your plans. You move smoothly from one project to the next with no wasted motion. Throughout the day you gain stamina and momentum as your successes build. People believe your promises because you always follow through. When you enter a meeting, you are prepared for whatever they throw at you. When at last you show your hand, you're a winner.

Christopher Robin, in *Winnie the Pooh*, gives my favorite definition of organization: "Organizing is what you do before you do something, so that when you do it, it's not all mixed up."

Here is my top ten list for personal organization:

1. SET YOUR PRIORITIES

Two things are difficult to get people to do. The first is to do things in order of importance, and the second is to *continue* doing things in order of importance. William Gladstone said, "He is a wise man who wastes no energy on pursuits for which he is not fitted; and he is wiser still who from among the things he can do well, chooses and resolutely follows the best."

Major events in my life, such as my speaking at conferences, are scheduled a year or two in advance. The last week of each month I spend two hours planning my schedule for the next thirty days. On paper I list all my major responsibilities according to importance and time needed to accomplish those tasks. This becomes the gauge to help me "keep on track" and keep moving. As each assignment is completed in its allotted time, I check it off my monthly list.

2. PLACE YOUR PRIORITIES IN YOUR CALENDAR

Once this list is written out on paper, I give it to my personal assistant, who writes it on my calendar. This protects me from outside pressures that clamor daily for my time. This also makes me accountable to someone else who can help me stay on track.

3. ALLOW A LITTLE TIME FOR THE UNEXPECTED

The kinds of work you do will determine the amount of time you set aside for interruptions. For example, the more you interact with people, the more time you must set aside. I set aside one-half day each week in my calendar for the unexpected.

4. DO PROJECTS ONE AT A TIME

A good general fights only on one front at a time. That is also true of a good leader. A feeling of being overwhelmed is the result of too many projects clamoring for your attention. For years I have followed this simple process:

> Itemize all that needs to be done.
> Prioritize things in order of importance.
> Organize each project.
> Emphasize only one project at a time.

5. ORGANIZE YOUR WORK SPACE

My work space is organized in two places: administrative and creative. My administrative office includes a room for small-group meetings, my work desk, and a desk for my personal assistant. This allows me to constantly communicate any details immediately to my key people. This office contains my calendar, computers, and files, and allows me easy access to administrative help. My creative office is separated from everyone. It contains my books, a copy machine, and my writing files. This secluded place is off-limits to my staff and allows me a proper environment for thinking, reading, and writing.

6. WORK ACCORDING TO YOUR TEMPERAMENT

If you are a morning person, organize your most important work for the morning hours. Obviously, if you are a late starter, do the opposite. However, be sure not to allow the weaknesses of your temperament to excuse you from what you know you need to do to work most effectively.

7. USE YOUR DRIVING TIME FOR LIGHT WORK AND GROWTH

My father gave me some great advice the day I became sixteen and received my driver's license. Climbing into the passenger side of the car, he placed a book in my glove compartment and said, "Son, never be in a car without a book. Whenever you are delayed in traffic, you can pull out this book and read." My car also contains many tapes for me to listen to and a notepad to jot down thoughts. My hands-free car phone also allows me to make calls to people on the way home from work. Recently while driving, I made twenty-one calls and saved hours of office time. Many times I take a staff person with me so we can discuss business and develop a closer relationship. I estimate that the average person could achieve eight additional hours of personal growth and work in each week by using driving time wisely.

8. Develop Systems That Work for You

Bobb Biehl says, "Systems—from to-do lists and calendars to libraries and computers—are your servants. They help you do things better and quicker, and by improving them, you decrease your time expenses and increase your results." Don't fight systems. Improve them.

9. Always Have a Plan for Those Minutes Between Meetings

Hours can be saved by making the best use of minutes. I keep a list of things to do that can be done anywhere in very short amounts of time. There are calls to make, memos to reply to or send, reports to scan, thank-you notes to write, and communications to share. Keep handy a list of things you can do in a short time.

10. Focus on Results, Not the Activity

Remember Peter Drucker's definition of efficiency (doing things right) versus effectiveness (doing the right things)? As you spend time on personal organization, be sure to keep your focus on doing the right things, that is, doing what is truly important. Then use this rule of thumb for organizing your overall work strategy:

Work where you are the strongest 80 percent of the time.
Work where you are learning 15 percent of the time.
Work where you are weak 5 percent of the time.

Welcome Responsibility

Winston Churchill said, "The price of greatness is responsibility." To increase your ability to take responsibility, do the following:

Be responsible for who you are. I believe in this. In fact, I'd like you to consider how it relates to research done by a psychologist who studied some people on the bottom.

The psychologist visited a prison and asked various inmates, "Why are you here?" The answers were very revealing, even though expected. There were many of them: "I was framed"; "They ganged up on me"; "It was a case of mistaken identity"; "It was not me—it was somebody else." The psychologist wondered if one could possibly find a larger group of "innocent" people anywhere else but in prison!

That reminds me of one of Abraham Lincoln's favorite stories about the man who murdered both his parents and then, when his sentence was about to be pronounced, pleaded for mercy on the grounds that he was an orphan! As the politician said to the judge, "It's not my fault, Your Honor, I never could have done all that stuff if the people hadn't elected me!"

Be responsible for what you do. It is rare to find a person who will be responsible, who will follow through correctly and finish the job. But when half-finished assignments keep returning to your desk to check up on, verify, edit, and upgrade, obviously someone is failing to take hold of the reins of responsibility.

> I am only one,
> But still I am one.
> I cannot do everything,
> But still I can do something;
> And because I cannot do everything
> I will not refuse to do the
> something that I can do.[3]

Be responsible for what you have received. John D. Rockefeller Jr. said, "I believe that every right implies a responsibility; every opportunity, an obligation; every possession, a duty." Winston Churchill said, "It is not enough that we do our best; sometimes we have to do what's required." And Jesus said, "Everyone to whom much is given, from him much will be required" (Luke 12:48).

Be responsible to those you lead. Great leaders never set themselves above their followers, except in carrying out responsibilities.

Coach Bo Schembechler tells about the third game of the 1970 season. His University of Michigan Wolverines were playing Texas A&M and they could not move the ball. All of a sudden, Dan Dierdorf, their offensive lineman—who was probably the best in the country at that time—came rushing over to the sidelines. Fed up with the team's performance, he yelled at Schembechler in front of everybody on the sidelines.

"Listen, coach! Run every play over me! Over me! Every play!" And they did. Michigan ran off-tackle six times in a row and marched right down the field. Michigan won the game.

When the game is on the line, great leaders always take responsibility for leading their teams to victory. This is my favorite "take responsibility" story.

The sales manager of a dog-food company asked his salespeople how they liked the company's new advertising program. "Great! Best in the business!" the salespeople responded.

"How do you like our new label and package?"

"Great! Best in the business!" the salespeople responded.

"How do like our sales force?"

They were the sales force. They had to admit they were good. "Okay, then," said the manager. "So we've got the best label, the best package, and the best advertising program being sold by the best sales force in the business. Tell me why we are in seventeenth place in the dog food business."

There was silence. Finally someone said, "It's those lousy dogs. They won't eat the stuff!"

ACCEPT ACCOUNTABILITY

Plato said, "The unexamined life is not worth living." Success and power have often crowded out of the leader's life a willingness to become accountable to others. Leaders in all areas of life are increasingly falling before the public because of this problem. Why does this happen?

HUMAN NATURE CANNOT HANDLE UNCHECKED POWER

Abraham Lincoln said, "Nearly all men can stand adversity, but if you want to test a man's character, give him power." Power can be compared to a great river; while within bounds it is both beautiful and useful. But when it overflows its bounds, it destroys. The danger of power lies in the fact that those who are vested with it tend to make its preservation their first concern. Therefore, they will naturally oppose any changes in the forces that have given them this power. History tells us that power leads to the abuse of power, and abuse of power leads to loss of power.

George Bush prayed in his inaugural address of 1989, "For we are given power not to advance our own purposes nor to make a great show in the world, nor a name. There is but one use of power, and it is to serve people."

LEADERS CAN EASILY BE SEPARATED FROM THEIR PEOPLE

When Harry Truman was thrust into the presidency at the death of FDR, Sam Rayburn gave him some fatherly advice: "From here on out you're going to have lots of people around you. They'll try to put a wall around you and cut you off from any ideas but theirs. They'll tell you what a great man you are, Harry. But you and I both know you ain't."

Hubert H. Humphrey said, "There is no party, no chief executive, no Cabinet, no legislature in this or any other nation, wise enough to govern without constant exposure to informed criticism." That is true for any person who occupies a leadership position.

DEVELOP INTEGRITY

The book *Profiles of Leadership* reveals the answers America's top business and government leaders gave when asked what quality they thought was most important to their success as leaders. Their unanimous answer: *integrity*.

Integrity is the human quality most necessary to business success according to the 1,300 senior executives who responded to a recent survey. Seventy-one percent put it at the top of a list of sixteen traits responsible for enhancing an executive's effectiveness. The dictionary defines integrity as "the state of being complete, unified." When people have integrity, their words and deeds match up. They are who they are, no matter where they are or who they're with. People with integrity are not divided (that's duplicity) or merely pretending (that's hypocrisy). They are "whole," and their lives are "put together." People with integrity have nothing to hide and nothing to fear. Their lives are open books.

Integrity in a leader must be demonstrated daily in a number of tangible ways. These are five that I strive to demonstrate to those I lead.

1. I will live what I teach. Deciding what to be is more important than deciding what to do. Often we ask young people "What are you going to do when you grow up?" But the more important question is, "What are you going to *be?*" The character decision must be made before a career is chosen.

Early in my years of leadership, I read this poem by Howard A. Walter and adopted its principles:

Character

I would be true, for there are those who trust me;
I would be pure, for there are those who care;
I would be strong, for there are those who suffer;
I would be brave, for there is much to dare.
I would be friend of all—the foe, the friendless;
I would be giving, and forget the gift;
I would be humble, for I know my weakness;
I would look up, and laugh, and love, and lift.

2. I will do what I say. If I promise something to a subordinate, colleague, or superior, I want to keep my word. The Center for Creative Leadership in Greensboro, North Carolina, released a study of twenty-one high-potential executives who were terminated from their companies or forced to retire early. The one universal character flaw or unforgivable sin which always led to downfall was betraying a trust; that is, not doing something that was promised.

3. I will be honest with others. If those who work with me ever catch me misrepresenting the facts or covering up a problem, I will instantly lose credibility. And it will not be easy to repair.

Dr. William Schultz, a noted psychologist who developed truth-in-management strategies at Proctor and Gamble and NASA, believes the key to productivity is "how well people work together," and he believes that nothing "increases compatibility like mutual trust and honesty." Dr. Schultz says, "If people in business just told the truth, 80 percent to 90 percent of their problems would disappear." Trust and honesty are the means that allow individuals to cooperate so that they can all prosper.

4. I will put what is best for others ahead of what is best for me. The organization I lead and those I work with must come first. When I put the organization's best interests ahead of mine, I keep integrity with those who hired me. When I put the interest of those I work with ahead of mine, I develop friendships and loyalty. Below is the leadership pyramid that I have always tried to follow.

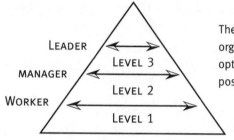

The higher a person rises in an organization, the less personal options and rights they should possess.

5. I will be transparent and vulnerable. Long ago I realized that in working with people, I have two choices. I can close my arms or I can open them. Both choices have strengths and weaknesses. If I close my arms, I won't get hurt, but I will not get much help either. If I open my arms, I likely will get hurt, but I will also receive help. What has been my decision? I've opened my arms and allowed others to enjoy the journey with me. My greatest gift to others is not a job, but myself. That is true of any leader.

PAY NOW, PLAY LATER

There are two paths that people can take. They can either play now and pay later, or pay now and play later. Regardless of the choice, one thing is certain. Life will demand a payment.

My father taught me this important discipline. Each week he would lay out the chores for the next seven days. Many of them could be done anytime during the week. Our goal was to complete them by Saturday noon. If completed, we could do something fun with the family. If not

completed, fun was forfeited and that individual stayed home to complete the chore. I needed to miss my deadline only a couple of times to
realize that I needed to "pay up front" and finish my work on time.

This lesson has been valuable to me, and I'm teaching it to my children, Elizabeth and Joel Porter. I want them to realize that there is no
such thing as a "free lunch," that life is not a gift—it is an investment.
The sooner they can take control of their desires and submit them to
life's demands, the more successful they will become. John Foster said,
"A man without decision of character can never be said to belong to
himself. He belongs to whatever can make captive of him." My friend
Bill Klassen often reminds me that "when we pay later, the price is
greater!"

"I've never known a man worth his salt who in the long run, deep
down in his heart, didn't appreciate the grind, the discipline," said
Vince Lombardi. "I firmly believe that any man's finest hour—this
greatest fulfillment to all he holds dear—is that moment when he has
worked his heart out in a good cause and lies exhausted on the field of
battle—victorious."

BECOME CHARACTER DRIVEN INSTEAD OF EMOTION DRIVEN

Most of the significant things done in the world were done by persons who were either too busy or too sick! "There are few ideal and
leisurely settings for the disciplines of growth," Robert Thornton
Henderson said. "Ninety percent of the work is done in this country by
people who don't feel well."

It is not doing the things we like to do, but doing the things we have
to do that causes growth and makes us successful. John Luther said,
"There's no such thing as a perfect job. In any position you'll find some
duties which, if they aren't onerous immediately, eventually will be."
Success depends not merely on how well you do the things you enjoy,
but how conscientiously you perform those duties you don't.

Tenor Luciano Pavarotti is such a winner. He is often described by
his admirers as "the new Caruso." In a newspaper interview, the six-

foot, three-hundred-pound tenor asked: "Do you want to know the hardest thing about being a singer? It is to sacrifice yourself every moment of your life, with not one exclusion. For example, if it is rain-ing, don't go out; eat this, do this, sleep ten hours a day. It is not a very free life. You cannot jump on a horse. You cannot go to swim."

Successful people are willing to do things unsuccessful people will not do. My observation is that one of those things that makes a differ-ence is this issue of being character driven instead of emotion driven. This is the difference:

CHARACTER-DRIVEN PEOPLE:	EMOTION-DRIVEN PEOPLE:
do right, then feel good	feel good, then do right
are commitment driven	are convenience driven
make principle-based decisions	make popular based decisions
let action control attitude	let attitude control action
believe it, then see it	see it, then believe it
create momentum	wait for momentum
ask, "What are my responsibilities?"	ask, "What are my rights?"
continue when problems arise	quit when problems arise
are steady	are moody
are leaders	are followers

The late Louis L'Amour is one of the best-selling authors of all time. Nearly 230 million copies of his books are in print worldwide, and every one of his more than one hundred books is still in print. When asked the key to his writing style, he responded, "Start writing, no matter what. The water does not flow until the faucet is turned on."

That's a good word for life. Sometimes, what we need to do is just to do something. Help someone. Sometimes, just getting into action will release power in our lives. We ought to adopt this as our motto for life: "The water does not flow until the faucet is turned on."

Good character is more to be praised than outstanding talent. Most talents are, to some extent, gifts. By contrast, good character is not given to us. We have to build it piece by piece—by thought, choice, courage, and determination. This will only be accomplished with a disciplined lifestyle.

Stephen Covey said:

> If I try to use human influence strategies and tactics of how to get other people to do what I want, to work better, to be more motivated, to like me and each other—while my character is fundamentally flawed, marked by duplicity or insincerity—then, in the long run, I cannot be successful. My duplicity will breed distrust and everything I do even using so-called good human relations techniques will be perceived as manipulative.
>
> It simply makes no difference how good the rhetoric is or even how good the intentions are: if there is little or no trust there is no foundation for permanent success. Only basic goodness gives life to technique.[4]

TEN

THE MOST IMPORTANT LESSON OF LEADERSHIP:
STAFF DEVELOPMENT

The growth and development of people is the highest calling of leadership. Chapter 7 emphasized the general development of people. This chapter will center on the development of a staff, but it is impossible to go into depth on this important subject in one chapter. The intent of this book is to help establish a leadership foundation. Therefore, I have dealt only with basics in the hope that I can help you develop the leader in you. I will write another book that will enable you to develop the leaders around you.

When I turned forty, I began to review my life. I made a list of all the things I was doing at that time. My list included:

senior pastor of a congregation of 3,500 attenders;
oversight and development of thirteen pastors;
president of Injoy, Inc., a company that develops resource materials for thousands of people;
a national and international speaking schedule with over four hundred engagements annually;
producing a monthly leadership tape for Injoy Life Club subscribers;
writing a book every eighteen months;

working on another education degree;

and most important—taking enough time for my wife, Margaret, and our two children, Elizabeth and Joel Porter.

After writing out my list, my conclusion was twofold: I didn't have any more hours, and therefore I couldn't work any harder; and my future growth in production would be determined by my ability to work through other people.

These two realities enabled me to search for and find the most important leadership lesson I've ever learned:

THOSE CLOSEST TO THE LEADER WILL DETERMINE THE LEVEL OF SUCCESS FOR THAT LEADER.

Niccolò Machiavelli said, "The first method for estimating the intelligence of a ruler is to look at the men he has around him." I'm not certain this subject is an issue of IQ, but I am sure that it is a test of leadership. Leaders who continue to grow personally and bring growth to their organizations will influence many and develop a successful team around them. The better the players, the better the leader. Few people are successful unless a lot of people want them to be. Andrew Carnegie said, "It marks a big step in your development when you come to realize that other people can help you do a better job than you could do alone."

Below is an illustration of what can happen to an organization when the key players slightly increase their potential while they work for the same team.

$$3 \times 3 \times 3 \times 3 \times 3 = \underline{243} + 25\% \text{ increase individually}$$
$$4 \times 4 \times 4 \times 4 \times 4 = \underline{1024} + 400\% \text{ increase together}$$

A great leader develops a team of people who increase production. The result? The leader's influence and effectiveness begin to multiply (working through others) instead of adding (working by oneself). That no man can sincerely try to help another without helping himself is, according to Ralph Waldo Emerson, one of the most beautiful compensations of this life.

David Jackson, founder and chief executive officer of Altos Computer Systems, said, "In my experience, the real turning point in a company is when you go from one to two people. Then, at least, there's someone to answer the phone while you eat your lunch."

All leaders have "war stories" of bad experiences in leading and developing staff. Perhaps this humorous illustration will help us laugh about our past experiences and allow us to get a second wind to begin building a winning team around us:

As nearly everyone knows, a leader has practically nothing to do except to decide what is to be done; tell somebody to do it; listen to reasons why it should not be done or why it should be done in a different way; follow up to see if the thing has been done; discover that it has not; inquire why; listen to excuses from the person who should have done it; follow up again to see if the thing has been done, only to discover that it has been done incorrectly; point out how it should have been done; conclude that as long as it has been done, it may as well be left where it is; wonder if it is not time to get rid of a person who cannot do a thing right; reflect that the person probably has a spouse and a large family, and any successor would be just as bad and maybe worse; consider how much simpler and better matters would be now if he had done it himself in the first place; reflect sadly that he could have done it right in twenty minutes, and, as things turned out, he has had to spend two days to find out why it has taken three weeks for somebody else to do it wrong.

In spite of all the problems that arise in the development of staff, two facts are certain. First, only as we develop a team do we continually succeed. A Chinese proverb says, "If you are planning for one year, grow rice. If you are planning for twenty years, grow trees. If you are planning for centuries, grow men." Second, only as we develop a team do we continually multiply.

A PICTURE OF A WINNING TEAM

Winning teams. . . .

- have great leaders
- pick good people
- play to win
- make other team members more successful
- keep improving

WINNING TEAMS HAVE GREAT LEADERS

Everything rises and falls on leadership. There are two ways you can get others to do what you want: You can compel them to do it, or you can persuade them. Compulsion is the method of slavery; persuasion is the method of free men.

Persuading requires an understanding of what makes people tick and what motivates them, that is, a knowledge of human nature. Great leaders possess that knowledge.

In a recent survey, seventy psychologists were asked: "What is the most essential thing for a supervisor to know about human nature?" Two-thirds said that motivation—an understanding of what makes people think, feel, and act as they do—is uppermost.

If you understand what motivates people, you have at your command the most powerful tool for dealing with them.

People Management has been studying the personal histories of tens of thousands of people since 1961. They found that, without exception, people repeat a pattern of behavior every time they accomplish something they think they do well and find deeply satisfying. They also found that excellent leaders underscore this behavior in the following ways.

EXCELLENT LEADERS CREATE THE RIGHT ENVIRONMENT

They believe in their team. This creates an environment for success. The best way to gain and hold the loyalty of your personnel is to show interest in and care for them by your words and actions. Sam Walton said, "Outstanding leaders go out of the way to boost the self-esteem of their personnel. If people believe in themselves, it's amazing what they can accomplish."

EXCELLENT LEADERS KNOW BASIC HUMAN NEEDS

Paul "Bear" Bryant, the legendary football coach at the University of Alabama, said there are five things winning team members need to know:

1. what is expected from each one;

2. that each will have an opportunity to perform;

3. how each one is getting along;

4. that guidance will be given where each needs it; and

5. that each will be rewarded according to his contribution.

EXCELLENT LEADERS KEEP CONTROL OF THE "BIG 3"

Any leader who wants to play an active role in all areas of the organization may be tempted to take on too many responsibilities. However, three areas are crucial to the leader's authority and success:

1. **Finance:** because the finance staff is a prime means of exercising executive control in any organization.

2. Personnel: because the selection of people will determine the organization.

3. Planning: because the plan determines the future of the organization.

EXCELLENT LEADERS AVOID THE "SEVEN DEADLY SINS."

1. Trying to be liked rather than respected.

2. Not asking team members for advice and help.

3. Thwarting personal talent by emphasizing rules rather than skills.

4. Not keeping criticism constructive.

5. Not developing a sense of responsibility in team members.

6. Treating everyone the same way.

7. Failing to keep people informed.

T. Boone Pickens said, "There are many ways to avoid mistakes, but the best way to sidestep the disasters is to be available. You don't have to make every decision, but you should always be accessible. If your people are smart, they will keep you informed, and if you're informed, you're a part of the decision. With that in place, it's easy for you to back your people and that eliminates second guessing."

WINNING TEAMS PICK GOOD PEOPLE

When building the staff for his newly conceived computer company, H. Ross Perot hired the best people he could find. His motto is, "Eagles don't flock. You have to find them one at a time." He was saying that you can't build a strong team on weak individuals.

Adlai E. Stevenson said that there are only three rules of sound administrators: Pick good people, tell them not to cut corners, and back them to the limits. Picking good people is the most important.

Bobb Biehl says that from 60 to 80 percent of the success of any company or organization is attributable to three factors:

- a clear direction

- the right team of players

- sound finances

That's why few things are as important as putting the right people in the right places.

Recently I read a humorous article entitled "Who Not to Hire." It said never hire anyone. . .

- who is accompanied by his or her (a) slave, (b) attorney with a tape recorder, (c) bodyguard, (d) teddy bear, (e) police escort, (f) mother.

- who brags about being smarter than any three of the jerks he or she has worked for previously.

- whose résumé runs longer than forty pages.

- whose résumé is printed in crayon.

- who hisses at your questions.

- who occasionally lapses into pig latin.

- who breaks into wracking sobs when asked to name a personal reference.

- who is unable to decide hair and eye colors.

- who is, by court order, on permanent intravenous sedation.

- who tries to impress you with his or her repertoire of "knock knock" jokes.

- who, under salary requirements, scrawls, "I want it all now!"

While you're laughing, remember that Murphy's Law would seem to conclude that the ideal résumé will turn up one day after the position is filled! Still, getting the right people in the right places is crucial to the success of your organization. There are five principles for picking people that will help you get the best candidates on your team.

1. THE SMALLER THE ORGANIZATION, THE MORE IMPORTANT THE HIRING

Small organizations often make the mistake of thinking that they can get by with inferior staff members because they are small. The opposite is true. In a firm of one hundred employees, if one is inferior, the loss is only 1 percent. But if the organization has a payroll of two, and one is inferior, the loss is 50 percent. However, the bright side is that it's much easier to pick one excellent person than a hundred.

2. KNOW WHAT KIND OF PERSON YOU NEED (PERSONAL REQUIREMENTS)

Listed below are the "Top 20" personal requirements I look for in a potential staff member:

1. Positive attitude—the ability to see people and situations in a positive way.

*2. High energy level—strength and stamina to work hard and not wear down.

3. Personal warmth—a manner that draws people to them.

4. Integrity—trustworthy, good solid character, words and walk are consistent.

5. Responsible—always "comes through," no excuses; job delegated-job done.

6. Good self-image—feels good about self, others, and life.

*7. Mental horsepower—ability to keep learning as the job expands.

8. Leadership ability—has high influence over others.

9. Followership ability—willingness to submit, play team ball, and follow the leader.

*10. Absence of personal problems—personal, family, and business life are in order.

11. People skills—the ability to draw people and develop them.

12. Sense of humor—enjoys life, fails to take self too seriously.

*13. Resilience—able to "bounce back" when problems arise.

*14. Track record—has experience and success, hopefully in two or more situations.

15. Great desire—hungers for growth and personal development.

16. Self-discipline—willing to "pay the price" and handle success.

17. Creativity—ability to see solutions and fix problems.

18. Flexibility—not afraid of change; fluid; flows as the organization grows.

19. Sees "Big Picture"—able to look beyond personal interest and see the total picture.

*20. Intuitive—able to discern and sense a situation without tangible data.

*These things probably cannot be taught. The others can be taught with a proper mentor, environment, and willingness by the staff member. Most of the qualities in the above list can be evaluated with a couple of interviews and tests.

3. KNOW WHAT THE JOB REQUIRES

A job has certain characteristics that require specific skills and personality traits. These ten general questions will help a leader pick the right person. Does the job require . . .

1. an up-front or a behind-the-scenes person?

2. a generalist or a specialist?

3. a producer or a maintainer?

4. a people person or a paper person?

5. a leader or a supporter?

6. a veteran or a rookie?

7. a creative thinker or an abstract thinker?

8. constant supervision or little supervision?

9. a team player or an individual?

10. short-term commitment or long-term commitment?

The more you know about the kind of person you need and what the job requires, the greater your odds of hiring the right individual. Kurt Einstren says, "Hiring the wrong persons costs your company at least two years' salary. Many times there is a much higher price that is paid, not in cash, but strained relationships, bad PR, and lack of trust."

Often I am asked in leadership conferences, "How do you know which staff person to hire?" I always laugh and say, "You never know for sure," and my track record underscores that comment! These are some guidelines I have tried to follow when looking for staff:

- Know what you need before you start looking for someone.

- Take time to search the field.

- Call many references.

- Have several interviews.

- Include your associates in some of the interviews and ask for their input.

- Interview the candidates' spouses.

- Check out the candidates' track records.

- If possible, have a trial run to see if the job and the potential staff match.

- Ask hard questions, such as, "Why did you leave?"; "What can you contribute?"; "Are you willing to pay the price?"

- Trust your instincts.

There is only so much you can put on paper. If it looks good on paper but feels bad inside, go slowly. In fact, back off and let an associate take over; then compare conclusions. Personally, I only hire a person if it looks good *and* feels good.

4. KNOW WHAT THE POTENTIAL STAFF MEMBER WANTS

People work harder, stay longer, and do better on the job when they like what they do. Realizing this truth, I always make sure the potential team player feels good about me as the leader, the other players on the team, and the vision and requirements of the team. I always say to them, "Don't come unless it feels right." I know that no amount of money, attention, privileges, and promises will motivate a staff member who really does not want to be on the team. It is also important that the spouse "feels good" about the job. Positive feelings of a staff member will slowly disappear if the spouse is unhappy.

5. WHEN YOU CANNOT AFFORD TO HIRE THE BEST, HIRE THE YOUNG WHO ARE GOING TO BE THE BEST

Then:

Believe in them—that will encourage risk.

Show them—that will build respect.

Love them—that will strengthen relationships.

Know them—that will personalize development.

Teach them—that will enhance growth.

Trust them—that will develop loyalty.

Expand them—that will provide challenges.

Lift them—that will ensure results.

WINNING TEAMS PLAY TO WIN

The difference between playing to win and playing to not lose is the difference between success and mediocrity. I grew up in Ohio and became a fan of Big Ten football. Over the years I observed that Big Ten teams usually lost the "big game" every year at the Rose Bowl. Why? Were Pac Ten teams consistently better? No, the margin of victory was not a result of talent. It was a result of how each team approached the game. Big Ten teams played conservatively, trying not to lose. Pac Ten teams played wide open, trying to win.

Each time new staff members join our team, I give them each a plaque and ask them to display it on the wall of their offices. The words on the plaque read, "I don't have to survive." At the presentation, I encourage them to be not-survivors. I remind them to take risks, make tough decisions, live on the edge, and make a difference. People who play it safe continually miss opportunities and seldom make progress. It's the same way in baseball—you cannot steal second base with your foot on first! This is a favorite poem of mine. It describes those bland, safe people.

> There was a very cautious man
> Who never laughed or played.
> He never risked, he never tried,
> He never sang or prayed.
> And when he one day passed away,
> His insurance was denied.
> For since he never really lived,
> They claimed he never really died.

A recent survey of workers across the United States revealed that nearly 85 percent of those interviewed said they could work harder on the job. More than half claimed they could double their effectiveness "if they wanted to."[1] Winning teams are seldom more talented than losing teams. But they are always more committed. They want to win. They pay the price and go after victory. The crowd in the bleachers may wonder how they got so lucky, but the team members know they played to win.

WINNING TEAMS MAKE THEIR TEAM MEMBER MORE SUCCESSFUL

In other words, because of the other members of the team, each player is better than the player would be if he or she played alone. Vince Lombardi, one of the all-time great head coaches, said, "Start by teaching the fundamentals. A player's got to know the basics of the game and how to play his position. Next, keep him in line. That's discipline. The men have to play as a team, not as a bunch of individuals. . . Then you've got to care for one another. You've got to *love* each other . . . Most people call it team spirit."[2]

Robert W. Keidel said that trying to change individual and/or corporate behavior without addressing the larger organizational context is bound to disappoint. Sooner or later bureaucratic structures will consume even the most determined of collaborative processes. As Woody Allen once said, "The lion and the lamb may lie down together, but the lamb won't get much sleep."

What to do? Work on the lion as well as the lamb by designing teamwork into the organization. Although the Boston Celtics have won sixteen championships, they have never had the league's leading scorer and never paid a player based on his individual statistics. The Celtics understand that virtually every aspect of basketball requires close collaboration.

There are significant ways to engage in better team building.

KNOW THE KEY TO EACH PLAYER

Every individual has a personal agenda, the "real reason" he or she wants to be on the team. That personal agenda is the key to motivating each player.

MAP OUT A TEAM MISSION

Lay out the vision. Develop organizational mottoes, names, symbols, and slogans. This will encourage pride in team memberships.

DEFINE THE ROLE OF EACH PLAYER

This will help avoid unnecessary rivalries by clearly identifying each person's role within the group. This will also avoid the "fairness" issue that is common with staffs. Each player will be appreciated for his or her contribution to the team.

CREATE A GROUP IDENTITY

Establish your groups' worth by examining and promoting its history and values. Create memories together as a group.

USE LIBERAL DOSES OF "WE" AND "OUR"

Team building involves getting the members to feel a sense of ownership in what they are doing as a group. When the group has done well, it is important to praise the entire effort without singling out individuals.

COMMUNICATE WITH EVERYONE

Don't be a fact hog. Share information with everyone who is affected, not with just the key players. People are usually "down on" what they are not "up on." As a leader, you will know you have succeeded when the members of your team put the interests of the group over their own.

Do you recall when Edmund Hillary and his Sherpa guide, Tenzing, made their historic climb of Mount Everest? Coming down from the peak, Hillary suddenly lost his footing. Tenzing held the line taut and kept them both from falling by digging his axe into the ice. Later Tenzing refused any special credit for saving Hillary's life; he considered it a routine part of the job. As he put it, "Mountain climbers always help each other."

WINNING TEAMS KEEP IMPROVING

Whenever an organization is through improving, it's through! Why is it that a professional football, basketball, or baseball team seldom repeats as the world champion in consecutive years? Mainly, it's because of the temptation to keep all the players, practices, and strategies the same as the previous year. Too many think that if they "stay put," they can stay on top. That's not true. Either the current players must keep growing and improving, or potentially better ones must be brought into the organization. Continued success is a result of continued improvement.

The first objective of the leader is to develop people, not to dismiss them.

Studies have shown that day-to-day coaching, rather than comprehensive annual appraisals, is most effective for improving performance. This coaching process has two crucial components: setting specific objectives and holding frequent progress reviews.

Objectives should specify end results, the exact extent of achievement the manager expects, and should be tied to a timetable. How many objectives should the employee be given? In our experience, a few are better than too many. If the subordinate is overloaded, expecting all the objectives to be accomplished is unreasonable. Remember, the objectives are the primary measuring stick.

By *end results*, we mean what should be observably different as a result of the subordinate's performance on the job. All too often employees expect to be evaluated on the basis of how much effort they are putting into the job, rather than what they are accomplishing. This is especially true of weak performers. It is critical that the manager make clear that certain outcomes are expected and the subordinate will be held accountable for them. The manager should make every effort to set mutually acceptable goals. If there is disagreement, however, the manager must unhesitatingly insist upon setting the objectives. Remember: performance, not just effort, is the yardstick for meeting objectives.

Frequent progress reviews accomplish three things. First, they serve as a continual reminder that reaching the objectives is important to the person's career. Second, reviews give the manager a chance to recognize positive movement toward objectives. Third, if progress is not forthcoming, the manager can listen to the reasons for lack of performance and attempt to get the subordinate on track. The review becomes a problem-solving session.

Whether or not the employee makes progress, holding reviews permits the manager or boss to remain in control of the process.[3] If you have more than three people reporting to you right now, chances are you are unhappy with at least one of them. The situation usually has one or more of these elements:

- The person is not doing a top-notch job, but not a terrible one either; so you keep him or her around.

- Finding someone else who can do the job means interviewing, hiring (taking a risk), and then training the new person. You do not have time for that either.

- The person definitely is not doing the job, but you like him or her (or more likely you feel sorry for him or her).

- You don't quite have all the documentation you need to fire this person. Your last review was too flowery, and you have not really said how unhappy you are with the individual's work.

The result? Nothing happens. But keep in mind that you and the person who needs to be dismissed are not the only two people in the equation. What too many leaders fail to realize are the facts:

- The situation is well-known to other workers in the organization. No one can keep below-par performance a secret.

- Your failure to fire will have a detrimental effect on your career. As a leader, your first and greatest responsibility is to the organization and its highest good. Whenever a person's leadership position puts the personal agenda of himself or herself ahead of the organization, that leader is a liability.

- The morale of the other employees suffers because you keep the below-par performer on the payroll while everyone else is pulling more than enough weight.

Remember, it isn't the people you fire who make your life miserable; it's the ones you don't. If you have serious doubts about a staff member and have worked with him or her without success, it is better to have that person working somewhere else.

How can dismissing a person be handled correctly? Bobb Biehl says the essence of doing it right is in maintaining this perspective: "When you appropriately fire a person from a position in which he is failing, you are actually releasing him from that failure—and freeing him to seek a position in which he can find success. With a proper release, it's even possible to instill in a person the excitement that comes from anticipating a new adventure."

Obviously the optimum scenario is to interview well, hire well, and then begin to develop your staff to reach their—and your—greatest potential. There are three phases of potential:

1. I maximize my potential (I pour my energy into myself).

2. I maximize the potential of others (I pour my energy into key people).

3. They maximize my potential (they pour their energy into me).

Producers excel only at phase 1.
Leaders excel at phases 1 and 2.
Fortunate leaders excel at phases 1 and 2 and experience phase 3.

Let's take a moment now to stop and consider your strengths as a leader. This evaluation will allow you to review those areas of importance to a leader we've discussed in the pages of this book, while reinforcing the areas you need to emphasize in your development. Just circle the number that corresponds with how you see your ability, right now.

1	2	3	4	5
Mastered	Strong	Satisfactory	Needs growth	Difficult

Common Strengths Outstanding Leaders Share

DREAMING 1 2 3 4 5
Never let go of a dream until you're ready to wake up and make it happen.

In working with leaders, I have often asked myself, "Does the man make the dream, or does the dream make the man?" My conclusion: both are equally true.

GOAL SETTING 1 2 3 4 5
A goal is a dream with a deadline.

If you don't know what you want and where you are going, you will get next to nothing and end up nowhere.

INFLUENCING 1 2 3 4 5
The very essence of all power to influence lies in getting the other person to participate.

People do not care how much you know until they know how much you care.

PERSONAL ORGANIZATION 1 2 3 4 5
"Organizing is what you do before you do something, so that when you do it, it's not all mixed up."—Christopher Robin in *Winnie the Pooh*.

PRIORITIZING 1 2 3 4 5
"He is a wise man who wastes no energy on pursuits for which he is not fitted; and he is wiser still who, from among the things he can do well, chooses and resolutely follows the best."—William Gladstone

PROBLEM SOLVING 1 2 3 4 5
"The majority see the obstacles; the few see the objectives; history records the successes of the latter, while oblivion is the reward of the former."—Alfred Armand Montapert

RISK TAKING 1 2 3 4 5
Risks are not to be evaluated in terms of the probability of success, but in terms of the value of the goal.

DECISION MAKING 1 2 3 4 5
Your decisions will always be better if you do what is right for the organization rather than what is right for yourself.

CREATIVITY   1   2   3   4   5

There is always a better way . . . your challenge is to find it.

"Man's mind, once stretched by a new idea, never regains its original dimensions."—Oliver Wendall Holmes

HIRING/FIRING   1   2   3   4   5

"There are only three rules of sound administration: pick good [people], tell them not to cut corners, and back them to the limit. Picking good [people] is the most important."—Adlai E. Stevenson

"When you appropriately fire a person from a position in which he is failing, you are actually releasing him from that failure—and freeing him to seek a position in which he can find success."—Bobb Biehl

EVALUATION   1   2   3   4   5

People who reach their potential spend more time asking, "What am I doing well?" rather than "What am I doing wrong?"

The person who knows how will always have a job; but the person who knows why will always be the boss.

If you are strong in or if you have mastered four areas, you are on Level #1. If you are strong in or if you have mastered eight, you are on Level #2. If you are strong in or if you have mastered every area, you are on Level #3, and that means you have a strong support team that has allowed you to grow beyond yourself.

At this point in my life, I am fortunate to be living on the Level #3. I've grown beyond my own resources and am multiplying instead of adding because of those closest to me. I will be forever grateful to them. With them I will continue to lead. Because of them I will continue to grow.

Some of these precious people are:

Margaret Maxwell—my wife and best friend. Marrying her is the best decision I ever made.
Stephen F. Babby—my colleague and the wisest person I know.

Dick Peterson—my close friend, whose goal in life is to help me.

Dan Reiland—my executive pastor, whose loyalty and energy are unequaled.

Barbara Brumagin—my personal assistant, who has a servant's heart and superior skills.

Melvin Maxwell—my father, who is my hero in life and mentor in leadership.

EPILOGUE

This world needs leaders . . .

who use their influence at the right times for the right reasons;
who take a little greater share of the
  blame and a little smaller share of the credit;
who lead themselves successfully before attempting
  to lead others;
who continue to search for the best answer,
  not the familiar one;
who add value to the people and organizations they lead;
who work for the benefit of others and not for personal gain;
who handle themselves with their heads and handle others
  with their hearts;
who know the way, go the way, and
  show the way;
who inspire and motivate rather than
  intimidate and manipulate;
who live with people to know their
  problems and live with God in order
  to solve them;

_____

The growth and
development
of people is
the highest
calling of
leadership.

_____

who realize that their dispositions are
    more important than their positions;
who mold opinions instead of following opinion polls;
who understand that an institution is
    the reflection of their character;
who never place themselves above others except in carrying
    responsibilities;
who will be as honest in small things as
    in great things;
who discipline themselves so they will
    not be disciplined by others;
who encounter setbacks and turn them
    into comebacks;
who follow a moral compass that points
    in the right direction regardless of the trends.

NOTES

INTRODUCTION

1. David Hartley-Leonard, "Perspectives," *Newsweek*, 24 August 1987, 11.
2. Contributed by Doug Lysen, *Reader's Digest*, February 1989.
3. John W. Gardner, "The Nature of Leadership," Leadership Papers #1, Independent Sector, January 1986.
4. Richard Kerr for United Technologies Corp. *Bits and Pieces*, March 1990.

CHAPTER 1

1. James C. Georges, ParTraining Corp., Tucker, GA, interviewed in *Executive Communications*, January 1987.
2. J. R. Miller, *The Building of Character* (New Jersey: AMG Publishers, 1975).
3. Warren Bennis and Burt Nanus, *Leaders* (New York: Harper and Row, 1985), 222.
4. Robert Dilenschneider, *Power and Influence: Mastering the Art of Persuasion* (New York: Prentice Hall, 1990).
5. E. C. McKenzie, *Quips and Quotes* (Grand Rapids: Baker, 1980).

6. Fred Smith, *Learning to Lead* (Waco: Word, 1986), 117.

7. John C. Maxwell, *Be a People Person* (Wheaton: Victor, 1989).

CHAPTER 2

1. R. Earl Allen, *Let It Begin in Me* (Nashville: Broadman Press, 1985).

2. William H. Cook, *Success, Motivation and the Scriptures* (Nashville: Broadman, 1974).

CHAPTER 3

1. Dwight D. Eisenhower, *Great Quotes from Great Leaders*, ed. Peggy Anderson (Lombard: Great Quotations, 1989).

2. CCM *Communicator*, newsletter of the Council of Communication, Spring 1988.

3. Peter Drucker, *Management, Tasks, Responsibilities and Practices* (New York: Harper & Row, 1974).

4. *Newsweek*, 24 August 1987, 11.

5. Joseph Bailey, "Clues for Success in the President's Job," *Harvard Business Review*, 1983.

6. James M. Kouzes and Barry Z. Posner, *The Leadership Challenge* (San Francisco: Jossey-Bass, 1987).

CHAPTER 4

1. Quoted in Paul Wharton, *Stories and Parables for Preachers and Teachers* (Mahwah: Paulist, 1986).

2. Howard Hendricks, *Teaching to Change Lives* (Portland: Multnomah, 1987), 32.

3. Robert Lacy, *Ford: The Man and the Machine* (New York: Little Brown, 1986).

4. Bobb Biehl, *Increasing Your Leadership Confidence* (Sisters, OR: Questar Publishers, 1989).

5. Melvin E. Page and H. Leon Abrams Jr., *Your Body Is Your Doctor* (New Canaan: Keats, 1972).

6. John Maxwell, *The Winning Attitude* (San Bernardino: Here's Life, 1984).

7. Winifield Arn, *Growth Report No. 5, Ten Steps for Church Growth* (New York: Harper & Row, 1977).

8. George F. Trusell, *Helping Employees Cope with Change: A Manager's Guidebook* (Buffalo: PAT Publishers, 1988).

9. Bennis and Nanus, *Leaders*.

10. Trusell, *Helping Employees Cope with Change*.

11. R. F. Caldwell, "The Face of Corporate Culture," *Santa Clara Today*, November 1984, 12.

12. Max DePree, *Leadership Is an Art* (New York: Doubleday, 1989), 87.

13. Ron Jenson, ed., *Higher Ground*.

CHAPTER 5

1. F. F. Fournies, *Coaching for Improved Work Performance* (New York: Van Nostrand Reinhold, 1978).

2. Taken from a quotation by MacDonald in A. C. Remley, *Leaves of Gold*, (Williamsport: Coslett Publishing, 1948).

3. Adapted from G. W. Target, "The Window," in *The Window and Other Essays* (Mountain View: Pacific Press Publishing Association, 1973), 5–7.

4. Beihl, *Increasing Your Leadership Confidence*.

5. Tom Wujec, *Pumping Ions: Games and Exercises to Flex Your Mind* (New York: Doubleday, 1988).

6. John K. Clemens, *Hartwick Humanities in Management Report* (Oneonta: Hartwick Institute, 1989).

CHAPTER 6

1. Chuck Swindoll, *Improving Your Serve* (Waco: Word, 1981).

2. Nell Mohney, "Beliefs Can Influence Attitudes," *Kingsport Times News*, 25 July 1986, 4B.

3. Norman Vincent Peale, *Power of the Plus Factor* (New York: Fawcett, 1988).

4. Anonymous, "Attitude," *Bartlett's Familiar Quotations*, ed. Emily Morison Beck (Boston: Little Brown, 1980).

5. Viktor Frankl, "Youth in Search of Meaning," *Moral Development Foundations*, Donald M. Joy, ed. (Nashville: Abingdon, 1983).

6. C. S. Lewis, *Mere Christianity* (New York: Macmillan, 1952), 86.

7. Donald Robinson, "Mind Over Disease," *Reader's Digest*, March 1990.

Chapter 7

1. Thomas Peters and Robert Waterman, *In Search of Excellence* (New York: Warner, 1984), 58.

2. Frankl, "Youth in Search of Meaning."

3. Stephen Ash, " The Career Doctor," cited in Michigan Department of Social Services, *No-Name Newsletter*, Fall 1986.

4. Richard Huseman and John Hatfield, *Managing the Equity Factor* (New York: Houghton Mifflin, 1989).

5. Henry David Thoreau, *Bartlett's Familiar Quotations*.

6. Ron Watts, La Croix United Methodist Church, Cape Girardeau, MO, personal communication.

7. Huseman and Hatfield, *Managing the Equity Factor*.

Chapter 8

1. Robert K. Greenleaf, *The Servant as Leader* (Mahwah: Paulist, 1977).

2. Biehl, *Increasing Your Leadership Confidence*.

3. Quoted in "Weekend," *Newsday*, 8, 1990.

4. Harry C. McKown, *A Boy Grows Up* (New York: McGraw-Hill, 1985).

5. George S. Patton, *Great Quotes from Great Leaders*, Peggy Anderson, ed. (Lombard: Great Quotations, 1989).

6. Ralph Waldo Emerson, *Bartlett's Familiar Quotations*.

7. Roger von Oech, *A Kick in the Seat of the Pants* (San Francisco: HarperCollins, 1986).

8. Denis Waitley and Reni L. Witt, *The Joy of Working* (New York: Dodd, Mead & Co., 1985).

CHAPTER 9

1. Harry S. Truman, *Great Quotes from Great Leaders*.
2. Edwin Markham, *Great Quotes from Great Leaders*.
3. Edward Everett Hale, *Bartlett's Familiar Quotations*.
4. Stephen Covey, *The Seven Habits of Highly Effective People: Restoring the Character Ethic* (New York: Simon and Schuster, 1989).

CHAPTER 10

1. Huseman and Hatfield, *Managing the Equity Factor*.
2. Vince Lombardi, *Great Quotes from Great Leaders*.
3. William J. Morin and Lyle Yorks, *Dismissal* (San Diego: Harcourt Brace Jovanovich, 1990).

DEVELOPING
the LEADERS
AROUND YOU

This book is dedicated to the men who have developed me:

To Larry Maxwell,
my brother, who encouraged in me the desire
to grow mentally;

To Glenn Leatherwood,
my junior high Sunday school teacher,
who inspired me to have a heart for God;

To my high school basketball coach,
Don Neff, who instilled in me the desire to win;

To Elmer Towns, pastor and friend,
who strengthened my desire to reach my potential;

And above all, to my father, Melvin Maxwell,
my lifelong mentor. I am a leader today because of the time
you spent developing me.

CONTENTS

CONTENTS

ONE

THE LEADER'S KEY QUESTION:
AM I RAISING UP POTENTIAL LEADERS?

One night, after working quite late, I grabbed a copy of *Sports Illustrated*, hoping its pages would lull me to sleep. It had the opposite effect. On the back cover was an advertisement that caught my eye and got my emotional juices flowing. It featured a picture of John Wooden, the coach who led the UCLA Bruins for many years. The caption beneath his picture read, "The guy who puts the ball through the hoop has ten hands."

John Wooden was a great basketball coach. Called "the Wizard of Westwood," he brought ten national basketball championships to UCLA in a span of twelve years. Two back-to-back championships are almost unheard of in the world of competitive sports, but he led the Bruins to *seven titles in a row*. It took a consistent level of superior play, good coaching, and hard practice. But the key to the Bruins's success was Coach Wooden's unyielding dedication to his concept of teamwork.

He knew that if you oversee people and you wish to develop leaders, you are responsible to: (1) appreciate them for who they are; (2) believe that they will do their very best; (3) praise their accomplishments; and (4) accept your personal responsibility to them as their leader.

Coach Bear Bryant expressed this same sentiment when he said:

> I'm just a plowhand from Arkansas, but I have learned how to hold a team together—how to lift some men up, how to calm others down, until finally they've got one heartbeat together as a team. There's always just three things I say: "If anything goes bad, I did it. If anything goes semi-good, then we did it. If anything goes real good, they did it." That's all it takes to get people to win.

Bear Bryant won people and games. Until a few years ago, he held the title of the winningest coach in the history of college football with 323 victories.

Great leaders—the truly successful ones who are in the top 1 percent—all have one thing in common. They know that acquiring and keeping good people is a leader's most important task. An organization cannot increase its productivity—but people can! The asset that truly appreciates within any organization is people. Systems become dated. Buildings deteriorate. Machinery wears. But people can grow, develop, and become more effective if they have a leader who understands their potential value.

> **Acquiring and keeping good people is a leader's most important task.**

The bottom line—and the essential message of this book—is that you can't do it alone. If you really want to be a successful leader, you must develop other leaders around you. You must establish a team. You must find a way to get your vision seen, implemented, and contributed to by others. The leader sees the big picture, but he needs other leaders to help make his mental picture a reality.

Most leaders have followers around them. They believe the key to leadership is gaining more followers. Few leaders surround themselves with other leaders, but the ones who do bring great value to their organizations. And not only is their burden lightened, but their vision is also carried on and enlarged.

WHY LEADERS NEED TO REPRODUCE LEADERS

The key to surrounding yourself with other leaders is to find the best people you can, then develop them into the best leaders they can be. Great leaders produce other leaders. Let me tell you why:

THOSE CLOSEST TO THE LEADER WILL DETERMINE THE SUCCESS LEVEL OF THAT LEADER

The greatest leadership principle that I have learned in more than thirty years of leadership is that those closest to the leader will determine the success level of that leader. A negative reading of this statement is also true: Those closest to the leader will determine the level of failure for that leader. In other words, the people close to me "make me or break me." The determination of a positive or negative outcome in my leadership depends upon my ability as a leader to develop those closest to me. It also depends upon my ability to recognize the value that others bring to my organization. My goal is not to draw a following that results in a crowd. My goal is to develop leaders who become a movement.

Stop for a moment and think of the five or six people closest to you in your organization. Are you developing them? Do you have a game plan for them? Are they growing? Have they been able to lift your load?

Within my organizations leadership development is continually emphasized. In their first training session, I give new leaders this principle: *As a potential leader you are either an asset or a liability to the organization.* I illustrate this truth by saying, "When there's a problem, a 'fire' in the organization, you as a leader are often the first to arrive at the scene. You have in your hands two buckets. One contains water and the other contains gasoline. The 'spark' before you will either become a greater problem because you pour the gasoline on it, or it will be extinguished because you use the bucket of water."

Every person within your organization also carries two buckets. The question a leader needs to ask is, "Am I training them to use the gasoline or the water?"

An Organization's Growth Potential Is Directly Related To Its Personnel Potential

When conducting leadership conferences, I often make the statement, "Grow a leader—grow the organization." A company cannot grow without until its leaders grow within.

> **Grow a leader— grow the organization.**

I am often amazed at the amount of money, energy, and marketing focus organizations spend on areas that will not produce growth. Why advertise that the customer is number one when the personnel have not been trained in customer service? When customers arrive, they will know the difference between an employee who has been trained to give service and one who hasn't. Slick brochures and catchy slogans will never overcome incompetent leadership.

In 1981 I became Senior Pastor of Skyline Wesleyan Church in San Diego, California. This congregation averaged 1,000 in attendance from 1969 to 1981, and it was on an obvious plateau. When I assumed leadership responsibilities, the first question I asked was, "Why has the growth stopped?" I needed to find an answer, so I called my first staff meeting and gave a lecture titled *The Leadership Line*. My thesis was, "Leaders determine the level of an organization." I drew a line across a marker board and wrote the number "1,000." I shared with the staff that for thirteen years the average attendance at Skyline was 1,000. I knew the staff could lead 1,000 people effectively. What I did not know was whether they could lead 2,000 people. So I drew a dotted line and wrote the number 2,000, and I placed a question mark between the two lines. I then drew an arrow from the bottom 1,000 to the top 2,000 line and wrote the word "change."

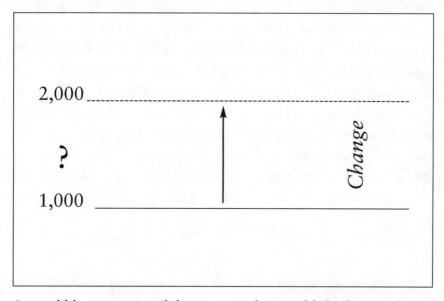

It would be my responsibility to train them and help them make the necessary changes to reach our new goal. When the leaders changed positively, I knew the growth would become automatic. Now, I had to help them change themselves, or I knew I would literally have to change them by hiring others to take their place.

From 1981 to 1995 I gave this lecture at Skyline on three occasions. The last time, the number 4,000 was placed on the top line. As I discovered, the numbers changed, but the lecture didn't. The

> **Everything rises and falls on leadership.**

strength of any organization is a direct result of the strength of its leaders. Weak leaders equal weak organizations. Strong leaders equal strong organizations. Everything rises and falls on leadership.

POTENTIAL LEADERS HELP CARRY THE LOAD

Businessman Rolland Young said, "I am a self-made man, but I think if I had it to do over again, I would call in someone else!" Usually leaders fail to develop other leaders either because they lack training or because they possess wrong attitudes about allowing and encouraging others to come alongside them. Often, leaders wrongly believe that they must compete with the people close to them instead of working with them. Great leaders have a different mind-set. In *Profiles in Courage*, President John F. Kennedy wrote, "The best way to go along is to get along with others." This kind of positive interaction can happen only if the leader has an attitude of inter-dependency with others and is committed to win-win relationships.

Take a look at differences between the two views leaders possess about people:

WINNING BY COMPETITIVENESS	WINNING BY COOPERATION
Look at others as enemies	Look at others as friends
Concentrate on yourself	Concentrate on others
Become suspicious of others	Become supportive of others
Win only if you are good	Win if you or others are good
Winning determined by your skills	Winning determined by the skills of many

Small victory	Large victory
Some joy	Much joy
There are winners and losers	There are only winners

Peter Drucker was correct when he said, "No executive has ever suffered because his people were strong and effective." The leaders around me lift my load in many ways. Here are two of the most important ones:

1. *They become a sounding board for me.* As a leader, I sometimes hear counsel that I don't want to hear but need to hear. That's the advantage of having leaders around you—having people who know how to make decisions. Followers tell you what you want to hear. Leaders tell you what you need to hear.

I have always encouraged those closest to me to give me advice on the front end. In other words, an opinion before a decision has potential value. An opinion after the decision has been made is worthless. Alex Agase, a college football coach, once said, "If you really want to give me advice, do it on Saturday afternoon between one and four o'clock, when you've got twenty-five seconds to do it, between plays. Don't give me advice on Monday. I know the right thing to do on Monday."

2. *They possess a leadership mind-set.* Fellow leaders do more than work with the leader, they think like the leader. It gives them the power to lighten the load. This becomes invaluable in areas such as decision making, brainstorming, and providing security and direction to others.

A majority of my time is spent away from the office speaking at conferences and events. Therefore, it is essential that I have leaders in my organizations who can carry on effectively while I am gone. And they do. It happens because I have spent my life finding and developing potential leaders. The results are very gratifying.

This leadership mind-set of sharing the load is wonderfully demonstrated by, of all things, geese, as illustrated by Tom Worsham:

When you see geese heading south for the winter flying along in a "V" formation, you might be interested in knowing that science has discovered why they fly that way. Research has revealed that as each bird flaps its wings, it creates an uplift for the bird immediately behind it. By flying in a "V" formation, the whole flock adds at least 71 percent greater flying range than if each bird flew on its own. (*People who share a common direction and sense of community get where they are going more quickly and easily because they are traveling on one another's thrust.*)

Whenever a goose falls out of formation, it suddenly feels the drag and resistance of trying to go it alone. It quickly gets back into formation to take advantage of the lifting power of the bird immediately in front. (*If we as people have as much sense as a goose, we will stay in formation and so will those who are headed the same way we are.*) When the lead goose gets tired, he rotates back in the "V" and another goose flies the point. (*It pays to take turns doing hard jobs.*)

The geese honk from behind to encourage those up front to keep up their speed. (*What do we say when we honk from behind?*)

And finally, when a goose gets sick, or is wounded by gunfire and falls out, two other geese fall out of formation and follow it down to help and protect it. They stay with the goose until it is either able to fly again or dead, and then they launch out on their own or with another formation to catch up with their group. (*If we have the sense of a goose, we will stand by each other like that.*)

Whoever was the first to call another person a "silly goose" didn't know enough about geese![1]

LEADERS ATTRACT POTENTIAL LEADERS

Birds of a feather really do flock together. I really believe that it takes a leader to know a leader, grow a leader, and show a leader. I have also found that it takes a leader to attract a leader.

Attraction is the obvious first step, yet I find many people in leadership positions who are unable to accomplish this task. True leaders are able to attract potential leaders because:

- Leaders think like them.

- Leaders express feelings that other leaders sense.

- Leaders create an environment that attracts potential leaders.

- Leaders are not threatened by people with great potential.

For example, a person in a leadership position who is a "5" on a scale of 1 to 10 will not attract a leader who is a "9." Why? Because leaders naturally size up any crowd and migrate to other leaders who are at the same or higher level.

Any leader who has only followers around him will be called upon to continually draw on his own resources to get things done. Without other leaders to carry the load, he will become fatigued and burnt out. Have you asked yourself lately, "Am I tired?" If the answer is yes, you may have a good reason for it, as this humorous story illustrates:

> It takes a leader to know a leader, grow a leader, and show a leader.

Somewhere in the world there is a country with a population of 220 million. Eighty-four million are over sixty years of age, which leaves 136 million to do the work. People under twenty years of age total 95 million, which leaves 41 million to do the work.

There are 22 million employed by the government, which leaves 19 million to do the work. Four million are in the Armed Forces, which leaves 15 million to do the work. Deduct 14,800,000, the number in state and city offices, and that leaves 200,000 to do the work. There are 188,000 in hospitals or insane asylums, so that leaves 12,000 to do the work.

It is of interest to note that in this country 11,998 people are in jail, so that leaves just two people to carry the load. That's you and me—and brother, I'm getting tired of doing everything myself!

Unless you want to carry the whole load yourself, you need to be developing leaders.

LEADERS WHO MENTOR POTENTIAL LEADERS MULTIPLY THEIR EFFECTIVENESS

Not long ago, at a conference where management expert Peter Drucker was speaking, thirty of my leaders and I were continually challenged to produce and mentor other leaders. Peter asked us, "Who will take your place?" He kept emphasizing, "There is no success without a successor."

I left that meeting with one resolve: *I was going to produce leaders who could produce other leaders.* No longer was it enough to grow by adding leaders. Now, my focus was upon *multiplying* those leaders. To accomplish this, I began to train my leaders to learn the fine art of setting parameters and priorities. I wanted them to gain a deep understand of our goals and then go out into our

organization and train others to someday replace them or help carry the load.

At that time, the board of my organization became my focus for developing leaders. In 1989 one-half of my board members

> **There is no success
> without a successor.**

were brand new, and the group faced major decisions on a $35 mil-
lion relocation project. I was concerned. Could decisions of such
magnitude be made by rookies? However, my fears subsided at the
next board retreat when I discovered that every new board member
had been mentored by former, experienced members. The old board
had heard me and implemented my teachings, and the new board
was now benefiting. The new members had come into their positions already running with the rest of us. It was then that I realized
an important lesson: *Leaders create and inspire new leaders by
instilling faith in their leadership abilities and helping them develop
and hone leadership skills they don't know they possess.*

My experience with the board shows what happens when people
work together—side by side. When people work for a common
cause, they no longer *add* to their growth potential. Their unity *multiplies* their strength. The following anecdote further illustrates my
point:

> At a Midwestern fair, many spectators gathered for an old-
> fashioned horse pull (an event where various weights are put on
> a horse-drawn sled and pulled along the ground). The grand-
> champion horse pulled a sled with 4,500 pounds on it. The runner-
> up was close, with a 4,400-pound pull. Some of the men wondered
> what the two horses could pull if hitched together. Separately they
> totaled nearly 9,000 pounds, but when hitched and working
> together as a team, they pulled over 12,000 pounds.

DEVELOPED LEADERS EXPAND AND ENHANCE THE FUTURE OF THE ORGANIZATION

I was once asked to speak at a conference on the subject, *How to Structure Your Organization for Growth*. I politely refused. I am convinced that structure can aid growth but not give it. Pollster George Barna said, "Great organizations may have great leaders and a poor structure, but I've never seen a great organization that had a great structure and a poor leader." Structure can mean the difference between a bad organization and a good one. But the difference between a good organization and a great one is leadership.

Henry Ford knew this. He said, "You can take my factories, burn up my buildings, but give me my people, and I'll bring my business right back again." What did Henry Ford know that so many other people in leadership positions don't know? He knew that buildings and bureaucracy are not essential to growth. A company must organize around what it is trying to accomplish, not around what is being done. I have seen people in an organization do things a particular way simply because the bureaucracy states it must be done that way, even when it hinders what the organization is trying to accomplish. Organize around tasks, not functions.

Too often we are like the community that built a new bridge:

> The residents of a small town built a new bridge. Then they decided that, if they had a new bridge, they'd better hire a watchman to keep an eye on it. So they did. Someone noted that the watchman needed a salary, so they hired an accountant. He in turn pointed out the need for a treasurer. With a watchman, an accountant, and a treasurer, they had to have an administrator, so residents appointed one. Congress then voted a cut in funding, and personnel had to be cut back. So, they fired the watchman!

Don't let the machinations or trappings of your organization make you lose sight of what's to be accomplished.

One of the things my father taught me was the importance of people above all other elements in an organization. He was the president of a college for sixteen years. One day, as we sat on a campus bench, he explained that the most expensive workers on campus were not the highest paid. The most expensive ones were the people who were nonproductive. He explained that developing leaders took time and cost money. You usually had to pay leaders more. But such people were an invaluable asset. They attracted a higher quality of person; they were more productive; and they continued to add value to the organization. He closed the conversation by saying, "Most people produce only when they feel like it. Leaders produce even when they don't feel like it."

THE MORE PEOPLE YOU LEAD, THE MORE LEADERS YOU NEED

Moses was the greatest leader in the Old Testament. How would you like to relocate one-and-a-half million complaining people? It was hard . . . and tiring. And as his nation grew, Moses became more tired, and the people's needs went unmet.

The problem? Moses was trying to do it all himself. His *Disorganization Chart* looked like the diagram on page 14.

Jethro, the father-in-law of Moses, suggested that he find, recruit, and train other leaders to assist him in his leadership responsibilities. Moses followed that advice, and soon he had other leaders helping him carry the load. The result? This needed change gave added strength to Moses and enabled all the needs of the people to be met.

> A leader's success can be defined as the maximum utilization of the abilities of those under him.

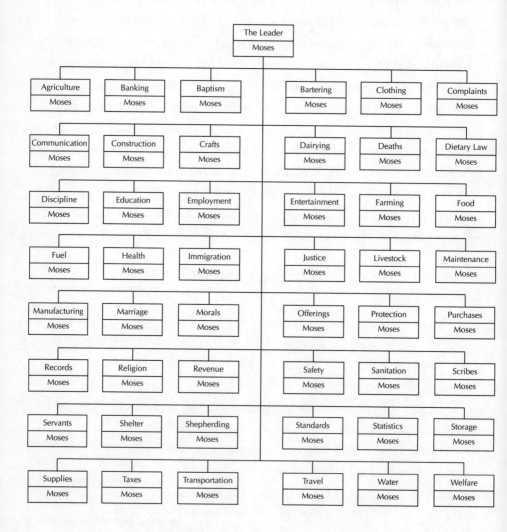

Zig Ziglar says, "Success is the maximum utilization of the ability that you have." I believe a leader's success can be defined as *the maximum utilization of the abilities of those under him.* Andrew Carnegie explained it like this: "I wish to have as my epitaph: 'Here lies a man who was wise enough to bring into his service men who knew more than he.'" It is my desire that the following pages help you do exactly that.

TWO

THE LEADER'S TOUGHEST CHALLENGE:
CREATING A CLIMATE FOR POTENTIAL LEADERS

Those who believe in our abilities do more than stimulate us—they create an atmosphere in which it becomes easier for us to succeed. Creating an environment that will attract leaders is vital to any organization. Doing that is the job of leaders. They must be active; they must generate activity that is productive; and they must encourage, create, and command changes in the organization. They must create a climate in which potential leaders will thrive.

LEADERS MUST BE ENVIRONMENTAL CHANGE AGENTS

The leaders in any organization must be the environmental change agents. They must be more like thermostats than thermometers. At first glance, a person could confuse these instruments. Both are capable of measuring heat. However, they are really quite different. A thermometer is passive. It records the temperature of its environment but can do nothing to change that environment. A thermostat is an active instrument. It determines what the environment will be. It effects change in order to create a climate.

The attitude of the leader, coupled with a positive atmosphere in the organization, can encourage people to accomplish great things. And consistent accomplishment generates momentum. Many times momentum is the only difference between a winning, positive growth climate and a losing, negative growth climate.

Leaders cannot afford to overlook the importance of momentum:

With momentum,	Leaders look better than they actually are.
With momentum,	Followers increase their performance.
Without momentum,	Leaders look worse than they actually are.
Without momentum,	Followers decrease their performance.

Momentum is the greatest of all change agents. More than 90 percent of the successful changes we've instituted in our organization have been the result of creating momentum before asking people to change.

To maximize the *value* of momentum, leaders must: (1) develop an appreciation for it *early*; (2) know the key ingredients of it *immediately*; and (3) pour resources into it *always*.

The next time you find it difficult to adjust the environment in your company, keep in mind this simple fact from the laws of physics:

Water boils at 212 degrees, but at 211 degrees, it is still just hot water. One extra degree, an increase of less than one-half of one percent, can make the difference between a pot of languishing liquid and a bubbling caldron of power. One degree can create a full head of

> **Momentum is the greatest of all change agents.**

steam—enough power to move a train weighing tons. That one degree is usually momentum.

Leaders in some organizations don't recognize the importance of creating a climate conducive to building potential leaders. They don't understand how it works. Advertising executive William Bernbach, who understands the difference it makes, once stated, "I'm always amused when other agencies try to hire my people away. They'd have to 'hire' the whole environment. For a flower to blossom, you need the right soil as well as the right seed." Until the leaders in an organization realize this, they will not succeed, regardless of the talented individuals they bring into the firm. The right atmosphere allows potential leaders to bloom and grow. That is why the atmosphere needs to be valued and developed first. Even when a leader from an organization with a poor climate steals away a potential leader who is beginning to bloom from the rich "greenhouse" environment of a healthy organization, the potential leader will not continue to grow and bloom. Unless, of course, the leader has already converted the environment of his or her own organization from "arctic" to "tropical."

To see the relationship between environment and growth, look at nature. An observation was made by a man who dives for exotic fish for aquariums. According to him, one of the most popular aquarium fish is the shark. The reason for this is that sharks adapt to their environment. If you catch a small shark and confine it, it will stay a size proportionate to the aquarium in which it lives. Sharks can be six inches long and fully mature. But turn them loose in the ocean and they grow to their normal size.

The same is true of potential leaders. Some are put into an organization when they are still small, and the confining environment ensures that they stay small and underdeveloped. Only leaders can control the environment of their organization. They can be the change agents who create a climate conducive to growth.

MODEL THE DESIRED STYLE OF LEADERSHIP

According to noted medical missionary Albert Schweitzer, "Example is not the main thing in influencing others . . . it is the only thing." Part of creating an appealing climate is modeling leadership. People emulate what they see modeled. Positive model—positive response. Negative model—negative response. What leaders do, potential leaders around them do. What they value, their people value. The leaders' goals become their goals. Leaders set the tone. As Lee Iacocca suggests, "The speed of the boss is the speed of the team." A leader cannot demand of others what he does not demand of himself.

As you and I grow and improve as leaders, so will those we lead. We need to remember that when people follow us, they can only go as far as we go. If our growth stops, our ability to lead will stop along with it. Neither personality nor methodology can substitute for personal growth. We cannot model what we do not possess. Begin learning and growing today, and watch those around you begin to grow. As a leader, I am primarily a follower of great principles and other great leaders.

FOCUS ON THE POTENTIAL OF THE LEADER AND THE ORGANIZATION

As stated before, those who believe in our abilities do more than stimulate us. They create an atmosphere in which it becomes easier to succeed. The opposite is also true. When a leader does not believe in us, success is very difficult for us to achieve. It becomes nearly impossible. As leaders, we cannot allow this to happen to those we lead if we expect our organizations to succeed.

To ensure success, identify the potential in each future leader and cultivate it in light of the needs of the organization. It produces a win-win situation. The mentoring leader wins because of the rising star working beneath him or her who can perform and produce. The organization wins because its mission is being fulfilled. The potential leader wins because he is being developed and improved. His future looks bright.

One of the best applications of this idea is expressed in what I call the 101 percent principle: *Find the one thing that you believe is the potential leader's greatest asset, and then give 101 percent encouragement in that area.* Focusing on a person's strengths promotes positive growth, confidence, and success as a potential leader.

Focus on the Potential Leader's Needs (Desires)

People often associate great achievement with a number of things: luck, timing, circumstance, or natural talent. The secret to a person's success often appears to be an elusive quality. The University of Chicago did a five-year study of leading artists, athletes, and scholars to determine what made them successful. Conducted by Dr. Benjamin Bloom, the research was based on anonymous interviews with the top twenty performers in various fields. Included were a variety of professionals such as concert pianists, Olympic swimmers, tennis players, sculptors, mathematicians, and neurologists. Bloom and his team of researchers probed for clues as to how these high achievers developed. For a more complete picture, they also interviewed their families and teachers. The report stated conclusively that drive, determination, and desire, not great natural talent, led to the extraordinary success of these individuals.

Great leaders know the desires of the people they lead. As much as potential leaders respect the knowledge and ability of their leaders, these are secondary matters to them. They don't care how much their leaders *know* until they know how much their leaders *care* . . . about their needs, their dreams, their desires. Once a leader is genuinely interested in the well-being of those around him, the determination and drive of the people in that group are activated in a remarkable way. The starting point of all achievement is drive, determination, and desire.

> It takes a leader with vision to see the future leader within the person.

Napoleon Bonaparte is known as one of history's greatest leaders. One of his leadership secrets was knowing the needs of his men. He first determined what his men wanted most. Then he did everything possible to help them get it. He knew this was a key to successful motivation. Most leaders do the opposite. They first decide what *they* want. Then they try to persuade others to want the same thing as much as they do.

LOOK FOR THE LEADER WITHIN THE PERSON

There is no future in any job. The future lies in the person who holds the job. It takes a leader with vision to see the future leader within the person. Michelangelo, when questioned about his masterpiece *David*, answered that the sculpture had always existed within the stone. He had simply chiseled away the rock around it. Leaders must have the same kind of vision when viewing potential leaders. Some of the qualities to look for in a person include the following:

Positiveness: the ability to work with and see
                       people and situations in a
                       positive way

Servanthood: the willingness to submit, play
                       team ball, and follow the leader

Growth potential: a hunger for personal growth
                       and development; the ability to
                       keep growing as the job expands

Follow-through: the determination to get the job
                       done completely and with
                       consistency

Loyalty: the willingness to always put the
                       leader and the organization
                       above personal desires

Resiliency: the ability to bounce back when
                       problems arise

Integrity: trustworthiness and solid
                       character; consistent words
                       and walk

"Big picture" mind-set: the ability to see the whole
                       organization and all of its needs

Discipline: the willingness to do what is
                       required regardless of personal
                       mood

Gratitude: an attitude of thankfulness that
                       becomes a way of life

When searching for these traits within a person, the leader should emulate gold prospectors. They are always on the lookout for potential gold mines. Every mountain is a possible opportunity to strike it rich. When they find traces of ore, they assume there is a vein and begin digging. The same is true in every organization. If you as a leader look for and find traces of gold in your people, start digging. You will uncover the mother lode!

PLACE AN EMPHASIS ON PRODUCTION, NOT POSITION AND TITLE

Organizations that place great emphasis on titles and position are teaching their employees to do the same. Employees in that type of environment can often become preoccupied with moving up the ladder to the next position or with receiving a more important-sounding title. When it comes down to it, titles are worth little. A lofty title doesn't help a poor producer. A lowly title doesn't hinder a super producer. Position, like a title, doesn't make a leader either.

In *Developing the Leader Within You*, I describe the five levels of leadership: position, permission, production, personnel development, and personhood. *Position* is the lowest level. A person who stands on his position will never have influence beyond his or her job description.

Seniority also provides little in and of itself. A survey was conducted by Accountemps, a temporary personnel service and placement organization. Executives and personnel directors were asked for the most influential factors in evaluating an employee for promotion. The results: 66 percent named specific accomplishments, 47 percent named general work habits and performance, and only 4 percent cited seniority as being important. Time on the job is no substitute for production in the job.

In an organization emphasizing production, attention and energy are devoted to doing the job and doing it well. There is a team atmosphere, with accomplishing the mission of the organization as the goal. That is the kind of climate where leaders emerge. As Charles Wilson, the former president of General Electric, said, "No matter what size the bottle, the cream always came to the top."

PROVIDE GROWTH OPPORTUNITIES

There is a story of a tourist who paused for a rest in a small town in the mountains. He went over to an old man sitting on a bench in front of the only store in town and inquired, "Friend, can you tell me something this town is noted for?" "Well," replied the old man, "I don't rightly know except that it's the starting point to the world. You can start here and go anywhere you want."

All people do not view their current location as the starting point to wherever they want to go in the world. We as leaders must encourage those around us to see themselves in such a place. Creating an environment for personal growth is critical. However, if the people around you are unaware they are in such an environment, they may not take advantage of it. That is one reason why it is important to *create opportunities for growth*. Another reason is that established leaders are in a position to know what opportunities a potential leader needs.

In order to create the right opportunities, we must look at the potential leaders around us and ask, "What does this person need in order to grow?" A generic formula will not work. If we don't fit the opportunity to the potential leader, we may find ourselves in the position of offering things that our people don't need.

Ernest Campbell, a faculty member at Union Theological Seminary, tells an enlightening story:

A woman went to a pet store and purchased a parrot to keep her company. She took her new pet home but returned the next day to report, "That parrot hasn't said a word yet!"

"Does it have a mirror?" asked the storekeeper. "Parrots like to be able to look at themselves in the mirror." So she bought the mirror and returned home.

The next day she was back, announcing that the bird still wasn't speaking.

"What about a ladder?" the storekeeper said. "Parrots enjoy walking up and down a ladder." So she bought a ladder and returned home.

Sure enough, the next day she was back with the same story—still no talk.

"Does the parrot have a swing? Birds enjoy relaxing on a swing." She bought the swing and went home.

The next day she returned to the store to announce the bird had died.

"I'm terribly sorry to hear that," said the storekeeper. "Did the bird ever say anything before it died?"

"Yes," the lady replied. "It said, 'Don't they sell any food down there?'"

Many leaders are like the lady in the story. They want their people to produce. When the people don't, the leaders provide them with all the things some expert says they are supposed to like. However, the leaders themselves never look at their people to see what they really need.

As you examine potential leaders and determine what each needs, keep in mind these ideas for growth opportunities:

• Expose the potential leader to people successful in his field.

• Provide a secure environment where the potential leader is free to take risks.

- Provide the potential leader with an experienced mentor.

- Provide the potential leader with the tools and resources she needs.

- Spend the time and money to train the potential leader in his areas of need.

The idea of building potential leaders through growth opportunities can be summed up in this poem by Edwin Markham:

We are blind until we see
That in the human plan
Nothing is worth the making
If it does not make the man.

Why build these cities glorious
If man unbuilded goes?
In vain we build the world
Unless the builder also grows.[1]

LEAD (DON'T MANAGE) WITH VISION

An important part of leadership involves casting vision. Some leaders forget to cast vision because they get caught up in managing. True leaders recognize a difference between leaders and managers. Managers are maintainers, tending to rely on systems and controls. Leaders are innovators and creators who rely on people. Creative ideas become reality when people who are in a position to act catch the vision of their innovative leader.

An effective vision provides guidance. It gives direction for an organization . . . direction that cannot effectively result from rules and regulations, policy manuals, or organizational charts. True direction for an organization is born with a vision. It begins when the leader accepts it. It gains acceptance when the leader models it. And it becomes reality when the people respond to it.

DO BIG THINGS

Nearly everything a leader does hinges on the type of vision he has. If his vision is small, so will be his results and his followers. A high-ranking French official who understood this concept once expressed it thus when addressing Winston Churchill: "If you are doing big things, you attract big men. If you are doing little things, you attract little men. Little men usually cause trouble." An effective vision attracts winners.

Too often people limit their own potential. They think small. They are afraid of risk. People no longer willing to stretch are no longer able to grow. As author Henry Drummond says, "Unless a man undertakes more than he possibly can do, he will never do all he can do."

SPEND MORE EFFORT ON THE "FARM TEAM" THAN ON THE FREE AGENTS

Once a leader has a vision, he needs to build a team to carry it out. Where does he find winners? It's not easy. In fact, most winners are made, not found. In major league baseball, teams generally recruit players in one of two ways. They either bring players up from their own minor league farm teams or go outside the organization in search of free agents. Time after time, baseball fans have seen their teams bring in expensive free agents with the expectation of winning a World Series. Time after time they are disappointed.

The "farm team" method involves bringing in the best undeveloped players who can be found and allowing them to start with the organization at their own level. They are coached and developed. Their managers and coaches discover their strengths and weaknesses and find the right positions for them. The players gain experience and have an opportunity to bring up their level of play. If their performance is good enough, they get promoted to the major league team.

The vast majority of the leadership in our organization is recruited and promoted from within. It has not always been easy, but there are tremendous advantages in using the farm-team method. The first is that you already know the individual's character and attitude. When you interview somebody on the outside, you take a risk. You have to base a hiring decision on what the potential employee and the recommendations tell you. Job descriptions on a resume address skills, not character. Most employers agree that character and attitude are the most important factors in hiring a new employee. Skills can be taught.

The second advantage is that a person promoted from within already knows the organization and its people. A successful employee who is considered for promotion has already caught the leader's vision. He shares the philosophy of the organization. He has spent time building relationships with the people. A person brought in from outside must spend time learning these things. Once hired, he may even be unwilling or unable to assimilate. When you hire people from within, they hit the ground running.

The third advantage is that a person brought up from the farm team is a proven performer. You have already seen his gifts and impact. You know he can hit the ball in your park. As a result, the risk is relatively small. With a free agent, you have had limited opportunity to observe him firsthand. It is possible that he may not be able to hit the ball in your park, because the conditions are different. Developing the talent on your farm team will require strategic action and a particular attitude from the team's leader. The leader must:

- Invest time and money in his potential leaders.

- Commit to promoting from within.

- Show his people that personal and professional growth within the organization are not only possible but also actual.

MAKE DIFFICULT DECISIONS

Willard C. Butch, chairman of the Chase Manhattan Corporation, was once given some advice by Marion Folsom, then a top Eastman Kodak Company executive: "Bill, you're going to find that 95 percent of all the decisions you'll ever make in your career could be made as well by a reasonably intelligent high school sophomore. But they'll pay you for the other five percent."

Some of the toughest decisions a leader faces concern poor performers. Great leaders make smart choices concerning them. A leader who does not effectively handle them will hurt:

- the organization's ability to achieve its purpose

- the morale of top performers

- his own credibility

- the low performers' self-image and potential effectiveness

To discover the proper course concerning a poor performer, a leader needs to ask himself, "Should this person be trained, transferred, or terminated?" The answer will determine the appropriate course of action.

If low performance is due to poor or undeveloped skills, it calls for training. Likewise, training can often benefit an employee needing to be taught the organization's philosophy or vision. Training is often the most positive of solutions, because it invests in the employee. It is also more economical to improve a current employee than start a new person from scratch.

Sometimes an employee is a low performer because he is expected to perform a job that does not match his gifts and abilities. If the employee has a good attitude and a desire to succeed, he can be transferred to a position matching his gifts. There he may flourish.

Terminating an employee is by far the most difficult of the tough decisions a leader faces. It is also one of the most important decisions he may make. In fact, removing poor performers from an organization is as important as finding good ones. Terminating a poor performer benefits the organization and everyone in it. It also gives the former employee the opportunity to reevaluate his or her potential and find the place and position where he or she can be a winner.

PAY THE PRICE THAT ATTRACTS LEADERS

Success always comes at a price. That is a lesson I learned a long time ago. My father taught me that a person can pay now and play later, or he can play now and pay later. Either way, he is going to pay.

Creating a climate for potential leaders also requires a leader to pay a price. It begins with personal growth. The leader must examine himself, ask himself the hard questions, and then determine to do the right thing regardless of atmosphere or mood. There are few ideal and leisurely settings for the disci-

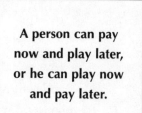

A person can pay now and play later, or he can play now and pay later.

plines of growth. Most of the significant things done in the world were done by persons who were either too busy or too sick to do them. Emotion-based companies allow the atmosphere to determine the action. Character-based companies allow the action to determine the atmosphere.

Successful leaders recognize that personal growth and the development of leadership skills are lifetime pursuits. Warren Bennis and Burt Nanus, in *Leaders: The Strategies for Taking Charge*, did a study of ninety top leaders in all fields. They found that "it is the capacity to develop and improve their skills that distinguishes leaders from their followers." They came to the conclusion that "leaders are perpetual learners."

Commitment to provide a climate where potential leaders may grow must start with the leader's commitment to personal growth. Answer the following questions to determine your current commitment level.

QUESTIONS ON COMMITMENT TO PERSONAL GROWTH

1. Do I have a game plan for personal growth?

    Yes   No

2. Am I the leader of that plan?

    Yes   No

3. Am I willing to change to keep growing, even if it means giving up my current position, if I am not experiencing growth?

    Yes   No

4. Is my life an example for others to follow?:

    Yes   No

5. Am I willing to pay the price to become a great leader?

Yes   No

A no on any of these questions should cause a leader to examine his plan and commitment to personal growth. A lack of commitment on the part of a leader makes it difficult for potential leaders around him to be developed. If you as a leader have not made this commitment, your future is limited, and you will never become a great leader. Now is the time to change.

The environment in which you work will influence you and those you lead. Answer the following questions to help determine your organization's dedication to developing leaders and providing a climate that promotes organizational and personal growth.

QUESTIONS TO ASK CONCERNING ORGANIZATIONAL GROWTH

1. Has the organization made a specific commitment to grow and develop people?

   Seldom   Sometimes   Usually

2. Is the organization willing to spend money to develop employees' growth?

   Seldom   Sometimes   Usually

3. Is the organization willing to make changes to keep itself and its people growing?

   Seldom   Sometimes   Usually

4. Does the organization support leaders willing to make the difficult decisions necessary for people's personal growth and the growth of the organization?

> Seldom   Sometimes   Usually

5. Does the organization place an emphasis on production rather than position or title?

> Seldom   Sometimes   Usually

6. Does the organization provide growth opportunities for its people?

> Seldom   Sometimes   Usually

7. Do organizational leaders have vision and share it with their people?

> Seldom   Sometimes   Usually

8. Does the organization think big?

> Seldom   Sometimes   Usually

9. Does the organization promote from within?

> Seldom   Sometimes   Usually

10. Are there other leaders in the organization willing to pay the price of personal sacrifice to ensure their growth and the growth of others?

> Seldom   Sometimes   Usually

If the majority of the answers to these questions is Seldom or Sometimes, a change is in order. If the organization is controlled by you, begin changing now. If you head a department in the organization, then you are in a position to make positive changes. Do as many things as your organization will allow to create a positive climate for potential leaders. If you are in a position only to make changes for yourself, try to find someone in the organization who will develop you—or change your job. Great leaders share themselves and what they have learned with the learners who will become tomorrow's leaders. A person can impress potential leaders from a distance, but only from up close can he impact them.

Here are a few closing thoughts on creating a climate for potential leaders. Sports records provide tangible evidence of the positive changes that can occur when the right climate has been established. One Olympic athlete, Parry O'Brien, won a gold medal at

> **Great leaders share themselves and what they have learned.**

the 1952 Olympics by throwing a 16-pound shot 57 feet. In 1953 he set a new world record by throwing the shot 59 feet, 3/4 inch. Experts at the time said O'Brien, the best in the world, might beat his record by a few inches if he practiced, but they were certain that no one would ever be able to break the 60-foot barrier.

Luckily, O'Brien didn't think like an expert. As an athlete he was determined to continue improving himself. He began experimenting with different styles and invented a new technique for his event, which would become the universal style of putting the shot until the mid-1970s.

In 1956 O'Brien won at the Olympics again—not by a few inches, but by a few *feet*. He also broke the unbreakable barrier by tossing the shot 60 feet, 11 inches. O'Brien set his final record in 1959 when he threw the shot 63 feet, 4 inches. From that time on, every competitive shot-putter has tossed the shot beyond that length. Today, the record is over 75 feet.

The same is true of the four-minute mile. No one, the experts said, would ever be able to run the mile in less than four minutes. Then, in 1954, a young medical student named Roger Bannister did the impossible by breaking that barrier. Today, every world-class runner can run the mile in less than four minutes. Why? Because one man decided to keep improving. One man decided to pay the price of personal growth. He was willing to lead. As a result, he created a climate for those achievers who followed him. Are you the type of leader who is willing to pay the price and create a climate in which your people can follow you and emerge as the leaders of tomorrow?

THREE

THE LEADER'S PRIMARY RESPONSIBILITY:
IDENTIFYING POTENTIAL LEADERS

There is something much more important and scarce than ability: It is the ability to recognize ability. One of the primary responsibilities of a successful leader is to identify potential leaders. It's not always an easy job, but it is critical.

Dale Carnegie was a master at identifying potential leaders. Once asked by a reporter how he had managed to hire forty-three millionaires, Carnegie responded that the men had not been millionaires when they started working for him. They had become millionaires as a result. The reporter next wanted to know how he had developed these men to become such valuable leaders. Carnegie replied, "Men are developed the same way gold is mined. Several tons of dirt must be moved to get an ounce of gold. But you don't go into the mine looking for dirt," he added. "You go in looking for the gold." That's exactly the way to develop positive, successful people. Look for the gold, not the dirt; the good, not the bad. The more positive qualities you look for, the more you are going to find.

> To develop positive, successful people, look for the gold, not the dirt.

SELECTING THE RIGHT PLAYERS

Professional sports organizations recognize the importance of selecting the right players. Every year, coaches and owners of professional baseball, basketball, and football teams look forward to the draft. To prepare for it, sports franchises spend much time and energy scouting new prospects. For instance, scouts from pro football organizations travel to regular-season college games, bowl games, senior-only bowl games, and camps to gain knowledge about prospective players. All of this enables the scouts to bring plenty of information back to the owners and head coaches so that when draft day arrives, the teams can pick the most promising players. Team owners and coaches know that the future success of their teams depends largely on their ability to draft effectively.

It's no different in business. You must select the right players in your organization. If you select well, the benefits are multiplied and seem nearly endless. If you select poorly, the problems are multiplied and seem endless.

Too often, leaders hire employees haphazardly. Because of desperation, lack of time, or just plain ignorance, they quickly grab any candidate who comes along. Then they hold their breath and hope everything works out. But hiring needs to be done strategically. Before you hire a new employee, your options are nearly limitless. Once you have made the hiring decision, your options are few. Hiring an employee is like skydiving: once you've jumped out of the plane, you're committed.

> **Hiring an employee is like skydiving: once you've jumped out of the plane, you're committed.**

The key to making the right choice depends on two things: (1) your ability to see the big picture, and (2) your ability to judge potential employees during the selection process.

It is a good idea to start with an inventory. I use this one because I always want to look inside as well as outside the organization to find candidates. I call this list the Five A's:

Assessment of needs:	What is needed?
Assets on hand:	Who are the people already in the organization who are available?
Ability of candidates:	Who is able?
Attitude of candidates:	Who is willing?
Accomplishments of candidates:	Who gets things done?

Notice that the inventory begins with an assessment of needs. The leader of the organization must base that assessment on the big picture. While he was manager of the Chicago Cubs, Charlie Grimm reportedly received a phone call from one of his scouts. The man was excited and began to shout over the telephone, "Charlie, I've landed the greatest young pitcher in the land! He struck out every man who came to bat. Twenty-seven in a row. Nobody even hit a foul until the ninth inning. The pitcher is right here with me. What shall I do?" Charlie replied, "Sign up the guy who got the foul. We're looking for hitters." Charlie knew what the team needed.

There is one situation that supersedes a needs analysis: when a truly exceptional person is available but doesn't necessarily match the current need, do whatever you can to hire him or her anyway. In the long run, that person will positively impact the organization. You see this kind of decision-making in sports. Football coaches generally draft players to fill specific needs. If they lack a strong running back, they draft the best running back available. But sometimes they get an opportunity to draft an "impact player," a superstar who can instantly change the whole complexion of the team. Incidentally, impact players usually possess not only athletic ability but also leadership skills. Even as rookies, they have all the qualities to be team captains. When I have an opportunity to hire someone who is exceptional—a superstar—I do it. Then I find a place for him or her. Good people are hard to find, and there is always room for one more productive person in an organization.

Usually we are not judging superstars, and the decisions are harder to make. How do pro sports teams evaluate potential players? Many use a grid that yields a score for each player based on his abilities. In the same way, we need to have a tool to help evaluate people's potential as leaders. Here is a list of twenty-five characteristics to help you rate and identify a potential leader.

ASSESSMENT OF CURRENT LEADERSHIP QUALITIES (FOR POTENTIAL LEADERS)

SCALE
0=Never   1=Seldom   2=Sometimes   3=Usually   4=Always

1. The person has influence.   0   1   2   3   4

2. The person has self-discipline.   0   1   2   3   4

3. The person has a good track record.   0   1   2   3   4

4. The person has strong people skills.   0   1   2   3   4

5. The person has the ability to solve problems.   0   1   2   3   4

6. The person does not accept the status quo.   0   1   2   3   4

7. The person sees the big picture.   0   1   2   3   4

8. The person has the ability to handle stress.   0   1   2   3   4

9. The person displays a positive spirit.   0   1   2   3   4

10. The person understands people.   0   1   2   3   4

11. The person is free of personal problems.   0   1   2   3   4

12. The person is willing to take responsibility.   0   1   2   3   4

13. The person is free from anger.   0   1   2   3   4

14. The person is willing to make changes.   0   1   2   3   4

15. The person has integrity.   0   1   2   3   4

16. The person is growing closer to God.   0   1   2   3   4

17. The person has the ability to see what has to be done next.   0   1   2   3   4

18. The person is accepted as a   0 1 2 3 4
    leader by others.

19. The person has the ability and   0 1 2 3 4
    desire to keep learning.

20. The person has a manner that   0 1 2 3 4
    draws people.

21. The person has a good self-image.   0 1 2 3 4

22. The person has a willingness to   0 1 2 3 4
    serve others.

23. The person has the ability to   0 1 2 3 4
    bounce back when problems arise.

24. The person has the ability to   0 1 2 3 4
    develop other leaders.

25. The person takes initiative.   0 1 2 3 4

Total Points:_____

When assessing a potential leader, pay more attention to the quality of the person as addressed by the characteristics than to the specific score. Since leaders grade differently, scores vary. Here is my grading scale:

90–100   Great leader (should be mentoring other good and great leaders)

80–89   Good leader (must keep growing and keep mentoring others)

70–79	Emerging leader (focus on growth and begin mentoring others)
60–69	Bursting with potential (excellent person to be developed)
Below 60	Needs growth (may not be ready to be mentored as a leader)

The "Below 60" category is often the most difficult to judge. Some people in this group will never become leaders. Others are capable of becoming great leader. The better leader the evaluator is, the better his judgment of a person's leadership potential. Thus, it is important that a successful leader do the interviewing and hiring of potential leaders.

In *Inc.* magazine, marketing expert I. Martin Jacknis identifies a trend he has seen in hiring. He terms it the *Law of Diminishing Expertise*. Simply stated, leaders tend to hire people whose ability and expertise are beneath their own. As a result, when organizations grow and more people are hired, the number of people with low expertise far exceeds the leaders who have great expertise.

Here's how this works. Let's say, for example, you are an outstanding leader with great vision, self-discipline, right priorities, and super problem-solving skills. You score a 95 on the Assessment of Current Leadership Qualities. So you decide to start your own business, called *Leader to Leader, Inc.* Your business does so well that you soon need four new employees. You would like to hire four 95s, but, chances are, 95s want to work for themselves (just as you do) and are not available. You need help, so you hire four 85s, not as skilled as you, but each a leader in his or her own right.

I must mention at this crucial stage in the company's development, you may have been tempted to hire less than 85s for your staff. You may be thinking to yourself, *The four people I hire just have to follow me and my direction, and the company will do fine. I can settle for a couple of followers who are 65s.* That is the critical error many leaders make. By selecting followers rather than potential leaders, the leader of an organization limits its potential for growth. But for the moment, let's say that you don't make that mistake, and you hire four leaders with scores of 85.

You and your team of leaders are doing great. The business can hardly keep up with demand. Then you land a national account. Your hard work has paid off, but you now estimate that you will need about one hundred employees working around the clock to carry the load. You now need to build a whole organization.

You begin with your faithful four employees. They're good leaders, they helped you make it, and you're dedicated to promoting from within. They are going to be your four managers. You decide the best way to structure the new organization is to have one manager overseeing sales, and each of the other three managers overseeing an eight-hour shift to keep production going twenty-four hours a day. Each manager will supervise two assistant managers and about twenty other employees.

The four managers hire their assistants who, consistent with the law of diminishing expertise, rate as 75s. The managers give the assistants the job of hiring the twenty employees. You guessed it. They hire 65s. As a result, almost overnight, the company whose staff leadership score averaged 87 and looked like this:

Leader to Leader, Inc. with five employees

now has a leadership score averaging 67 and looks like this:

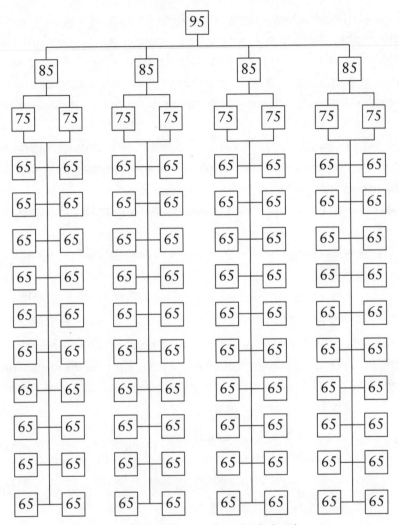

Leader to Leader, Inc. with nearly one hundred employees

The whole complexion of *Leader to Leader, Inc.* has changed. And if the original four you hired had not been leaders, you would have been in even worse trouble.

This is a slightly exaggerated example. Most companies don't go from five to one hundred employees overnight. But the organizations of great leaders expand quickly. What's important is that you can actually see the impact hiring has on an organization. In this example, what was once an organization comprised of high producers is now an organization overwhelmed with marginal producers. If the sales department lands another national account, another expansion will occur. In the next expansion, the assistant mangers, who are 75s, will probably be promoted to become new managers, and the company will take another downturn, possibly putting its average in the mediocre 50s.

Fortunately, there are ways to combat the trend toward mediocrity:

1. Make Hiring the Responsibility of a Highly Developed Leader
   Since undeveloped people hire less developed people, improve the source.

2. Hire the Most Highly Developed Leaders You Can Get
   Don't settle for poor performers. Keep in mind that one great person will always out-produce and out-perform two mediocre people.

3. Commit to Modeling Leadership
   Let all the people in the organization know what is expected of them. Many potential leaders will try to reach a standard they can see.

4. Commit to Developing Those Around You
   If you develop the potential leaders around you, by the next expansion, the dedicated assistant managers who were 75s will be 85s and ready to lead.

I would say that David Ogilvy, founder of the giant advertising agency Ogilvy and Mather, understood the law of diminishing expertise, based on the information Dennis Waitley gives about him in *The New Dynamics of Winning*. He states that Ogilvy used to give each new manager in his organization a Russian doll. The doll contained five progressively smaller dolls. A message inside the smallest one read: "If each of us hires people who are smaller than we are, we shall become a company of dwarfs. But if each of us hires people who are bigger then we are, Ogilvy and Mather will become a company of giants." Commit to finding, hiring, and developing giants.

QUALITIES TO LOOK FOR IN A LEADER

To hunt for leaders, you first need to know what they look like. Here are ten leadership qualities to seek in anyone you hire:

CHARACTER

The first thing to look for in any kind of leader or potential leader is strength of character. I have found nothing more important than this quality. Serious character flaws cannot be ignored. They will eventually make a leader ineffective—every time.

Character flaws should not be confused with weaknesses. We all have weaknesses. They can be overcome through training or experience. Character flaws cannot be changed overnight. Change usually takes a long period of time and involves significant relational investment and dedication on the part of the leader. Any person that you hire who has character flaws will be the weak link in your organization. Depending on the nature of the character flaw, the person has the potential to destroy the organization.

> **Character flaws cannot be ignored. They will eventually make a leader ineffective.**

259

Some of the qualities that make up good character include: honesty, integrity, self-discipline, teachability, dependability, perseverance, conscientiousness, and a strong work ethic. The words of a person with right character match the deeds. His reputation is solid. His manner is straightforward.

The assessment of character can be difficult. Warning signs to watch for include:

- a person's failure to take responsibility for his actions or circumstances

- unfulfilled promises or obligations

- failure to meet deadlines

You can tell much about a person's ability to lead others from how well he manages his own life.

Finally, look at his interactions with others. You can also tell much about a person's character from his relationships. Examine his relationships with superiors, colleagues, and subordinates. Talk to your employees to find out how the potential leader treats them. This will give you additional insight.

INFLUENCE

Leadership is influence. Every leader has these two characteristics: (A) he is going somewhere and (B) he is able to persuade others to go with him. Influence by itself is not enough. That influence must be measured to determine its *quality*. When looking at a potential employee's influence, examine the following:

What is the leader's level of influence? Does that person have followers due to position (he uses the power of his job title), permission (he has developed relationships which motivate), production (he and his followers consistently produce results), personnel development (he has developed others around him), or personhood (he transcends the organization and develops people on a world-class scale)?

Who influences the leader? Who is he following? People become like their models. Is his model ethical? Does his model have the right priorities?

Whom does he influence? Likewise, the quality of the follower will indicate the quality of the leader. Are his followers positive producers or a bunch of mediocre yes-men?

Stuart Briscoe, in *Discipleship for Ordinary People*, tells the story of a young clergyman who officiated at the funeral of a war veteran. The veteran's military friends wanted to participate in the service to honor their comrade, so they requested that the young pastor lead them down to the casket for a moment of remembrance and then out through a side door. The occasion failed to have the desired effect when the clergyman led them through the wrong door. In full view of the other mourners, the men marched with military precision into a broom closet and had to beat a hasty and confused retreat. Every leader must know where he is going. And every follower had better be sure he's behind a leader who knows what he's doing.

POSITIVE ATTITUDE

A positive attitude is one of the most valuable assets a person can have in life. My belief in this is so strong that I wrote an entire book on the subject, *The Winning Attitude: Your Key to Personal Success*. So often, what people say their problem is really isn't their problem. Their problem is the attitude which causes them to handle life's obstacles poorly.

The individual whose attitude causes him to approach life from an entirely positive perspective is someone who can be called a no-limit person. In other words, the person doesn't accept the normal limitations of life as most people do. He or she is determined to walk to the very edge of his potential, or his product's potential, before he accepts defeat. People with positive attitudes are able to go places where others can't. They do things that others can't. They are not restricted by self-imposed limitations.

A person with a positive attitude is like a bumblebee. The bumblebee should not be able to fly, because the size, weight, and shape of its body in relationship to its wingspread makes flying aerodynamically impossible. But the bumblebee, being ignorant of scientific theory, flies anyway and makes honey every day.

This no-limit mind-set allows a person to start each day with a positive disposition, as did an elevator operator I once read about. One Monday morning, in a full elevator, the man began humming a tune. One passenger, irritated by the man's mood, snapped, "What are you so happy about?" "Well, sir," replied the operator happily, "I ain't never lived this day before." Not only does the future look bright when the attitude is right, but the present is much more enjoyable too. The positive person understands that the journey is as enjoyable as the destination.

Think of the attitude like this:

> It is the advance man of our true selves.
> Its roots are inward, but its fruit is outward.
> It is our best friend or our worst enemy.
> It is more honest and more consistent than our words.
> It is an outward look based on past experiences.
> It is a thing which draws people to us or repels them.
> It is never content until it is expressed.
> It is the librarian of our past.
> It is the speaker of our present.
> It is the prophet of our future.[1]

Attitude sets the tone, not only for the leader with the attitude, but also for the people following him.

EXCELLENT PEOPLE SKILLS

A leader without people skills soon has no followers. Andrew Carnegie, a fantastic leader, is reported to have paid Charles Schwab a salary of $1 million a year simply because of his excellent people skills. Carnegie had other leaders who understood the job better and whose experience and training were better suited to the work. But they lacked the essential human quality of being able to get others to help them, and Schwab could get the best out of his fellow workers. People may admire a person who has only talent and ability, but they will not follow him—not for long.

Excellent people skills involve a genuine concern for others, the ability to understand people, and the decision to make positive inter-action with others a primary concern. Our behavior toward others determines their behavior toward us. A successful leader knows this.

EVIDENT GIFTS

Every person God creates has gifts. One of our jobs as leaders is to make an assessment of those gifts when considering a person for employment. I think of every job candidate as a "wanna be" leader. My observation is that there are four types of wanna-bes:

Never be. Some people simply lack the ability to do a particular job. As I mentioned before, all people are gifted. However, not all are gifted for the particular task at hand. A *never be* who is directed into an area where he is not gifted becomes frustrated, often blames others for his lack of success, and eventually burns out. Redirected, he has a chance of reaching his potential.

Could be. A *could be* is a person with the right gifts and abilities but lacking self-discipline. He may even be a person with superstar abilities who just can't get himself to perform. This person needs to develop the self-discipline to "just do it."

Should be. A *should be* is someone with raw talent (gifts) but few skills for harnessing that ability. He needs training. Once he is given help in developing those skills, he will begin to become the person he was created to be.

Must be. The only things a *must be* lacks is opportunity. He has the right gifts, the right skills, and the right attitude. He has the drive to be the person he was created to be. It is up to you to be the leader who gives him that opportunity. If you don't he will find someone else who will.

God creates all people with natural gifts. But he also makes them with two ends, one to sit on and one to think with. Success in life is dependent on which one of these ends is used the most, and it's a toss-up: heads you win, and tails you lose!

Proven Track Record

Poet Archibald MacLeish once said, "There is only one thing more painful than learning from experience, and that is not learning from experience." Leaders who learn this truth develop successful track records over time. Everyone who breaks new ground, who strives to do something, makes mistakes. People without proven track records either haven't learned from their mistakes or haven't tried.

I've worked with many talented people who've established tremendous track records. When I first started my organization, two men in particular stood out as first-rate leaders capable of the highest quality of leadership (they score in the top category on the Assessment of Current Leadership Qualities). Dick Peterson, who worked with IBM for years, quickly demonstrated that experience had not been wasted on him. Dick already had a proven track record when I asked him to team with me in 1985 to start one of my companies, INJOY. In the beginning, we were long on potential and short on resources. Dick's hard work, planning, and insight turned a shoestring business operating out of his garage into an enterprise producing materials and influencing tens of thousands of leaders nationally and internationally every year. For fifteen years Dick served as the president of INJOY and helped get the company off the ground.

Dan Reiland has quite a different story. Dan was totally a product of the farm team. He started as a church member at Skyline—the church I led as senior pastor for fourteen years. After attending seminary, he returned to the church as an intern.

> **A proven leader always has a proven track record.**

He was not the best intern we ever had. In fact, at one point I thought he wasn't going to make it. But through his hard work and mentoring on my part, he soon became one of the finest pastors on staff and developed an outstanding track record. Because of that record I asked him to become the executive pastor of the church and continued to train him. When I left the pastorate in 1995 to lead INJOY full time, Dan came with me to serve as a vice president, and he became a nationally recognized church consultant. Recently Dan returned to full-time ministry as the executive pastor of Crossroads Community Church. And no matter where Dan is leading he excels in his ability to develop other leaders.

Management expert Robert Townsend notes, "Leaders come in all sizes, ages, shapes, and conditions. Some are poor administrators, some not overly bright. But there is one clue for spotting them. Since most people *per se* are mediocre, the true leader can be recognized because somehow or other, his people consistently turn in superior performances." Always check a candidate's past performance. A proven leader always has a proven track record.

CONFIDENCE

People will not follow a leader who does not have confidence in himself. In fact, people are naturally attracted to people who convey confidence. An excellent example can be seen in an incident in Russia during an attempted coup. Army tanks had surrounded the government building housing President Boris Yeltsin and his pro-democracy supporters. High-level military leaders had ordered the tank commander to open fire and kill Yeltsin. As the army rolled into position, Yeltsin strode from the building, climbed up on a tank, looked the commander in the eye, and thanked him for coming over to the side of democracy. Later the commander admitted that they had not intended to go over to his side. Yeltsin had appeared so confident and commanding that the soldiers talked after he left and decided to join him.

Confidence is characteristic of a positive attitude. The greatest achievers and leaders remain confident regardless of circumstances. There's a wonderful story about baseball great Ty Cobb's confidence: When Cobb was seventy years old, a reporter asked, "What do you think you'd hit if you were playing these days?" Cobb, a lifetime .367 hitter, said, "About .290, maybe .300." The reporter said, "That's because of the travel, the night games, the artificial turf, and all the new pitches like the slider, right?" "No," said Cobb, "it's because I'm seventy." Strong confident leaders recognize and appreciate confidence in others.

Reprinted with special permission of King Features Syndicate

Confidence is not simply for show. Confidence empowers. A good leader has the ability to instill within his people confidence in himself. A great leader has the ability to instill within his people confidence in themselves.

SELF-DISCIPLINE

Great leaders always have self-discipline—without exception. Unfortunately, our society seeks instant gratification rather than self-discipline. We want instant breakfast, fast food, movies on demand, and quick cash from ATMs. But success doesn't come instantly. Neither does the ability to lead. As General Dwight D. Eisenhower said, "There are no victories at bargain prices."

Because we live in a society of instant gratification, we cannot take for granted that the potential leaders we interview will have self-discipline—that they will be willing to pay the price of great leadership. When it comes to self-discipline, people choose one of two things: the pain of discipline which comes from sacrifice and growth or the pain of regret which comes from the easy road and missed opportunities. Each person in life chooses. In *Adventures in Achievement*, E. James Rohn says that the pain of discipline weighs ounces. Regret weighs tons.

There are two areas of self-discipline we must look for in potential leaders. The first is in the emotions. Effective leaders recognize that their emotional reactions are their own responsibility. A leader who decides not to allow other people's actions to dictate his reactions experiences an empowering freedom. As the Greek philosopher Epictetus said, "No person is free who is not master of himself."

> A great leader has the ability to instill within his people confidence in themselves.

The second area concerns time. Every person on the planet is given the same allotment of minutes in a day. But each person's level of self-discipline dictates how effectively those minutes are used. Disciplined people are always growing, always striving for improvement, and they maximize the use of their time. I have found three things that characterize disciplined leaders:

- They have identified specific long- and short-term goals for themselves.

- They have a plan for achieving those goals.

- They have a desire that motivates them to continue working to accomplish those goals.

Progress comes at a price. When you interview a potential leader, determine whether he or she is willing to pay the price. The author of the popular cartoon comic strip *Ziggy* recognized this when he drew the following scene:

As our friend Ziggy, in his little automobile, drove down a road, he saw two signs. The first stated in bold letters, THE ROAD TO SUCCESS. Farther down the road stood the second sign. It read, PREPARE TO STOP FOR TOLLS.

EFFECTIVE COMMUNICATION SKILLS

Never underestimate the importance of communication. It consumes enormous amounts of our time. One study, reported by D. K. Burlow in *The Process of Communication*, states that the average American spends 70 percent of his active hours each day communicating verbally. Without the ability to communicate, a leader cannot effectively cast his vision and call his people to act on that vision. President Gerald Ford once said, "Nothing in life is more important than the ability to communicate effectively." A leader is not capable of reaching his potential without effective communication skills.

A leader's ability to convey confidence and his ability to communicate effectively are similar. Both require action on his part and a response from the follower. Communication is positive *interaction*. When communication is one-sided, it can be comical. You may have heard the story of the frustrated judge preparing to hear a divorce case:

> Liking people is the beginning of the ability to communicate.

"Why do you want a divorce?" the judge asked. "On what grounds?"

"All over. We have an acre and a half," responded the woman.

"No, no," said the judge. "Do you have a grudge?"

"Yes, sir. Fits two cars."

"I need a reason for the divorce," said the judge impatiently.

"Does he beat you up?"

"Oh, no. I'm up at six every day to do my exercises. He gets up later."

"Please," said the exasperated judge. "What is the reason you want a divorce?"

"Oh," she replied. "We can't seem to communicate with each other."

When I look at a potential leader's communication skills, I look for the following.

A genuine concern for the person he's talking to. When people sense that you have a concern for them, they are willing to listen to what you have to say. Liking people is the beginning of the ability to communicate.

The ability to focus on the responder. Poor communicators are focused on themselves and their own opinions. Good communicators focus on the response of the person they're talking to. Good communicators also read body language. When I interview a potential employee, and he can't read in my body language that I'm ready to move on to another subject, it sends up a red flag.

The ability to communicate with all kinds of people. A good communicator has the ability to set a person at ease. He can find a way to relate to nearly anyone of any background.

Eye contact with the person he's speaking to. Most people who are being straight with you are willing to look you in the eye. Personal integrity and conviction make communication credible.

A warm smile. The fastest way to open the lines of communication is to smile. A smile overcomes innumerable communication barriers, crossing the boundaries of culture, race, age, class, gender, education, and economic status.

If I expect a person to lead, I must also expect him to be able to communicate.

Discontent with the Status Quo

I've told my staff before that *status quo* is Latin for "the mess we're in." Leaders see what is, but more important, they have vision for what could be. They are never content with things as they are. To be leading, by definition, is to be in front, breaking new ground, conquering new worlds, moving away from the status quo. Donna Harrison states, "Great leaders are never satisfied with current levels of performance. They constantly strive for higher and higher levels of achievement." They move beyond the status quo themselves, and they ask the same of those around them.

> A leader who loves the status quo soon becomes a follower.

Dissatisfaction with the status quo does not mean a negative attitude or grumbling. It has to do with willingness to be different and take risks. A person who refuses to risk change fails to grow. A leader who loves the status quo soon becomes a follower. Raymond Smith, former CEO and Chairman of the Bell Atlantic Corporation, once remarked, "Taking the safe road, doing your job, and not making any waves may not get you fired (right away, at least), but it sure won't do much for your career or your company over the long haul. We're not dumb. We know that administrators are easy to find and cheap to keep. Leaders—risk takers—are in very short supply. And ones with vision are pure gold."

Risk seems dangerous to people more comfortable with old problems than new solutions. The difference between the energy and time that it takes to put up with the old problems and the energy and time it takes to come up with new solutions is surprisingly small.

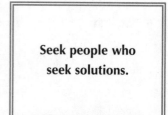

Seek people who seek solutions.

The difference is attitude. When seeking potential leaders, seek people who seek solutions.

Good leaders deliberately seek out and find potential leaders. Great leaders not only find them, but also transform them into other great leaders. An ability to recognize ability and a strategy for finding leaders make it happen. What is your plan for locating and identifying potential leaders?

FOUR

THE LEADER'S CRUCIAL TASK:
NURTURING POTENTIAL
LEADERS

Many organizations today fail to tap into their potential. Why? Because the only reward they give their employees is a paycheck. The relationship between employer and employee never develops beyond that point. Successful organizations take a different approach. In exchange for the work a person gives, he receives not only his paycheck, but also nurturing from the people for whom he works. And nurturing has the ability to transform people's lives.

Once you have identified potential leaders, you need to begin the work of building them into the leaders they can become. To do this you need a strategy. I use the *BEST* acronym as a reminder of what people need when they get started with my organization. They need me to:

B *elieve in them.*

E *ncourage them.*

S *hare with them.*

T *rust them.*

> **Nurturing has the ability to transform people's lives.**

The *BEST* technique is the beginning of the next element of developing the leaders around you: nurturing potential leaders.

Nurturing benefits everyone. Who wouldn't be more secure and motivated when his leader *believes* in him, *encourages* him, *shares* with him, and *trusts* him? People are more productive when nurtured. Even more important, nurturing creates a strong emotional and professional foundation within workers who have leadership potential. Later, using training and development, a leader can be built on that foundation.

The nurturing process involves more than just encouragement. It also includes modeling. In fact, the leader's major responsibility in the nurturing process is modeling . . . leadership, a strong work ethic, responsibility, character, openness, consistency, communication, and a belief in people. Even when he is in the process of giving to the people around him, he is also modeling. The modeling process is at its best when a leader chooses a model of his own to emulate and then becomes a model to his team members. As eighteenth-century writer Oliver Goldsmith once said, "People seldom improve when they have no other model but themselves to copy." We leaders must provide ourselves as models to copy.

Mark Twain once joked, "To do right is wonderful. To teach others to do right is even more wonderful—and much easier." I have a corollary to Twain's idea: "To lead others to do right is wonderful. To do right and then lead them is more wonderful—and harder." Like Twain, I recognize that the self-disciplines of doing right and then teaching others to do right are made difficult by human nature. Everyone can find excuses for not giving to those around them. Great leaders know the difficulties and nurture their people anyway. They know that there are people who will respond positively to what they give, and they focus on those positive results.

Here are the things I have found a leader must do to nurture the potential leaders around him.

CHOOSE A LEADERSHIP MODEL FOR YOURSELF

As leaders, you and I are first responsible for finding good models for ourselves. Give careful thought to which leaders you will follow because they will determine your course. I have developed six questions to ask myself before picking a model to follow:

DOES MY MODEL'S LIFE DESERVE A FOLLOWING?

This question relates to quality of character. If the answer is not a clear yes, I have to be very careful. I will become like the people I follow, and I don't want models with flawed character.

DOES MY MODEL'S LIFE HAVE A FOLLOWING?

This question looks at credibility. It is possible to be the very first person to discover a leader worth following, but it doesn't happen very often. If the person has no following, he or she may not be worth following.

If my answer to either of the first two questions is no, I don't have to bother with the other four. I need to look for another model.

WHAT IS THE MAIN STRENGTH THAT INFLUENCES OTHERS TO FOLLOW MY MODEL?

What does the model have to offer me? What is his best? Also note that strong leaders have weaknesses as well as strengths. I don't want to inadvertently emulate the weaknesses.

DOES MY MODEL PRODUCE OTHER LEADERS?

The answer to this question will tell me whether the model's leadership priorities match mine in regard to developing new leaders.

IS MY MODEL'S STRENGTH REPRODUCIBLE IN MY LIFE?

If I can't reproduce his strength in my life, his modeling will not benefit me. For instance, if you admire Shaquille O'Neil's ability as a basketball center, but you're only 5 feet, 9 inches tall and weigh 170 pounds, you are not going to be able to reproduce his strengths. Find appropriate models . . . but strive for improvement. Don't be too quick to say that a strength is not reproducible. Most are. Don't limit your potential.

IF MY MODEL'S STRENGTH IS REPRODUCIBLE IN MY LIFE, WHAT STEPS MUST I TAKE TO DEVELOP AND DEMONSTRATE THAT STRENGTH?

You must develop a plan of action. If you only answer the questions and never implement a plan to develop those strengths in yourself, you are only performing an intellectual exercise.

The models we choose may or may not be accessible to us in a personal way. Some may be national figures, such as a president. Or they may be people from history. They can certainly benefit you, but not the way a personal mentor can.

GUIDELINES FOR MENTORING RELATIONSHIPS

When you find someone who can personally mentor you, use these guidelines to help develop a positive mentoring relationship with that person:

ASK THE RIGHT QUESTIONS

Give thought to questions you will ask before you meet with your mentor. Make them strategic for your own growth.

CLARIFY YOUR LEVEL OF EXPECTATIONS

Generally, the goal of mentoring is improvement, not perfection. Perhaps only a few people can be truly excellent—but all of us can become better.

ACCEPT A SUBORDINATE, LEARNING POSITION

Don't let ego get in the way of learning. Trying to impress the mentor with your knowledge or ability will set up a mental barrier between you. It will prevent you from receiving what he is giving.

RESPECT THE MENTOR, BUT DON'T IDOLIZE HIM

Respect allows us to accept what the mentor is teaching. But making the mentor an idol removes the ability to be objective and critical—faculties we need for adapting a mentor's knowledge and experience to ourselves.

IMMEDIATELY PUT INTO EFFECT WHAT YOU ARE LEARNING

In the best mentoring relationships, what is learned comes quickly into focus. Learn, practice, and assimilate.

BE DISCIPLINED IN RELATING TO THE MENTOR

Arrange for ample and consistent time, select the subject matter in advance, and do your homework to make the sessions profitable.

REWARD YOUR MENTOR WITH YOUR OWN PROGRESS

If you show appreciation but make no progress, the mentor experiences failure. Your progress is his highest reward. Strive for growth, then communicate your progress.

DON'T THREATEN TO GIVE UP

Let your mentor know you have made a decision for progress and that you are a persistent person—a determined winner. Then he will know he is not wasting his time.

There is no substitute for your own personal growth. If you are not receiving and growing, you will not be able to give to the people you nurture and develop.

BUILD TRUST

I have learned that trust is the single most important factor in building personal and professional relationships. Warren Bennis and Burt Nanus call trust "the glue that binds followers and leaders together." Trust implies accountability, predictability, and reliability. More than anything else, followers want to believe in and trust their leaders. They want to be able to say, "Someday I want to be like him or her." If they don't trust you, they cannot say it. People first must believe in you before they will follow your leadership.

Trust must be built day by day. It calls for consistency. Some of the ways a leader can betray trust include: breaking promises, gossiping, withholding information, and being two-faced. These actions destroy the environment of trust necessary for the growth of potential leaders. And when a leader breaks trust, he must work twice as hard to regain it. As Christian leader Cheryl Biehl once said, "One of the realities of life is that if you can't trust a person at all points, you can't truly trust him or her at any point."

Every fall I look forward to seeing poor Charlie Brown try to placekick a football. He always ends up on his face or back because Lucy, his holder, jerks the ball away at the last moment. After she pulls the ball away, Lucy often tells Charlie she is trying to teach him not to be so trusting. But he keeps on trying to kick the football anyway, year after year. Why? Charlie really does want to trust people. Lucy is not a leader, and she never will be. Leadership can only function on the basis of trust; Lucy is untrustworthy.

> **Leadership can only function on the basis of trust.**

People will not follow a leader they do not trust. It is the leader's responsibility to actively develop that trust in him from the people around him. Trust is built on many things:

T *ime.* Take time to listen and give feedback on performance.

R *espect.* Give the potential leader respect and he will return it with trust.

U *nconditional Positive Regard.* Show acceptance of the person.

S *ensitivity.* Anticipate the feelings and needs of the potential leader.

T *ouch.* Give encouragement—a handshake, high five, or pat on the back.

Once people trust their leader as a person, they become able to trust his leadership.

SHOW TRANSPARENCY

All leaders make mistakes. They are a part of life. Successful leaders recognize their errors, learn from them, and work to correct their faults. A study of 105 executives determined many of the characteristics shared by successful executives. One particular trait was identified as the most valuable: They admitted their mistakes and accepted the consequences rather than trying to blame others.

We live among people who try to make someone else responsible for their actions or circumstances. People don't want to reap the consequences of their actions. You can see this attitude everywhere. Television advertisements invite us daily to sue "even if you were at fault in an accident" or "declare bankruptcy" to avoid creditors. A leader who is willing to take responsibility for his actions and be honest and transparent with his people is someone they will admire, respect, and trust. That leader is also someone they can learn from.

OFFER TIME

People cannot be nurtured from a distance or by infrequent, short spurts of attention. They need you to spend time with them—planned time, not just a few words on the way to a meeting. I make it a priority to stay in touch with the leaders in my organization. I plan and perform training sessions for my staff, I schedule one-on-one time for mentoring, and I schedule meetings where team members can share information. Often I'll take a potential leader to lunch. I frequently check with my people to see how their area of responsibility is progressing and give assistance if needed.

> **Time spent with a potential leader is an investment.**

We live in a fast-paced, demanding world, and time is a difficult thing to give. It is a leader's most valuable commodity. Peter Drucker wrote, "Nothing else, perhaps, distinguishes effective executives as much as their tender loving care of time." Time is valuable, but time spent with a potential leader is an investment. When you give of yourself, it benefits you, the organization, and the receiver. Nurtur-ing leaders must maintain a giving attitude. Norman Vincent Peale expressed it well when he said that the man who lives for himself is a failure; the man who lives for others has achieved true success.

BELIEVE IN PEOPLE

When you believe in people, you motivate them and release their potential. And people can sense intuitively when a person really believes in them. Anyone can see people as they are. It takes a leader to see what they can become, encourage them to grow in that direction, and believe that they will do it. People always grow toward a leader's expectations, not his criticism and examina-tions. Examinations merely *gauge* progress. Expectations *promote* progress. You can hire people to work for you, but you must win their hearts by believing in them in order to have them work with you.

> When you believe in people, you motivate them and release their potential.

GIVE ENCOURAGEMENT

Too many leaders expect their people to encourage themselves. But most people require outside encouragement to propel them forward. It is vital to their growth. Physician George Adams found encourage-ment to be so vital to a person's existence that he called it "oxygen to the soul."

New leaders need to be encouraged. When they arrive in a new situation, they encounter many changes and undergo many changes themselves. Encouragement helps them reach their potential; it empowers them by giving them energy to continue when they make mistakes.

Use lots of positive reinforcement with your people. Don't take acceptable work for granted; thank people for it. Praise a person every time you see improvement. And personalize your encouragement any time you can. Remember, what motivates one person may leave another cold or even irritated. Find out what works with each of your people and use it.

UCLA basketball coach John Wooden told players who scored to give a smile, wink, or nod to the player who gave them a good pass. "What if he's not looking?" asked a team member. Wooden replied, "I guarantee he'll look." Everyone values encouragement and looks for it—especially when his leader is a consistent encourager.

EXHIBIT CONSISTENCY

Consistency is a crucial part of nurturing potential leaders, just as it is in any other kind of nurturing. When we are consistent, our people learn to trust us. They are able to grow and develop because they know what to expect from us. They can answer the question, "What would my leader do in this situation?" when they face difficult decisions. They become secure because they know what our response to them will be, regardless of circumstances.

Perhaps you've heard the story about the farmer who had experienced several bad years. He went to see the manager of his bank:

> "I've got some good news and some bad news to tell you. Which would you like to hear first?" the farmer asked.

"Why don't you tell me the bad news first and get it over with?" the banker replied.

"Okay. With the bad drought and inflation and all, I won't be able to pay anything on my mortgage this year, either on the principal or the interest."

"Well, that is pretty bad."

"It gets worse. I also won't be able to pay anything on the loan for all that machinery I bought, not on the principal or interest."

"Wow, is that ever bad!"

"It's worse than that. You remember I also borrowed to buy seed and fertilizer and other supplies. Well, I can't pay anything on that either—principal or interest."

"That's awful and that's enough! Tell me what the good news is."

"The good news," replied the farmer with a smile, "is that I intend to keep on doing business with you."[1]

Fortunately, most of our potential leaders do better than our friend the farmer. Unlike him, they won't need consistent support for quite so long before they are able to turn things around. When we believe in our potential leaders, and we consistently support and encourage them, we give them the added strength they need to hang in there and perform well for us.

HOLD HOPE HIGH

Hope is one of the greatest gifts leaders can give to those around them. Its power should never be underestimated. It takes a great leader to give hope to people when they can't find it within themselves. Winston Churchill recognized the value of hope. He was prime minister of England during some of the darkest hours of World War II.

He was once asked by a reporter what his country's greatest weapon had been against Hitler's Nazi regime. Without pausing for a moment he said: "It was what England's greatest weapon has always been—hope."

> **It is the leader's job to hold hope high.**

People will continue working, struggling, and trying if they have hope. Hope lifts morale. It improves self-image. It reenergizes people. It raises their expectations. It is the leader's job to hold hope high, to instill it in the people he leads. Our people will have hope only if we give it to them. And we will have hope to give if we maintain the right attitude. Clare Boothe Luce, in *Europe in the Spring*, quotes Battle of Verdun hero Marshal Foch as saying, "There are no hopeless situations: there are only men who have grown hopeless about them."

Maintaining hope comes from seeing the potential in every situation and staying positive despite circumstances. Dr. G. Campbell Morgan tells the story of a man whose shop burned to the ground in the great Chicago fire. He arrived at the ruins the next morning carrying a table and set it up amid the charred debris. Above the table he placed this optimistic sign: "Everything lost except wife, children, and hope. Business will resume as usual tomorrow morning."

ADD SIGNIFICANCE

No one wants to spend his time doing work that is unimportant. People want to do work that matters. Workers often say things like, "I want to feel that I've achieved, that I've accomplished, that I've made a difference. I want excellence. I want what I do to be important work. I want to make an impact." People want significance.

It is the leader's job to add significance to the lives of the people he leads: One of the ways we can do this is to make them a part of something worthwhile. Too many people simply fall into a comfortable niche in life and stay there rather than pursue goals of significance. Leaders can't afford to do that. Every leader must ask himself, "Do I want survival, success, or significance?" The best leaders desire significance and expend their time and energy in pursuit of their dreams. As former *Washington Post* CEO Katharine Graham said, "To love what you do and feel that it matters—how could anything be more fun?"

Moishe Rosen teaches a one-sentence mental exercise that is an effective tool in helping a person identify his dream. He asks a person to fill in the blanks:

If I had _____

I would _____

The idea is that if you had anything you wanted—unlimited time, unlimited money, unlimited information, unlimited staff (all the resources you could ask for)—what would you do? Your answer to that question is your dream.

Acting on your dream adds significance to your life. There is a classic example of this from history. Everyone has heard the story of Isaac Newton's discovery of the law of gravity after observing the fall of an apple. What few people know is that Edmund Halley, the astronomer who discovered Halley's Comet, is almost single-handedly responsible for Newton's theories becoming known. Halley challenged Newton to think through his original notions. He corrected Newton's mathematical errors and prepared geometrical figures to support his work. Not only did he encourage Newton to write his great work, *Mathematical Principles of Natural Philosophy*, but he edited the work, supervised its publication, and financed its printing, even though Newton was wealthier and could easily afford the printing costs.

Halley encouraged Newton to act on his dream, and it added immeasurable significance to Newton's life. Newton began to reap the rewards of prominence almost immediately. Halley received little credit, but he must have gained great satisfaction in knowing he had inspired revolutionary ideas in the advancement of scientific thought.

Identify and pursue your dream. Make it personal, attainable, measurable, visible, and expandable. The desire for significance can stretch us to our very best. And being a part of the achievement of our dream can enrich the lives of those around us.

Another way to add significance to the lives of the people you lead is to show them the big picture and let them know how they contribute to it. Many people get so caught up in the task of the moment that they cannot see the importance of what they do.

A member of my staff who was once dean of a vocational college told me about a day he was showing around a new employee. As he introduced each person and described each person's position, the receptionist overheard him say that hers was a very important position. The receptionist commented, "I'm not important. The most important thing I do each day is fill out a report."

"Without you," the dean replied, "this school wouldn't exist. Every new student who comes here talks to you first. If they don't like you, they won't like the school. If they don't like the school, they won't come to school here, and we would soon run out of students. We would have to close our doors."

"Wow! I never thought of it that way," she replied. The dean immediately saw her appear more confident, and she sat up taller behind her desk as she answered the phone. The leader of her department had never explained to her the significance of her job. He had never explained her value to the organization. By seeing the big picture, she had significance added to her life.

PROVIDE SECURITY

Norman Cousins said, "People are never more insecure than when they become obsessed with their fears at the expense of their dreams." People who focus on their fears don't grow. They become paralyzed. Leaders are in a position to provide followers with an environment of security in which they can grow and develop. A potential leader who feels secure is more likely to take risks, try to excel, break new ground, and succeed. Great leaders make their followers feel bigger than they are. Soon the followers begin to think, act, and produce bigger than they are. Finally, they become what they think they are.

Henry Ford once said, "One of the great discoveries a man makes, one of his great surprises, is to find he can do what he was afraid he couldn't do." A nurturing leader provides the security a potential leader needs to make that discovery.

REWARD PRODUCTION

People rise to our level of expectations. They try to give us what we reward. If you want your people to produce, then you must reward production.

Thomas J. Watson, Sr., the founder of IBM, was famous for carrying a checkbook as he walked through offices and plants. Whenever he saw somebody doing an exceptional job, he wrote out a check to that person. It may have been for $5, $10, or $25. The amounts were small, but the impact of his action was tremendous. In many cases, people never cashed the checks. They framed them and put them on their walls. They found their reward not in the money, but in the personal recognition of their production. That's what gives significance and leads a person to give his personal best.

Even a person who is industrious and hardworking will finally get demoralized if production is discouraged rather than rewarded. You probably remember the children's story of the little red hen, the one who wanted help baking bread. Here is a modern version:

> Once upon a time there was a little red hen who scratched about the barnyard until she uncovered some grains of wheat. She called her neighbors and said, "If we plant this wheat, we shall have bread to eat. Who will help me plant it?"
>
> "Not I," said the cow.
>
> "Not I," said the duck.
>
> "Not I," said the pig.
>
> "Not I," said the goose.
>
> "Then I will," said the little red hen, and she did. The wheat grew tall and ripened into golden grain. "Who will help me reap my wheat?" asked the little red hen.
>
> "Not I," said the duck.
>
> "That's out of my classification," said the pig.
>
> "I'd lose my seniority," said the cow.
>
> "I'd lose my unemployment compensation," said the goose.
>
> "Then I will," said the little red hen, and she did.
>
> At last, it came time to bake the bread. "Who will help me bake the bread?" asked the little red hen.
>
> "That would be overtime for me," said the cow.
>
> "I'd lose my welfare benefits," said the duck.
>
> "If I'm to be the only helper, that would be discrimination," said the goose.

"Then I will," said the little red hen. She baked five loaves and held them up for her neighbors to see. They all wanted some. In fact, they demanded a share. But the little red hen said, "No, I can eat the five loaves myself."

"Excess profits!" yelled the cow.

"Capitalist leech!" cried the duck.

"I demand equal rights!" shouted the goose.

The pig just grunted. Then the others hurriedly painted picket signs and marched around, shouting obscenities.

The government agent came and said to the little red hen, "You must not be greedy."

"But I earned the bread," said the little red hen.

"Exactly," said the agent. "That is the wonderful free enterprise system. Anyone in the barnyard can earn as much as he wants. But, under government regulations, the productive workers must divide their product with the idle."

They all lived happily ever after. But the little red hen's neighbors wondered why she never again baked bread.[2]

We leaders must be certain that our people don't feel like the little red hen. We must never be like the government agent. We must give positive acknowledgment and encouragement to the producers, and we must be careful not to reward the idle. Take a hard look at your organization. What are you rewarding?

ESTABLISH A SUPPORT SYSTEM

Develop a support system for employees. Nothing hurts morale more than asking people to do something and not giving them resources to accomplish it. I believe every potential leader needs support in five areas:

EMOTIONAL SUPPORT

Provide a "yes you can" atmosphere. Even when support is lacking in other areas, a person can forge ahead when given emotional support. This support costs the least and yields an incredible return.

SKILLS TRAINING

One of the fastest ways to build people up is to train them. People receiving training perceive that the organization believes in them. And they are more productive because they are more highly skilled.

MONEY

Stingy leaders produce stingy workers. It is difficult for people to give of themselves when their leader does not give of himself. If you pay peanuts, expect to get monkeys. Invest money in people; it always yields the highest return on your investment.

> **Invest money in people; it always yields the highest return on your investment.**

EQUIPMENT

To do the job right, you need the right tools. Too often a poor leader looks at things from a short-term perspective. Investing in the right equipment will give your people the time to be more productive, and it will keep up their morale.

PERSONNEL

Provide the people needed to get the job done. And provide good people. Personnel problems can eat up the time and energy of a potential leader, leaving little time for production.

Create a support system for all the people around you. But increase it for any individual only as he grows and is successful. I have found the familiar 80/20 principle that I discussed at length in *Developing the Leader Within You* holds especially true here. The top 20 percent of the people in the organization will perform 80 percent of the organization's production. So when structuring your support system, provide the top 20 percent producers with 80 percent of the total support.

People who have a support system have the environment and the tools to succeed. They are a part of a cooperative environment. A business training exercise, described in a speech by Tom Geddie of Central and Southwest Services, is a wonderful illustration of what can happen in a cooperative environment:

Draw an imaginary line on the floor, and put one person on each side. The purpose is to get one person to convince the other, without force, to cross the line. U.S. players almost never convince one another, but their Japanese counterparts simply say, "If you'll cross the line, so will I." They exchange places and they both win.

The Japanese recognize the important of cooperation and mutual support. It has been a key to their success in the last fifty years. It can be a key to your success and to that of the leaders around you.

DISCERN AND PERSONALIZE THE POTENTIAL LEADER'S JOURNEY

Teddy Roosevelt once had a little dog that was always getting in fights and always getting licked. Somebody said, "Colonel, he's not much of a fighter." Teddy replied, "Oh, he's a good fighter. He's just a poor judge of dogs."

Leaders must be good at judging others. Leadership expert Peter Drucker has often said, "It is important to disciple a life, not teach a lesson." Discipleship of another person involves discerning where that person is, knowing where he is supposed to go, and giving him what he needs to get there. The person and the assignments he is given must match. As Drucker says, people are much like flowers. One, like a rose, needs fertilizer. Another, more like a rhododendron, doesn't. If you don't give flowers the care they need, they'll never bloom. The leader must be able to tell which is which.

> **Spend 80 percent of your time on the most promising 20 percent of the potential leaders around you.**

In the previous chapter, we discussed the identification of potential leaders. Everyone you recruit for your organization should be a potential leader, but you should not try to personally mentor everyone in your organization. Lead and nurture everyone within your influence, but spend 80 percent of your time on the most promising 20 percent of the potential leaders around you. Here are some guidelines for selecting the right people to mentor and develop:

SELECT PEOPLE WHOSE PHILOSOPHY OF LIFE IS SIMILAR TO YOURS

It will be difficult to develop someone whose values are too different from yours.

CHOOSE PEOPLE WITH POTENTIAL YOU GENUINELY BELIEVE IN

If you don't believe in them, you won't give them the time they need. And they will discern your lack of confidence in them. Belief in their potential, on the other hand, will empower them. Some of the nation's greatest professional athletes have come from tiny colleges that receive no publicity. All those ball players needed was for pro scouts to recognize the potential that the right opportunity could bring out. The secret of mentoring in any field is to help a person get where he or she is willing to go.

DETERMINE WHAT THEY NEED

Determining what potential leaders need involves looking at their strengths and weaknesses objectively. Their strengths indicate the directions they need to go, what they can become. Their weaknesses show us what we need to help them improve. Encouraging them in their strengths and helping them overcome their weaknesses will move them closer to reaching their potential.

EVALUATE THEIR PROGRESS CONSTANTLY

People need feedback, especially early in their development. Ben Franklin said, "The eye of the master will do more work than both his hands." He knew that a leader's ability to evaluate is his greatest strength. An honest mentor will be objective. If necessary, he or she will encourage the person to stay on course, to seek another direction, or even to enter into a relationship with another mentor.

BE COMMITTED, SERIOUS, AND AVAILABLE TO THE PEOPLE YOU MENTOR

The development of the potential leaders will be a reflection of your commitment to them: poor commitment equals poor development; great commitment equals great development.

Danny Thomas said, "All of us are born for a reason, but all of us don't discover why. Success in life has nothing to do with what you gain in life or accomplish for yourself. It's what you do for others." By personalizing each person's journey, you are helping him to maximize his potential. You are giving him a chance to discover his purpose. You also maximize his contribution to you and your organization.

Most people agree that nurturing is important to the development of children. However, they often fail to see its importance in the workplace. They assume that potential leaders will nurture themselves. If we as leaders do not nurture the potential leaders around us, they will never develop into the types of leaders we desire. As Ralph Waldo Emerson said, "It is one of the most beautiful compensations of this life that no man can sincerely try to help another without helping himself." When you nurture the people around you, everyone wins.

FIVE

THE LEADER'S DAILY REQUIREMENT: EQUIPPING POTENTIAL LEADERS

At this point you know how to identify potential leaders, how to create a climate in which they can be nurtured, and how to nurture them in some basic ways. It is time to look more specifically at how to prepare them for leadership within the organization. That preparation process is called equipping.

Equipping is similar to training. But I prefer the term "equipping" because it more accurately describes the process potential leaders must go through. Training is generally focused on specific job tasks; for instance, you train a person to use a copy machine or to answer a phone in a particular way. Training is only a part of the equipping process that prepares a person for leadership.

When I think of equipping a potential leader, I think of preparing an unskilled person to scale a tall mountain peak. His preparation is a process. Certainly he needs to be outfitted with equipment, such as cold-weather clothing, ropes, picks, and spikes. He also needs to be trained how to use that equipment.

A mountain climber's preparation, though, involves much more than simply having the correct equipment and knowing how to use it. The person must be conditioned physically to prepare him for the difficult climb. He must be trained to be a part of a team. Most important, he must be taught to *think* like a mountain climber. He needs to be able to look at a peak and *see* how it is to be conquered. Without going through the complete equipping process, he not only won't make it to the top of the mountain, but he also might find himself stranded on the side of the mountain, freezing to death.

> **Equipping, like nurturing, is an ongoing process.**

Equipping, like nurturing, is an ongoing process. You don't equip a person in a few hours or a day. And it can't be done using a formula or a videotape. Equipping must be tailored to each potential leader.

The ideal equipper is a person who can impart the vision of the work, evaluate the potential leader, give him the tools he needs, and then help him along the way at the beginning of his journey.

The equipper is a *model*—a leader who does the job, does it well, does it right, and does it with consistency.

The equipper is a *mentor*—an advisor who has the vision of the organization and can communicate it to others. He or she has experience to draw upon.

The equipper is an *empowerer*—one who can instill in the potential leader the desire and ability to do the work. He or she is able to lead, teach, and assess the progress of the person being equipped.

> **Equipping must be tailored to each potential leader.**

To see how your discernment skills measure up, take a look at this chart of potential leader characteristics adapted from author and leadership consultant Bobb Biehl:[1]

PERFORMANCE FACTORS	FAR EXCEEDS JOB REQUIREMENTS	EXCEEDS JOB REQUIREMENTS	MEETS JOB REQUIREMENTS	NEEDS SOME IMPROVEMENT	DOES NOT MEET MINIMUM REQUIREMENTS
Quality	Leaps tall buildings with a single bound	Must take running start to leap over tall buildings	Can only leap over a short building or medium with no spires	Crashes into buildings when attempting to jump over them	Cannot recognize building at all, much less jump
Timeliness	Is faster than a speeding bullet	Is as fast as a speeding bullet	Not quite as fast as a speeding bullet	Would you believe a slow bullet?	Wounds self with bullet when attempting to shoot gun
Initiative	Is stronger than a locomotive	Is stronger than an elephant	Is stronger than a bull	Shoots the bull	Smells like a bull
Adaptability	Walks on water consistently	Walks on water in emergencies	Washes with water	Drinks water	Passes water in emergencies
Communication	Talks with God	Talks with the angels	Talks to self	Argues with self	Loses those arguments

EQUIPPING QUESTIONS

Effective equipping begins with asking questions. We ask them to determine the direction our equipping efforts must take. If we don't, we may find ourselves teaching the wrong people the wrong things for the wrong purpose. I begin the process with analysis of the organization, myself, and the potential leaders. To get the information I need, I ask three sets of questions:

QUESTIONS ABOUT THE ORGANIZATION

These questions will determine what equipping needs to be done and the direction it should take to best serve the organization:

What is the statement of purpose for the organization? The development of leaders in an organization must begin with a review of the organization's purpose. (Presumably, the purpose of your organization is already in writing. If not, write it down. Or ask someone in authority to provide you with a statement of purpose.) Don't even consider performing equipping or training that does not contribute to the fulfillment of the organization's purpose.

What is the primary need of the organization? If you know what the organization needs most in order to fulfill its purpose, then you know its primary equipping need. Define that need as specifically as possible.

Is there a training program in place to meet that need? If there isn't, you know where to start. If there is, then use the ideas in this chapter to improve it.

What areas within the organization have the greatest growth potential? When you train and equip to prepare for growth, you play to your strengths. You are being proactive rather than reactive. You are putting yourself in a position to meet the future totally prepared.

Do those potential growth areas have the needed leaders to accomplish the task? Without leaders ready to make things happen, the area of growth potential will never move from "potential" to reality. If the leaders don't already exist, they will have to be equipped and developed.

QUESTIONS ABOUT MYSELF

The questions concerning the organization indicate the direction the equipping must take. This next set of questions will make clear how the equipping will be done. As the leader, I set the tone for the equipping process.

Am I willing to pour my life into others? Giving to potential leaders is a way of life for the best leaders. They do it daily. The development of their people is more important than the development of their own status. They are willing to share the credit when things go right. Equipping involves sacrifice.

Am I committed to an equipping organization? Equipping requires commitment. It takes time and effort on the part of an organization's leadership. Everyone knows it's quicker and easier for a leader to do a job himself than it is for him to teach other people to do it. But doing it yourself is a short-term solution. The longer, harder road of equipping others pays in the long run, but it requires commitment from everyone in the organization.

Am I effective in the areas I need to equip? This is a tough question that requires an honest answer. If the answer is "no," the leader must locate a person, inside or outside the organization, effective in those areas who can do some of the training. Either that, or he had better go out and get himself equipped.

Have I developed a prospect list of potential leaders? As I mentioned in Chapter Three, a good leader is always looking for potential leaders. You always begin with the best people you can. As you nurture them, a group of people with the most potential will emerge. From that group, draw up a prospect list of potential leaders to be considered for equipping and development.

What assumptions have I made that need to be changed? People often get a false first impression of other people. Many times leaders build their expectations of the people they will develop on assumptions from those false first impressions. When you are aware that you have made some assumptions, you can go beyond the superficial and move to a new level in your relationships with your potential leaders. It allows you to better understand where they are, what they need, and what you can provide them.

QUESTIONS ABOUT THE POTENTIAL LEADER

Once you have identified the organization's equipping needs, examined yourself, and developed a prospect list, you are ready to select the people to be equipped. The goal now is to narrow the field of prospective leaders down to the few people with the most potential. Ask yourself these questions about each person to find the ones with the highest potential:

Is this person compatible philosophically with the organization and my leadership? If the answer is no, don't even consider equipping or mentoring this person. There must be compatibility first; otherwise, no amount of training in the world will make this person the type of leader you want and need.

Does this person show a potential for growth? Potential for growth does not guarantee growth, but a lack of growth potential guarantees no growth will occur. If the person does not appear to have the desire and the ability to grow, look for another candidate.

Are there lingering questions I have about this person? The time to have lingering questions answered is before the person is selected for equipping. Take time to interview, then do follow-up interviews to answer other questions that occur to you later. You may want to have someone you respect in your organization do an interview as well. He or she will sometimes see things you missed. If you can positively answer 95 percent of your questions about this person, then the person is probably a good candidate. The one exception is character. If you have any lingering questions concerning his character, don't choose him for development.

Am I selecting this person because of obvious strengths or because I don't see any glaring weaknesses? When you look at a potential leader and don't see even one great strength, don't choose him for equipping and development—even if you see no great weaknesses. As tempting as it may be to select that person, don't do it. Why? Because if you do, you are asking for mediocrity.

Management expert Peter Drucker, in *The Effective Executive*, explains that Abraham Lincoln made this mistake early in his presidency when selecting generals. He sought men without glaring weaknesses. As a result, the well-equipped Union army fared poorly against the Confederates. Lincoln once remarked irritably that if General McClellen didn't plan to use the army, he would like to borrow it for a while.

The Confederate army was staffed with generals who, although they had obvious weaknesses, were picked for their great and obvious strengths. These strengths, properly developed and applied, gave them victory after victory. Lincoln finally learned this lesson and selected as leader of the Union army Ulysses Grant, a great general, but also an alcoholic. When you look for potential leaders, select people with obvious strengths even if you see weaknesses.

What is the potential leader's fit? There are two kinds of "fit" to consider. First, a person's gifts and abilities must fit the job he is to perform. Consider such gifts and abilities as temperament, background, job experiences, skills, personality, and passion. People need to be trained and developed primarily in their areas of strength. And most of the work they are asked to do should be in those areas. I often talk about the 80/20 principle, and it applies here as well. A person should be spending 80 percent of his time doing things that require his greatest gifts and abilities. This will help keep him fulfilled.

The second has to do with how well he will fit into the team. No matter how great the player, if he can't play with the team, he won't help the organization. The addition of a new team member always changes the chemistry of the team.

> A person should be spending 80 percent of his time doing things that require his greatest gifts and abilities.

It's obvious in sports: A good team is made up of people with different talents playing different positions to accomplish one goal. (Can you imagine a whole basketball team of seven-foot centers who specialize in blocking shots—no shooting guards, no shooting or rebounding forwards, and no playmakers—just centers? What a disaster.)

Teams outside of sports need to be created strategically too. They must have the right chemistry. When each player brings his particular style and talents to the team, and they come together with respect and appreciation for one another, it can create a wonderful and powerful team.

If you haven't already stopped to answer these questions, I want to encourage you to do so right now. Write down your answers. If you have your own organization, you cannot afford to let any more time go by without preparing for your organization's future. Even if you are not the CEO of the organization, you can still apply these principles. Do it now!

HOW TO EQUIP FOR EXCELLENCE

Now that you know who you are going to equip and for what you are going to equip them, you are ready to get started. The steps that follow will take you through the whole process. They begin with building relationships with your potential leaders. From that foundation, you can build programs for their development, supervise their progress, empower them to do the jobs, and finally get them to pass on the legacy.

DEVELOP A PERSONAL RELATIONSHIP WITH THE PEOPLE YOU EQUIP

All good mentoring relationships begin with a personal relationship. As your people get to know and like you, their desire to follow your direction and learn from you will increase. If they don't like you, they will not want to learn from you, and the equipping process slows down or even stops.

To build relationships, begin by listening to people's life stories, their journeys so far. Your genuine interest in them will mean a lot to them. It will also help you to know their personal strengths and weaknesses. Ask them about their goals and what motivates them. Find out what kind of temperaments they

> **All good mentoring relationships begin with a personal relationship.**

have. You certainly don't want to equip and develop a person whose greatest love is numbers and financial statements for a position where he would be spending 80 percent of his time dealing with disgruntled customers.

One of the best ways to get to know people is to see them outside of the business world. People are usually on their guard at work. They try to be what others want them to be. By getting to know them in other settings, you can get to know who they really are. Try to learn as much as you can about the people and do your best to win their hearts. If you first find their hearts, they'll be glad to give you their hands.

SHARE YOUR DREAM

While getting to know your people, share your dream. It helps them to know you and where you're going. There's no act that will better show them your heart and your motivation.

Woodrow Wilson once said,

> We grow by dreams. All big individuals are dreamers. They see things in the soft haze of a spring day, or in the red fire on a long winter's evening. Some of us let those great dreams die, but others nourish and protect them; nourish them through bad days until they bring them to the sunshine and light which comes always to those who sincerely hope that their dreams will come true.

I have often wondered, "Does the person make the dream or does the dream make the person?" My conclusion is both are equally true.

All good leaders have a dream. All great leaders share their dream with others who can help them make it a reality. As Florence Littauer suggests, we must:

Dare to dream:	Have the desire to do something bigger than yourself.
Prepare the dream:	Do your homework; be ready when the opportunity comes.
Wear the dream:	Do it.
Share the dream:	Make others a part of the dream, and it will become even greater than you had hoped.

ASK FOR COMMITMENT

In his book *The One Minute Manager*, Ken Blanchard says, "There's a difference between interest and commitment. When you are interested in doing something, you do it only when it is convenient. When you are committed to something, you accept no excuses." Don't equip people who are merely interested. Equip the ones who are committed.

Commitment is the one quality above all others that enables a potential leader to become a successful leader. Without commitment, there can be no success. Football coach Lou Holtz recognized the difference between being merely involved and being truly committed. He pointed out, "The kamikaze pilot that was able to fly 50 missions was involved—but never committed."

To determine whether your people are committed, first you must make sure they know what it will cost them to become leaders. That means that you must be sure not to undersell the job—let them know what it's going to take. Only then will they know what they are committing to. If they won't commit, don't go any further in the equipping process. Don't waste your time.

SET GOALS FOR GROWTH

People need clear objectives set before them if they are to achieve anything of value. Success never comes instantaneously. It comes from taking many small steps. A set of goals becomes a map a potential leader can follow in order to grow. As Shad Helmsetter states in *You Can Excel in Time of Change*, "It is the goal that shapes the plan; it is the plan that sets the action; it is the action that achieves the result; and it is the result that brings the success. And it all begins with the simple word *goal*." We, as equipping leaders, must introduce our people to the practice of setting and achieving goals.

Lily Tomlin once said, "I always wanted to be somebody, but I should have been more specific." Many people today find themselves in the same situation. They have some vague idea of what success is, and they know they want to achieve it. But they haven't worked out any kind of plan to get there. I have found that the greatest achievers in life are people who set goals for themselves and then work hard to reach them. What they *get* by reaching the goals is not nearly as important as what they *become* by reaching them.

When you help your people set goals, use the following guidelines:

Make the goals appropriate. Always keep in mind the job you want the people to do and the desired result: the development of your people into effective leaders. Identify goals that will contribute to that larger goal.

Make the goals attainable. Nothing will make people want to quit faster than facing unachievable goals. I like the comment made by Ian MacGregor, former AMAX Corporation chairman of the board: "I work on the same principle as people who train horses. You start with low fences, easily achieved goals, and work up. It's important in management never to ask people to try to accomplish goals they can't accept."

Make the goals measurable. Your potential leaders will never know when they have achieved their goals if they aren't measurable. When they are measurable, the knowledge that they have been attained will give them a sense of accomplishment. It will also free them to set new goals in place of the old ones.

Clearly state the goals. When goals have no clear focus, neither will the actions of the people trying to achieve them.

Make the goals require a "stretch." As I mentioned before, goals have to be achievable. On the other hand, when goals don't require a stretch, the people achieving them won't grow. The leader must know his people well enough to identify attainable goals that require a stretch.

> **The leader must know his people well enough to identify attainable goals that require a stretch.**

Put the goals in writing. When people write down their goals, it makes them more accountable for those goals. A study of a Yale University graduating class showed that the small percentage of graduates who had written down their goals accomplished more than all of the other graduates combined. Putting goals in writing works.

It is also important to encourage your potential leaders to review their goals and progress frequently. Ben Franklin set aside time every day to review two questions. In the morning he asked himself, "What good shall I do today?" In the evening he asked, "What good have I done today?"

COMMUNICATE THE FUNDAMENTALS

For people to be productive and satisfied professionally, they have to know what their fundamental responsibilities are. It sounds so simple, but Peter Drucker says one of the critical problems in the workplace today is that there is a lack of understanding between the employer and employee as to what the employee is to do. Often employees are made to feel they are vaguely responsible for everything. It paralyzes them. Instead, we need to make clear to them what they *are* and *are not* responsible for. Then they will be able to focus their efforts on what we want, and they will succeed.

Look again at how a basketball team works. Each of the five players has a particular job. There is a shooting guard whose job is to score points. The other guard is a point guard. His job is to pass the ball to people who can score. Another player is a power forward who is expected to get rebounds. The small forward's job is to score. The center is supposed to rebound, block shots, and score. Each person on the team knows what his job is, what his unique contribution to the team must be. When each concentrates on his particular responsibilities, the team can win.

One of the best ways to clarify expectations is to provide your people with job descriptions. In the description, identify the four to six primary functions you want the person to perform. Avoid long laundry lists of responsibilities. If the job description can't be summarized, the job is probably too broad. Also try to make clear what authority they have, the working parameters for each function they are to perform, and what the chain of authority is within the organization.

Another essential that has to be communicated to new leaders is how they are to prioritize. I tell people that everything they do is either an "A" or a "B" priority. The concept helps them understand what is most important.

"A" priorities are ones that move the organization, department, or job function forward. They break ground, open doors to new opportunities, or develop new markets. They promote growth within people or the organization. "B" priorities are concerned with maintenance. They are required for things to continue running smoothly, such as answering letters or phone calls, and taking care of details. They are things that cannot be neglected, but they don't add value to the organization. I have found that people often expend their best on "B" priorities because they seem urgent, and they give "A" priorities what's left over. I always encourage my people to give 80 percent of their time and energy to the "A" priorities and the remaining 20 percent to the "B" group.

Finally, a leader must communicate to his or her people that their work has value to the organization and to the individual leader. To the employee, this often is the most important fundamental of all.

PERFORM THE FIVE-STEP PROCESS OF TRAINING PEOPLE

Part of the equipping process includes training people to perform the specific tasks of the jobs they are to do. The approach the leader takes to training will largely determine his people's success or failure. If he takes a dry, academic approach, the potential leaders will remember little of what's taught. If he simply throws the people into the job without any direction, they may feel like this employee of Hagar the Horrible:

Reprinted with special permission of King Features Syndicate

The best type of training takes advantage of the way people learn. Researchers tell us that we remember 10 percent of what we hear,

50 percent of what we see, 70 percent of what we say, and 90 percent of what we hear, see, say, and do. Knowing that, we have to develop an approach to how we will train. I have found the best training method to be a five-step process:

Step 1: I model. The process begins with my doing the tasks while the person being trained watches. When I do this, I try to give the person an opportunity to see me go through the whole process. Too often when leaders train, they begin in the middle of the task and confuse the people they're trying to teach. When people see the task performed correctly and completely, it gives them something to try to duplicate.

Step 2: I mentor. During this next step, I continue to perform the task, but this time the person I'm training comes alongside me and assists in the process. I also take time to explain not only the *how* but also the *why* of each step.

Step 3: I monitor. We exchange places this time. The trainee performs the task and I assist and correct. It's especially important during this phase to be positive and encouraging to the trainee. It keeps him trying and it makes him want to improve rather than give up. Work with him until he develops consistency. Once he's gotten down the process, ask him to explain it to you. It will help him to understand and remember.

Step 4: I motivate. I take myself out of the task at this point and let the trainee go. My task is to make sure he knows how to do it without help and to keep encouraging him so he will continue to improve. It is important for me to stay with him until he senses success. It's a great motivator. At this time the trainee may want to make improvements to the process. Encourage him to do it, and at the same time learn from him.

Step 5: I multiply. This is my favorite part of the whole process. Once the new leaders do the job well, it becomes their turn to teach others how to do it. As teachers know, the best way to learn something is to teach it. And the beauty of this is it frees me to do other important developmental tasks while others carry on the training.

GIVE THE "BIG THREE"

All the training in the world will provide limited success if you don't turn your people loose to do the job. I believe that if I get the best people, give them my vision, train them in the basics, and then let go, I will get a high return from them. As General George S. Patton once remarked, "Never tell people how to do things. Tell them what to do and they will surprise you with their ingenuity."

You can't turn people loose without structure, but you also want to give them enough freedom to be creative. The way to do that is to give them the big three: *responsibility, authority,* and *accountability.*

For some people, responsibility is the easiest of the three to give. We all want the people around us to be responsible. We know how important it is. As author/editor Michael Korda said, "Success on any major scale requires you to accept responsibility. . . . In the final analysis, the one quality that all successful people have . . . is the ability to take on responsibility."

What is more difficult for some leaders is allowing their people to keep the responsibility after it's been given. Poor managers want to control every detail of their people's work. When that happens, the potential leaders who work for them become frustrated and don't develop. Rather than desiring more responsibility, they become indifferent or avoid responsibility altogether. If you want your people to take responsibility, truly give it to them.

With responsibility must go authority. Progress does not come unless they are given together. Winston Churchill, while addressing the House of Commons during the Second World War, said, "I am your servant. You have the right to dismiss me when you please. What you have no right to do is ask me to bear responsibility without the power of action." When responsibility and authority come together, people become genuinely empowered.

There's an important aspect of authority that needs to be noted. When we first give authority to new leaders, we are actually *giving them permission* to have authority rather than *giving them authority* itself. True authority has to be earned. George Davis, in *Magic Shortcuts to Executive Success*, notes:

> Authority is not something we buy, are born with, or even have delegated to us by our superiors. It is something we earn—and we earn it from our subordinates. No manager has any real authority over his people until he has proved himself worthy of it—in the eyes of his people—not his own, nor those of his superiors.

We must give our people permission to develop authority. That is our responsibility. They, in turn, must take responsibility for earning it.

I have found there are different levels of authority:

Position. The most basic kind of authority comes from a person's position on the organizational chart. This type of authority does not extend beyond the parameters of the job description. This is where all new leaders start. From here they may either earn greater authority, or they can minimize what little authority they have been given. It's up to them.

Competence. This type of authority is based on a person's professional capabilities, the ability to do a job. Followers give competent leaders authority within the leader's area of expertise.

Personality. Followers will also give authority to people based on their personal characteristics, such as personality, appearance, and charisma. Authority based on personality is a little broader than competence-based authority, but it is not really more advanced because it tends to be superficial.

Integrity. Authority based on integrity comes from a person's core. It is based on character. When new leaders gain authority based on their integrity, they have crossed into a new stage of their development.

Spirituality. In secular circles, people rarely consider the power of spiritual-based authority. It comes from people's individual experiences with God and from His power working through them. It is the highest form of authority.

Leaders must earn authority with each new group of people. However, I have found that once leaders have gained authority on a particular level, it takes very little time for them to establish that level of authority with another group of people. The higher the level of authority, the more quickly it happens.

Once responsibility and authority have been given to people, they are empowered to make things happen. But we also have to be sure they are making the right things happen. That's where accountability comes into the picture. True responsibility on the part of new leaders includes a willingness to be held accountable. If we are providing them the right climate (as described in Chapter Two), our people will not fear accountability. They will admit mistakes and see them as a part of the learning process.

The leader's part of accountability involves taking the time to review the new leader's work and give honest, constructive criticism. It is crucial that the leader be supportive but honest. It's been said that when Harry Truman was thrust into the presidency upon the death of President Franklin D. Roosevelt, Speaker of the House Sam Rayburn gave him some fatherly advice: "From here on out you're going to have lots of people around you. They'll try to put a wall around you and cut you off from any ideas but theirs. They'll tell you what a great man you are, Harry. But you and I both know you ain't." Rayburn was holding President Truman accountable.

GIVE THEM THE TOOLS THEY NEED

Giving responsibility without resources is ridiculous; it is incredibly limiting. Abraham Maslow said, "If the only tool you have is a hammer, you tend to see every problem as a nail." If we want our people to be creative and resourceful, we need to provide resources.

Obviously, the most basic tools are pieces of equipment, such as copying machines, computers, and whatever else simplifies someone's work. We must be sure not only to provide everything necessary for a job to be done, but also equipment that will allow jobs, especially "B" priorities, to be done more quickly and efficiently. Always work toward freeing people's time for important things.

Tools, however, include much more than equipment. It is important to provide developmental tools. Spend time mentoring people in specific areas of need. Be willing to spend money on things like books, tapes, seminars, and professional conferences. There is a wealth of good information out there, and fresh ideas from outside an organization can stimulate growth. Be creative in providing tools. It will keep your people growing and equip them to do the job well.

CHECK ON THEM SYSTEMATICALLY

I believe in touching base with people frequently. I like to give mini-evaluations all the time. Leaders who wait to give feedback only during annual formal evaluations are asking for trouble. People need the encouragement of being told they're doing well on a regular basis. They also need to hear as soon as possible when they are not doing well. It prevents a lot of problems with the organization, and it improves the leader.

How often I check on people is determined by a number of factors:

The importance of the task. When something is critical to the success of the organization, I touch base often.

The demands of the work. I find that if the work is very demanding, the person performing it needs encouragement more often. He may also need questions answered or need help solving difficult problems. Occasionally, when the job is really tough, I tell the person to take a break—demanding work can lead a person to burnout.

The newness of the work. Some leaders have no problem tackling a new task, no matter how different it is from previous work. Others have great difficulty adapting. I check often on the people who are less flexible or creative.

The newness of the worker. I want to give new leaders every possible chance to succeed. So I check on newer people more often. That way I can help them anticipate problems and make sure that they have a series of successes. By that they gain confidence.

The responsibility of the worker. When I know I can give a person a task and it will always get done, I may not check on that person until the task is complete. With less responsible people, I can't afford to do that.

My approach to checking on people also varies from person to person. For instance, rookies and veterans should be treated differently. But no matter how long people have been with me, there are some things I always do:

Discuss feelings. I always give my people an opportunity to tell me how they feel. I also tell them how I'm feeling. It clears the air and makes it possible for us to get down to business.

Measure progress. Together, we try to determine their progress. I often ask questions to find out what I need to know. If people are hitting obstacles, I remove the ones I can.

Give feedback. This is a critical part of the process. I always give them some kind of evaluation. I'm honest, and I do my homework to make sure I'm accurate. I give constructive criticism. This lets them know how they're doing, corrects problems, encourages improvements, and speeds the work.

Give encouragement. Whether the person is doing well or poorly, I always give encouragement. I encourage poor performers to do better. I encourage peak performers. I praise milestones. I try to give hope and encouragement when people are experiencing personal issues. Encouragement keeps people going.

Though it doesn't happen very often, I occasionally have a person whose progress is repeatedly poor. When that happens, I try to determine what's gone wrong. Usually poor performance is a result of one of three things: (1) a mismatch between the job and the person; (2) inadequate training or leadership; or (3) deficiencies in the person performing the work. Before I take any action, I always try to determine what the issues are. I line up my facts to be sure there really is a deficiency in performance and not just a problem with my perception. Next I define as precisely as possible what the deficiency is. Finally, I check with the person who is not performing to get the other side of the story.

Once I've done my homework, I try to determine where the deficiency is. If it's a mismatch, I explain the problem to the person, move him to a place that fits, and reassure him of my confidence in him. If the problem involves training or leadership issues, I back up and redo whatever step hasn't been performed properly. Once again, I let the person know what the problem was and give him plenty of encouragement. If the problem is with the person, I sit down with him and

DEVELOPING THE LEADERS AROUND YOU

let him know about it. I make it clear where his failures are and what he must do to overcome them. Then I give him another chance. But I also begin the documentation process in case I have to fire him. I want him to succeed, but I will waste no time letting him go if he doesn't do what it takes to improve.

CONDUCT PERIODIC EQUIPPING MEETINGS

Even after you've completed most of your people's training and are preparing to take them into their next growth phase—development—continue to conduct periodic equipping meetings. It helps your people stay on track, helps them keep growing, and encourages them to begin taking responsibility for equipping themselves.

When I prepare an equipping meeting, I include the following:

Good news. I always start on a positive note. I review the good things that are happening in the organization and pay particular attention to their areas of interest and responsibility.

Vision. People can get so caught up in their day-to-day responsibilities that they lose sight of the vision that drives the organization. Use the opportunity of an equipping meeting to recast that vision. It will also give them the appropriate context for the training you are about to give.

Content. Content will depend on their needs. Try to focus training on areas that will help them in the "A" priority areas, and orient the training on the people, not the lesson.

Administration. Cover any organizational items that give the people a sense of security and encourage their leadership.

Empowerment. Take time to connect with the people you equip. Encourage them personally. And show them how the equipping session empowers them to perform their jobs better. They will leave the meeting feeling positive and ready to work.

The entire equipping process takes a lot of time and attention. It requires more time and dedication from the equipping leader than mere training. But its focus is long term, not short term. Rather than creating followers or even adding new leaders, it multiplies leaders. As I explained in the section on the five-step process of equipping, it is not complete until the equipper and the new leader select someone for the new leader to train. It is only then that the equipping process has come full circle. Without a successor, there can be no success.

Leaders who are equipping others have the greatest possibility of success, no matter what type of organization they're in. When a leader is dedicated to the equipping process, the whole level of performance within the organization rises dramatically. Everyone is better prepared to get the work done. More important, the best-equipped people will be ready for the final growth stage that creates the very best leaders— development. As Fred A. Manske, Jr. said, "The greatest leader is willing to train people and develop them to the point that they eventually surpass him or her in knowledge and ability." The following chapter will show you how to take that step.

SIX

THE LEADER'S LIFELONG COMMITMENT: DEVELOPING POTENTIAL LEADERS

If you have done all the things I've discussed so far in this book—created a great environment, nurtured your people, and equipped the best people around you—your achievements have already surpassed those of the majority of managers in the work force today. You can consider yourself a better-than-average leader. If you go no further, though, you will never become a *great* leader. No matter how hard or how smart you work, you will never become one of the best of the best. Why? Because the very best leaders, the top 1 percent, take their people the next step and develop them so they can reach their potential. The growth and development of people is the highest calling of leadership.

You're probably wondering why most leaders don't take this final step. They don't because it's hard work. I once heard the story of a preacher who quit the ministry after twenty years and became a funeral director. When asked why he made the change, he replied, "Well, I spent three years trying to straighten out Fred, and Fred is still an alcoholic. And I spent six

> **The growth and development of people is the highest calling of leadership.**

months trying to straighten out Susan's marriage, and she filed for divorce. Then I spent over two-and-a-half years trying to straighten out Bob's drug problem, and he's still an addict. Now at the funeral home, when I straighten them out—they stay straight."

Living, breathing human beings require continual attention. And development is demanding work. It takes more attention and commitment than either nurturing or equipping. To see the differences in emphasis in nurturing, equipping, and developing, look at the following table:

NURTURING	EQUIPPING	DEVELOPING
Care	Training for Work	Training for Personal Growth
Focus Is on Need	Focus Is on Task	Focus Is on Person
Relational	Transactional	Transformational
Service	Management	Leadership
Maintains Leadership	Adds Leadership	Multiplies Leadership
Establishing	Releasing	Empowering
Helping	Teaching	Mentoring
Need Oriented	Skill Oriented	Character Oriented
What They Want	What the Organization Needs	What They Need
A Desire	A Science	An Art
Little or No Growth	Short-Term Growth	Long-Term Growth
All	Many	Few

Take a look at the qualities associated with developing leaders. They are based on what the potential leaders need, on their growth. The process is designed to build into them, to bring out their best qualities, to develop their character, and to help them discover and reach their potential.

Because the development of leaders requires time, attention, and commitment, a developer can only work with a few people at a time, as the last entry in the table indicates. Nurture all of your people, and equip many. But develop only a few—the few who are ready and willing.

There is another important difference between equipping and developing people. Equipping is essentially a step-by-step process. You can take people through specific steps to equip them. That is the *science* of equipping. Leadership development is more of an *art*. It is not a series of specific steps that you take people through. Instead, there are aspects that must be addressed throughout the whole process.

Here are the twelve actions a leader must take to develop potential leaders into the best they can be.

ASK THE THREE MOTIVATION QUESTIONS

All growth begins with motivation. You as the developer must find your potential leaders' motivations and harness them. Begin by asking these questions:

WHAT DO THEY WANT?

Everyone wants something. Even the person who appears not to be motivated has desires. You need to find out what your people want. Sometimes they will tell you. Other times you need to use discernment. Since you will have already built relationships with them, use information that you've learned during your personal interactions with them. No matter how, you need to find out what will motivate them to develop.

Do They Have a Way of Getting What They Want?

Whenever people want something but see no way to get it, they will not be motivated. One of your jobs as the leader is to determine how your potential leaders can achieve what they desire and show them a way to do it. Because you have already traveled the road of achievement, you may be able to see the way more clearly and can help point the way. Sometimes you may even have the power to create a way for them to achieve what they want on a personal level.

Will They Be Rewarded if Successful?

Sometimes even people who have goals and see ways of achieving them lack motivation. Why? Because they don't believe the rewards will outweigh the work required to achieve them. As their leader, you can share from your own experience that the rewards are worth the effort. You are also in a position to show them how their personal goals and desires coincide with those of the organization. When both have the same goals, the rewards are multiplied.

For example, if the goal of one of your people is to become an outstanding salesperson, that goal also benefits the organization, and the organization will reward it (in commission or salary). As a result, if that person achieves that goal, he will receive the personal benefits to himself as well as the monetary rewards from the organization. The rewards are multiplied.

> **Good leaders are good listeners.**

Ask the questions to find your people's motivation, and then harness that motivation to help them develop.

BE A GOOD LISTENER

Good leaders are good listeners. Listening to your people will add to your success and to their development. When you listen to their ideas and opinions, especially before you make decisions, you give them a chance to increase their contribution. Each time you use their ideas and give them credit, they will feel valued, and they will be encouraged to keep contributing. This is one of the best ways to get them to start thinking creatively. They will also develop judgment and begin to understand the reasons why you use some of their ideas and choose not to use others. They will learn to see things more clearly and more in terms of the big picture.

The critical aspect of this process is that you genuinely seek their advice and then listen to their views actively and positively. If you are simply going through the motions, your people will know it. Likewise, never criticize the person making a suggestion, even if it's a poor one. People who feel belittled will soon stop

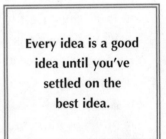

Every idea is a good idea until you've settled on the best idea.

making suggestions, and you may miss out on their next great idea because you've discouraged them from contributing. Try to adopt this attitude: every idea is a good idea until you've settled on the best idea.

DEVELOP A PLAN FOR PERSONAL GROWTH

One of the things I enjoy most is doing conferences around the country. I especially love the five or six leadership conferences sponsored each year through our organization INJOY. One of the most important things I talk about at those conferences is personal growth.

I often invite anyone in the audience who has already created a personal plan for growth to come up during the break to tell me about it. Do you know that in all the years I have been doing that, not once has anyone come up to me. Why? Because not one had created a personal growth plan for himself.

People think personal growth is a natural result of being alive. Well it's not. Growth is not automatic; it does not necessarily come with experience, nor simply as a result of gathering information. Personal growth must be deliberate, planned, and consistent.

One of the best things you can do for the people you are developing, besides modeling personal growth yourself, is to help them develop their own personal plans for growth. I want to emphasize that growth requires a *plan*. As my friend Zig Ziglar says, "You were born to be a winner, but to be a winner you must plan to win and prepare to win." Growing is the same. You have to create a plan and follow it.

I have devoted the greater part of my life to my own personal development and the creation of materials for the personal development of others. I have created leadership development lessons every month since 1985, and sent them out to people across the country through INJOY and Maximum Impact, because my greatest desire is to help others reach their potential. That is why I hold leadership conferences. Let me outline for you a plan for growth that I give people at these conferences. Help your people adapt it to their needs. And use it yourself if you aren't already using another plan that works for you.

PRACTICAL STEPS FOR PERSONAL GROWTH

SET ASIDE TIME DAILY FOR GROWTH

There are two important concepts in this step. First, time for growth must be *planned*. Getting sidetracked is one of the easiest things in the world to do. Growth time that is not strategically planned into the day soon disappears because our lives are busy. People must find a time that works for them and schedule it into their calendar. Then they must guard that time as they would any other appointment. Second, the time set aside must be set aside daily—for no fewer than five days a week. Educators report that people learn more effectively in shorter regular sessions than long, infrequent blocks of time. A daily discipline pays dividends. Here is the weekly plan that I recommend at my conferences:

Monday:	One hour with God
Tuesday:	One hour listening to a leadership tape
Wednesday:	Another hour with the same tape (including time filing notes on highlights and reflecting on what has been learned)
Thursday:	One hour reading a leadership book
Friday:	Another hour with the same book (including time filing notes on highlights and reflecting on what has been learned)

Besides the daily plan, I also recommend going through materials during times that other people normally consider wasted time. For instance, whenever I travel, I take along books and magazines that may not be as meaty as my daily reading but that have good material. If I'm waiting in an airport or flying on a plane, I'm also reviewing material and clipping out useful articles and quotes.

FILE QUICKLY WHAT YOU LEARN

Every good piece of information a person finds needs to be processed and filed. I have used this system for more than thirty-five years. As I find good articles or quotes, I clip and file them. This has two advantages. First, whenever I need materials for a talk or seminar, I have thirty-five years of collected resources to draw upon. Second, each time I reduce an article down to its one most relevant sentence or paragraph, I have processed through all the information, digested it, summarized it, and learned it.

APPLY QUICKLY WHAT YOU LEARN

Simply knowing a thing will not make it a part of you. To do that, you must apply it. Each time you learn something new, it's good to ask yourself, "Where, when, and how can I use this?" I prefer to do more than simply make a mental connection with the things I learn, so I use this system:

- Select one thing each week that I've learned.

- Put it on a 3 x 5 card. (I keep it in front of me for a week.)

- Share it with my wife.

- Share it with someone else within twenty-four hours.

- Teach it to someone else. (I put it in a lesson.)

GROW WITH SOMEONE

I have a number of people around me who share things with me and whom I deliberately share things with. When you share what you are learning with others, it increases your insight, builds your relationship with them, gives you a common vision, and holds you accountable. It also creates worthwhile conversation.

PLAN YOUR GROWTH AND FOLLOW IT FOR A YEAR

The five-day plan outlined previously was designed to be followed throughout the year. Using that plan, you can easily read twelve books and listen to fifty-two tapes per year. At the end of a year, you will have tremendous resources to draw on and will have grown tremendously. If you want to become an expert in a subject, according to Earl Nightengale, spend an hour a day for five years focusing on that subject.

There's one more thing I must say about developing a plan for your people's growth: Start them today! People may tell you that they are too old to start now, that they're too busy to start now, or that the timing isn't right. Personal growth is like investing. It's not your *timing*. It's your *time in*. Get them going now.

> **Personal growth is like investing. It's not your *timing*. It's your *time in*.**

KEEP THE GROWTH GOING

We live in a competitive society that focuses on making it. Baseball players live for the day they make it to the big leagues. Business people climb the corporate ladder with the hope of someday being the CEO or chairman of the board. A few of the businesses that use network-marketing techniques propose the idea that if a person builds a big enough organization, he or she can sit back and let others do the work. The individual will have made it; he will have arrived. But the idea of arriving is an illusion. Our society is filled with people who arrive somewhere only to find themselves as discontented as they were before they succeeded. The point of the journey is not arriving. The point is what you learn and whom you become along the way. Having goals is positive. Thinking that our journey is over once we achieve some of them is a danger we all face.

John Wooden, one of the most successful basketball coaches of all time, focused on the growing process. In *Six Timeless Marketing*

Blunders, William L. Shanklin writes about Wooden's approach to coaching. Shanklin tells that while Wooden coached UCLA, he did not stress winning. He emphasized preparation, teamwork, a willingness to change, and the desire for each person to perform at peak potential. His focus was on the process, not the end product.

The same thing is true in industry. From a quality-control expert I heard, "In quality control, we are not concerned about the product. We are concerned about the process. If the process is right, the product is guaranteed." The same is true when it comes to personal growth.

As the developers of leaders, we must keep our people growing. We must model growth, encourage it, and reward it. We must show our people how to keep growing for the long haul. They are to be like trees which grow their entire lives. There is no such thing as a full-grown tree. The day a tree stops growing is the day it dies.

USE THE FOUR-STAGE PROCESS OF ADAPTATION

It takes most people time to adopt new ideas and adapt to new situations. They usually have to go through four stages before new concepts become their own. I have found that they usually accept things in this order:

VISUALLY

Most people are visual. They usually have to see something new in order to understand it.

EMOTIONALLY

After people see something new, then they respond to it emotionally. Give them time to work through their emotions before going on to the next phase.

EXPERIENTIALLY

Once people understand something and have accepted it emotionally, they are ready to give it a try. Experience enables them to reach the final phase.

CONVICTIONALLY

After people see something, accept it emotionally, and experience it positively, it becomes truly a part of their thinking, their belief systems.

If you are aware of these phases, you will be able to bring people along in their development without as many obstacles.

FOLLOW THE IDEA GRID

Even though you will be helping your people create a personal growth plan and encouraging them to do as much growing as possible on their own, you will also need to teach them yourself. Ideally, you will share with them what you are learning in your own development. I continue to do this with the people in my organization. The best method I have found is represented in the following acronym:

I *nstruction*

D *emonstration*

E *xposure*

A *ccountability*

First I instruct my people in a life-related context. Any idea or theory that cannot be applied to real life is useless. Besides, if it can't be applied to real life, I wouldn't be able to demonstrate it, which is my next step. By actually living and demonstrating any idea before

I present it to others, I am able to test it, better able to learn it, and better qualified to teach it. Next I expose my people to actual experience. Once they have heard and seen it, they are ready to try it themselves. Finally, I make sure there is accountability for them, either with me or with each other. If you don't set some kind of accountability, your people may think the ideas are great, but they may forget to use them. And when people are held accountable for using them, the ideas become a part of them.

GIVE THEM VARIED EXPERIENCES

People resist change. If given a chance to do something comfortable and easy that they've done before versus the chance to do something difficult and new, most people will take the safe, easy route. As leaders, we can't let our people become complacent.

Varied experiences add incredibly to people's development. It keeps them growing, stretching, and learning. The broader people's base of experience, the better they will be at handling new challenges, solving problems, and overcoming difficult situations. In my organization, we have a three-year rule. Our leaders must change a significant number of their major duties and responsibilities every three years. It forces them to gain new skills. It gives newer leaders the opportunity to develop by having them step into new areas of responsibility. It allows older leaders to tackle new challenges. And it enhances everyone's creativity.

It is often tempting for us to leave successful people where they are—to keep them in the same jobs. But we must keep in mind that we are doing more than just getting the job done well. We are building leaders, and that takes extra effort and time. Angus J. MacQueen tells a story about James Garfield that illustrates this point. He says that prior to becoming President of the Unites States, Garfield was principal of Hiram College in Ohio. When a father asked if the course of study couldn't be simplified so his son might finish school sooner, Garfield replied, "Certainly. But it all depends upon what you want to make of your boy. When God wants to make an oak tree, He takes a hundred years. When He wants to make a squash, He requires only two months." Give your leaders deep, broad roots by growing them slowly and varying their experiences.

STRIVE FOR EXCELLENCE

Vince Lombardi, a great leader and one of the best ever to coach professional football, once said, "The quality of a person's life is in direct proportion to their commitment to excellence, regardless of their chosen field of endeavor." Lombardi recognized the importance of striving for excellence. And he was able to instill that desire in the people he coached.

When you strive for excellence, you prompt your people to shoot for the top. When a leader's goal is acceptability rather than excellence, then even the best people in the organization will produce what is merely acceptable. The rest may not even produce the minimum. When excellence is the standard, the best will hit the mark, and the others will at least hit the board.

Another advantage of focusing on excellence is that it shows your people's character. The success of any organization will not reach beyond the character of its leaders. Excellence breeds character, and character breeds excellence. Demand excellence from your people,

> **Excellence breeds character, and character breeds excellence.**

and they will develop into people who also demand excellence of themselves and the people they lead.

IMPLEMENT THE LAW OF EFFECT

Educational psychologist E. L. Thorndyke did work in behavior modification around the turn of the century. It led him to discover what he called the Law of Effect. Simply stated, it is this: "Behaviors immediately rewarded increase in frequency; behaviors immediately punished decrease in frequency."

We must ask ourselves what is being rewarded in our organizations. Do we reward personal growth and development? If so, our people will be growing.

Several years ago I developed a list of behaviors and qualities that I expect from the people in my organization, and I determined to reward those behaviors. I call it the RISE program:

R *ewards*

I *ndicating*

S *taff*

E *xpectations*

In other words I decided to give rewards to staff members to indicate they were meeting or exceeding expectations. The qualities I value most highly and reward are a positive attitude, loyalty, personal growth, leadership reproduction, and creativity. Notice that personal growth is on the list. I want to encourage you to decide what you value, determine to reward it in your people, and put personal growth on your list. You will find that once you set up a positive reward system for achieving the right goals, your people will become their own best managers, and they will develop as leaders.

CARE ENOUGH TO CONFRONT

Rewarding the positive takes effort, but it is pretty easy to do. Confronting negative behavior is tougher. Many people avoid confrontation. Some fear being disliked and rejected. Others are afraid confrontation will make things worse by creating anger and resentment in the person they confront. But when a person's behavior is inappropriate, *avoiding confrontation always worsens the situation.*

First, the organization suffers because the person is not acting in its best interest. Second, you suffer because the person's deficiencies reduce your effectiveness. And finally, when a person is acting inappropriately and isn't told, you have robbed him of an important opportunity to learn and grow in his development process. Any time a leader avoids a confrontation, he should ask himself whether he is holding back for his own good or for the good of the organization. If it is for himself, he is acting under selfish motives.

Confrontation, in its best form, is a win-win situation. In this country we have been conditioned to believe that conflict always produces a winner and a loser. But that does not have to be true. To produce a win-win, we must approach confrontation with the right attitude. Think of confrontation as a chance to help and develop your people. And never confront in anger or out of a desire to show power. Do it with respect and the other person's best interest at heart. Here are ten guidelines I use to make sure I'm doing just that:

CONFRONT ASAP

The longer I wait, the less likely I am to do what must be done. Another benefit to confronting immediately is that I am not likely to have to argue with the person over details.

SEPARATE THE PERSON FROM THE WRONG ACTION

I am to address myself to the action and confront it, not the person. I must continue to support and encourage the person.

CONFRONT ONLY WHAT THE PERSON CAN CHANGE

If I ask a person to change something he can't, he will become frustrated and it will strain our relationship.

GIVE THE PERSON THE BENEFIT OF THE DOUBT

I always try to start from the assumption that people's motives are right and work from there. If I can give them the benefit of the doubt, I do—especially in areas that are open to interpretation or are unclear.

BE SPECIFIC

The person I'm confronting can only address and change what is specifically identified. If I can't identify specifics, I may be making some false assumptions.

AVOID SARCASM

Sarcasm indicates anger with people, not their actions. When confronting, I avoid sarcasm.

AVOID WORDS LIKE *ALWAYS* AND *NEVER*

When I tell a person never to do a certain behavior, I am asking him to cling blindly to a rule, even in situations when it's not the best thing to do. I'd rather encourage him to use his head and take the right course of action in any given situation, based on right principles.

TELL THE PERSON HOW YOU FEEL ABOUT WHAT WAS DONE WRONG

If the person's actions have offended me, I tell him right then and there. I don't want to be going back over old ground later in order to vent emotions.

GIVE THE PERSON A GAME PLAN TO FIX THE PROBLEM

I always want to help the person succeed, not fail. If I can help him fix the problem, everybody wins.

AFFIRM HIM OR HER AS A PERSON AND A FRIEND

I prepare to confront in the same way that I fix a sandwich. I put the confrontation in the middle like meat. On both sides I put affirmation and encouragement.

Positive confrontation is a sure sign that you care for a person and have his best interests at heart. Each time you build up your people and identify their problems, you give them an opportunity to grow.

> Positive confrontation is a sure sign that you care for a person.

MAKE THE HARD DECISIONS

In Chapter Two I pointed out that leaders must be willing to make difficult decisions in order to create a climate that encourages development. Some of those difficult decisions concern letting employees go. But there are hard decisions to be made during your leaders' development process too.

People respond differently to development, and I have found from personal experience that each person who does grow will plateau at one of six levels of development:

LEVEL 1. SOME GROWTH

Some people experience growth at a very slow rate and their growth lacks direction. These people improve almost imperceptibly. They may be competent, but they will never shine in their jobs.

LEVEL 2. GROWTH THAT MAKES THEM CAPABLE IN THEIR JOB

Many people mistakenly believe that simply doing their job well is the final goal in their development. It's not. Without a good developer or a strong desire for personal growth, many people stop here in the growth process.

LEVEL 3. GROWTH THAT MAKES THEM ABLE TO REPRODUCE THEMSELVES IN THEIR JOB

At this level of growth, people are beginning to add to their value because they are able to train others in their area of expertise. Some people who are technically strong but have marginal leadership skills are able to do this. Others with strong leadership skills can do it despite marginal technical abilities. People who are strong in both areas often move up to the next level.

LEVEL 4. GROWTH THAT TAKES THEM TO A HIGHER-LEVEL JOB

The jump from Level 3 to Level 4 is difficult. It requires that people are willing to dedicate themselves to growing both personally and professionally. As they are able to broaden their thinking and experience, they become more capable and valuable to their organization and leaders.

LEVEL 5. GROWTH THAT ALLOWS THEM TO TAKE OTHERS HIGHER

It is at this level that great leaders begin to emerge. These people are true developers of people, and they no longer add value to their leaders and organization—they *multiply* it.

LEVEL 6. GROWTH THAT ALLOWS THEM TO HANDLE ANY JOB

People who develop to this level are rare. If you have the privilege of helping people to this level, treat them with the greatest love and respect. These people are leaders who could make it anywhere. And they have skills and abilities that transcend any particular field or industry. In your lifetime if God blesses you with one or more of these people, together you will have the ability to make an impact far beyond your own individual capabilities.

Take a look at the figure on the next page. As you can see, the pool of people at each level is represented by a circle. The higher the level, the fewer people at that level. You will also notice that each successive jump gets more difficult as the levels get higher. Each takes more commitment, dedication, and tenacity than the one before.

The reason I write about hard decisions is that you will have to make hard decisions concerning every person you develop other than the person who makes it to Level 6. When you are a developer of people, you meet each person on the level where you find him, usually on Level 1, then you begin a journey. Your job is to walk alongside that person and help him for as long as he is willing to keep going and growing. When that person stops growing, that's when you have to do something difficult: You have to leave that person behind. Your relationship can continue, but your development of that person won't.

That is one of the difficult things about being a developer of people. We give people so much time, attention, and love that leaving one behind can be like letting go of one of our children. But you can't force a person to keep growing to the highest level. You have to make the hard decision of leaving that person on his own plateau. It's difficult, but it's a price worth paying in order to develop people.

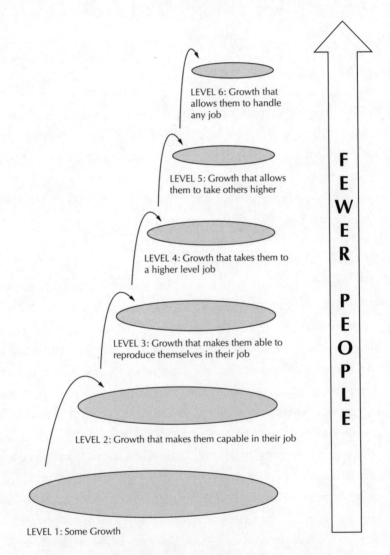

LEVEL 6: Growth that allows them to handle any job

LEVEL 5: Growth that allows them to take others higher

LEVEL 4: Growth that takes them to a higher level job

LEVEL 3: Growth that makes them able to reproduce themselves in their job

LEVEL 2: Growth that makes them capable in their job

LEVEL 1: Some Growth

FEWER PEOPLE

Pools of people at each level of growth

BE PERSONALLY SECURE

To be a great developer of people, you must be personally secure, because taking your people to the height of their potential may mean they will pass you by. As I mentioned in Chapter One, Andrew Carnegie wanted to be remembered as "a man who was wise enough to bring into his service men who knew more than he." It takes a very secure person to face that possibility, but without such a mind-set, you may be competing with your people instead of developing them.

As you prepare to lead and develop the people around you, I'd like you to keep in mind something Harvey Firestone said: "It is only as we develop others that we permanently succeed." All of the certificates of recognition we receive in life will fade. The monuments we build will crumble. The trophies will corrode. But what we do for others will make a lasting impact on our world.

SEVEN

THE LEADER'S HIGHEST RETURN:
FORMING A DREAM TEAM
OF LEADERS

Anyone who has ever experienced being on a team—from playing on a professional sports team to being a member of the junior high band—knows that being a part of a successful team can be one of the most rewarding experiences in life. And on the right team, it can also be one of the most powerful.

First, just what is a team? We know it's more than simply a group of people. If that's all it were, then people waiting at a trolley stop would make up a team. But they don't. I need to add that to be a team, a group must have a *common goal*, although that's not enough. Our people at the trolley stop have the common goal of waiting for the trolley car that will take them somewhere. Even if they had the same destination, it would help, but it would not be enough to make them a team. There must be *cooperation*, but once again, that doesn't complete the whole picture. Add *communication*—there is no team without communication.

Let's look again at our people waiting for the trolley to see how an ordinary group may act compared to a team. It's a hot, humid summer day. The group at the stop includes businesspeople in suits, mothers with toddlers and infants in strollers, construction workers, and homeless people. Finally, a crowded trolley pulls up to the stop. When everyone sees that the cars are packed, they all scramble. Each person runs to get a spot. A woman with a stroller does her best to herd her four children to the door of one of the cars, but she can't find a place with enough room to fit her whole family. By the time she tries another car, the doors close and the trolley moves away. She will have to wait thirty minutes for the next trolley.

The same trolley pulls into the next stop. Waiting is a team of twelve high school basketball players on a field trip with their coach. When they see how crowded the trolley cars are, they prepare to scramble too. One player shouts, "I'll check the first car to see if there's room." Another says, "I'll take the last one." The coach holds open the door to the full middle car because he knows that the trolley can't leave while a door is open. The player at the last car shouts, "There's room back here" as he holds that door open. Yet another player goes to find the teammate who went forward. As they reassemble in the last car, the coach counts to make sure everyone has made it.

As important as teamwork is, and as powerful as it can be to the success of an organization, many leaders don't teach their people how to work in teams. Management consultant Kenneth Blanchard observed:

> As I work in companies around the country, I often ask people what percent of their time do they spend in groups. Although managers report 60 to 90 percent of their time is usually spent in group activities, they also say they get little or no training in skills needed to work efficiently in groups. I know of few companies that focus training on this important skill.

Many leaders think that building a team and developing team-work is only for sports. They don't realize that they can build a team within their organization. Nor do they have any idea how to approach the task.

Developing leaders is wonderful: it's fulfilling and rewarding. But developing a team of leaders—that's incredible. A good team is always greater than the sum of its parts, but teams of *leaders* increase their effectiveness exponentially. With the right leaders teamed together, there is nothing they can't accomplish. Anyone who is developing leaders can also develop them into a team. It is the last development task that will yield the highest return.

THE QUALITIES OF A DREAM TEAM

In all my years of people development and team building, I have found that all successful teams share some common characteristics. If you, as the team leader or coach, can cultivate these qualities in your group of leaders, they will become a cohesive team capable of leaping tall buildings or performing any other required task. Here are those characteristics:

THE TEAM MEMBERS CARE FOR ONE ANOTHER

All great teams begin with this quality. It is the foundation upon which everything is built. Teams that don't bond can't build. Why? Because they never become a cohesive unit.

One of the best descriptions of this quality that I've ever come across was given by South Carolina football coach Lou Holtz. He said that he had once watched a television program that examined why men died for their country. In the program, which looked at United

States Marines, the French Foreign Legion, and the British Commandos, it was noted that men died for their country because of the love they had for their fellow man. In the show, they interviewed a soldier who had been wounded in combat and was recovering in a hospital when he heard his unit was going back out on a dangerous mission. The soldier escaped from the hospital and went with them, only to be wounded again. When asked why he did it, he said that after you work and live with people, you soon realize your survival depends on one another.

> **Teams that don't bond can't build.**

For a team to be successful, the teammates have to know they will look out for one another. When a team member cares about no one but himself, the whole team suffers. Uncaring people on a team remind me of a couple of guys in a story I once read: Two shipwrecked men sat together at one end of a lifeboat, doing nothing. As they watched intently, the people at the other end of the boat were bailing furiously. One man then said to the other, "Thank God that hole isn't in *our* end of the boat!"

I have found that one of the best ways to get members of a team to care about one another is to get them together outside of a work context in order to build relationships. Every year in our organization we plan retreats and other events that put our people together in social settings. And during those times, we also make sure they spend part of their time with staff members they don't know very well. That way they're not only building relationships, they're being prevented from developing cliques.

THE TEAM MEMBERS KNOW WHAT IS IMPORTANT

One of the things I enjoy most about a team experience is how the team functions as a single unit. All of its parts have a common goal and purpose. This quality is developed by making sure each team member knows what is important to the team. This quality, like the previous one, is foundational to team building. Without it team members cannot truly work together.

In a sport such as basketball, the players on a team recognize that scoring is what is important. When a team is more effective at scoring than the opponent, it wins. Because the team members know that, they spend their time improving and perfecting their ability to score. That is their focus. In contrast, in many organizational settings, the team members don't know what it means to "score." They may have a list of duties, but they don't know how those duties go together to make a score. It would be the equivalent of a basketball player who knew how to set a pick, dribble, pass, or toss up a ball, but who never knew all these skills were used together to score baskets. Without that knowledge, every time a player who was a good ball handler got the ball, he might dribble it until the shot clock ran out. That player could be the finest dribbler in all the world, and his ball handling could give spectators great joy. But the team would fail to score every time he touched the ball, and they would never win a game. On the other hand, if he knew dribbling was merely a tool used by a player so the team could score, then his attitude, actions, and effectiveness would change dramatically. And the whole team's success would follow in the wake of those changes.

You can see what happens if just one player on a basketball team doesn't know what is important to the team. It makes him ineffective. And when he is in the game, it is impossible for the team to succeed. The same is true in any organization. Anyone who doesn't know what's important to the team not only fails to contribute to the team, but actually *prevents the team from achieving success*. That is why it is so important for the leader of the team to identify what is important to the team and to communicate that information to her team members.

THE TEAM MEMBERS COMMUNICATE WITH ONE ANOTHER

The third foundational quality of an effective team is communication. Just as it is important for the team leader to communicate what is important to the team, the individual members of the team must communicate with one another. Without it, the players are likely to work against each other. Important tasks can be left undone, and team members can find themselves duplicating work.

Anyone who has played basketball is familiar with the situation in which two players go up for a rebound and fight one another for the ball, only to find that they are on the same team. On teams where players communicate with one another, a third player will shout, "Same team!" to make sure they don't lose the ball while trying to take it away from one another. That is what communication on the team is all about: letting each other know what's going on so the team's best interest is protected.

The same is true in nonsporting organizations. Clear and formal lines of communication must be established. But even more important, an atmosphere of positive communication must be established and encouraged on a daily basis. People on the team must be made to feel that they are in an environment where it is safe to offer suggestions or criticism without feeling threatened, freely trade information in the spirit of cooperation, and discuss ideas without being negatively criticized. Open communication among teammates increases productivity.

THE TEAM MEMBERS GROW TOGETHER

Once the members of the team care for one another, have a common goal, and communicate with one another, they are ready to start growing. Growth within a team is much like growth within a marriage. It is important and necessary. Without it, the team and its individual members do not improve. But like marriage, the growth should include shared experiences and periods of communication so team members stay connected to one another. In a marriage, when growth is not continuously interactive, eventually the two people's lives develop parallel but very separate courses. They cease to function together as a team. If much time passes, their two courses move farther and farther apart until neither one knows what the other is doing. Finally they won't care for each other, their goals will be different, and they will stop communicating. Their team is likely to fall apart.

In an organization, it is the team leader's responsibility to orchestrate the team's growth. He must make sure his people grow both personally and professionally. And he must ensure that their growth happens together—as a team.

When I work on growing my team members, I take several different approaches. First, we all learn together on a regular basis, at least once a month. In this way, I *know* there are some things everyone in the organization knows, and they share the common experience of learning these things together, regardless of their position or responsibilities.

Second, I regularly build small teams of learners. I periodically have groups of three or four work together on a project that requires them to learn. It builds strong relational bonds between those people. It's a good idea, by the way, to vary the members of these teams so that different people are learning to work together. It also gives you an idea about the particular chemistry of different groups as they work together.

Finally, I frequently send different people to conferences, workshops, and seminars. When they return, I ask them to teach others in the organization what they've learned. It gets everyone used to teaching and learning from each other. Shared experiences and the give-and-take of communication are the greatest ways to promote team growth.

THERE IS A TEAM FIT

As people who care about each other grow together and work toward a common goal, they get to know each other better. They start to appreciate each other's strengths and become aware of each other's weaknesses. They begin to recognize and appreciate each player's unique qualities. And that leads to the development of a team "fit."

The type of fit a team has depends on many things. It is more than just the way a group of people with particular talents come together. We have probably all seen teams made up of talented players at each position who should have been able to play well together but couldn't. Despite their talents, they didn't have the right chemistry.

> **A good team fit requires an attitude of partnership.**

A good team fit requires an attitude of partnership. Every team member must respect the other players. They must desire to contribute to the team, and they must come to expect a contribution from every other person. Above all, they must learn to trust each other. It is trust that makes it possible for them to rely on one another. It allows them to make up for each other's weaknesses instead of trying to exploit them. It enables one team member to say to the other, "You go ahead and do this task because you are better at it than I am," without shame or manipulation. Trust allows team members to begin working as a single unit, to begin accomplishing the things that together they recognize as important. Once the players know and trust one another, and develop a fit, the team's personality will begin to emerge.

THE TEAM MEMBERS PLACE THEIR INDIVIDUAL RIGHTS BENEATH THE BEST INTEREST OF THE TEAM

Once team members believe in the goals of their team and begin to develop genuine trust in one another, they will be in a position to demonstrate true teamwork. Their mutual trust will make it possible for them to place their own rights and privileges beneath the best interest of the team.

Notice that I mention the team members will be in a *position* to demonstrate true teamwork. That does not necessarily mean that they will. For there to be teamwork, several things must happen. First, they must genuinely believe that the value of the team's success is greater than the value of their own individual interests. They will be able to believe it only if they care about one another and if their leader has effectively cast the vision of what is important. Then they will recognize that their success will come with the team's success.

Second, for team members to place their individual rights beneath the team's best interest, personal sacrifice must be encouraged and then rewarded—by the team leader and the other members of the team. As this happens, the people will come to identify themselves more and more with the team. At that point they will recognize that individualism wins trophies, but teamwork wins pennants.

> **Individualism wins trophies, but teamwork wins pennants.**

EACH TEAM MEMBER PLAYS A SPECIAL ROLE

As the team fit becomes stronger and each person is willing to put the team first, people begin to recognize their different roles on the team. They can do this because they know what must be accomplished to win, and they know their teammates' capabilities. With that knowledge and some encouragement from the team leader, people will gladly assume appropriate roles. Philip Van Auken, in *The Well-Managed Ministry*, recognizes this as the *Niche Principle*. He says, "People who occupy a special place on the team feel special and perform in a special way. Team niches humanize teamwork."

In an ideal situation, each person's role is built on his or her greatest strengths. That way each person's talents can be maximized. But it doesn't always work exactly that way. Because the team's success is what is most important, sometimes the team members must be flexible. For example, anyone who follows professional basketball has heard of Magic Johnson. He played for the Los Angeles Lakers during the 1980s, when they were one of the best teams. His greatest talent was his ability to make plays happen, especially assists using incredible look-away passes. But Johnson was a player who was always willing to fill whatever role the team needed. Over several seasons, he started in NBA championship games as a guard, forward, and center. He may be the only professional basketball player who has ever done that.

The important thing is that all the team members take a role that fits the goals and needs of the organization as well as their own personal talents and abilities. When any role is not filled, the whole team suffers. The situation can be like the one in a story that management consultant James Lukaszewski told in one of his speeches:

[One day a farmer] was sitting on his porch noticing a highway department truck pulling over on the shoulder of the road. A man got out, dug a sizeable hole in the ditch, and got back into the vehicle. A few minutes later, the other occupant of the truck got out, filled up the hole, tamped the dirt, and got back in the truck. Then they drove forward on the shoulder about fifty yards and repeated the process—digging, waiting, refilling. After a half-dozen repetitions, the farmer sauntered over to them. "What are you doing?" he asked.

"We're on a highway beautification project," the driver said. "And the guy who plants the trees is home sick today."

As team leaders, we must recognize what roles need to be filled by our team members for the team to accomplish its goal. And when we see a role not being filled, we must make adjustments to the team to make sure the job gets done.

AN EFFECTIVE TEAM HAS A GOOD BENCH

In sports, the bench may be the most misunderstood resource of the team. Many "starting" players believe that they are important while the people on the bench are not. They believe they could do without them. Others who spend much of their time on the bench don't recognize their own contribution. Some mistakenly believe they don't have to bother preparing the way the starters do, that they don't have to be ready to play. But the truth is that a good bench is indispensable. Without a good bench, a team will never succeed.

The first thing a good bench gives is depth. In sports, many teams can produce a winning season. But when the level of competition goes up, such as in a play-off or a national tournament, a team without depth just can't make it. If the team does not have good reserve players, it will not be able to go the distance. I have yet to see a championship team that did not have a good bench. In fact, developing a good bench is what much of this book is about: selecting, equipping, and developing people to do their best and get the job done when they are needed.

Having a pool of good players able to play different roles gives the team leader great flexibility in any situation. In basketball, for instance, a coach will start a game with one group of people when playing against an opponent whose players are particularly tall. He may have another lineup when playing a particularly quick opponent. Some combinations of players will be great defensively. Others may be great at executing a run-and-gun offense. Which players he puts in the game will often depend on who his opponent is. Team leaders in other organizations will have the same kinds of options when they have a strong bench. With depth, the team can handle a variety of situations and demands with grace and effectiveness.

Another property of a team's bench is that it sets the tone for the whole team's level of play. This is true because the team's preparation depends on the bench. In sports, teams practice against their own players. If the starters practice only against weak players, their performance will not improve. But a good bench causes them to do their best all the time, to constantly improve. The same is true in any organization. If the level of play in the organization is high every day, then the team's performance will be top-notch when it really counts.

Finally, a good bench is a requirement for a successful team because it provides a place for a weary player to rest. On successful teams, when one of the players cannot make it any further due to fatigue or injury, his teammates carry the load and give him a rest. This is possibly the finest quality of teamwork—the willingness of one player to step up his level of play and go the extra mile for his teammate in a time of need. It is the ultimate indication of a player's desire to put the team and its goals first.

THE TEAM MEMBERS KNOW EXACTLY WHERE THE TEAM STANDS

In sports, the ability to know where their team stands at every moment during a game separates the great players from the adequate players. That quality, as much as talent, enables a player to move from one level of play up to the next, such as from college to the pros. Coaches have different terms for this quality. A football coach, for instance, might call it *football sense*. A basketball coach might call it *court sense* or *vision*. It is the ability to know how many seconds are left on the clock, how many points they are down, and which players are hot or hurt on each team. It is a quality that makes players, and therefore teams, great.

Outside of sports, the quality could be called *organizational sense*. It is the ability to know what is happening within the organization, how the organization stands in reference to its goals, how it stacks up against the competition, how the different players are doing, and how much more they can give in order to get the team where it needs to go. Not all team members are equally gifted with this sense. It is the job of the team leader to keep all of the

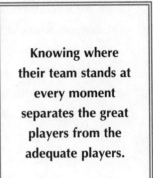

Knowing where their team stands at every moment separates the great players from the adequate players.

players informed. He must get them to check on the team's progress and listen to the other players to know where the team stands. If all the team members are informed of where the team stands, they are in a better position to know what it is going to take for the team to succeed.

THE TEAM MEMBERS ARE WILLING TO PAY THE PRICE

Time after time, success comes down to sacrifice—willingness to pay the price. The same is true of a winning team. Each member of the team must be willing to sacrifice time and energy to practice and prepare. He must be willing to be held accountable. He must be willing to sacrifice his own desires. He must be willing to give up part of himself for the team's success.

Success comes down to sacrifice— willingness to pay the price.

It all comes down to the desire and dedication of the individuals on the team. It's as true in business as it is in sports. It's even true in war. In an interview with David Frost, General Norman Schwarzkopf, commander of the Allied forces in the Gulf War, was asked, "What's the greatest lesson you've learned out of all this?" He replied:

I think that there is one really fundamental military truth. And that's that you can add up the correlation of forces, you can look at the number of tanks, you can look at the number of airplanes, you can look at all these factors of military might and put them together. But unless the soldier on the ground, or the airman in the air, has the will to win, has the strength of character to go into battle, believes that his cause is just, and has the support of his country . . . all the rest of that stuff is irrelevant.

Without each person's conviction that the cause is worth the price, the battle will never be won, and the team will not succeed. There must be commitment.

When you build a team within your organization, you will be capable of a level of success you never thought possible. Teamwork for a worthwhile vision makes it possible for common people to attain uncommon results. And when the team members are not common people, but leaders, their accomplishments can multiply. All the team needs is the right coach. And becoming that coach is the subject of the next chapter.

EIGHT

THE LEADER'S GREATEST JOY:
COACHING A DREAM TEAM
OF LEADERS

In 1992 American sports journalists could talk about nothing but the Dream Team—the United States Olympic basketball team composed of Michael Jordan, Larry Bird, Magic Johnson, Charles Barkley, and other basketball greats. Some players on that team have been called the best ever to play the game of basketball. When people watched them play, the question was not whether they would win or lose. The question was, "What magnificent plays will I see, and how big a margin will the team win by?" The team was such an assembly of stars that even the players on the opposing teams were asking them for their autographs.

All coaches dream of having a team like that—players who know the game inside and out, who have the talent, the desire, and the discipline to compete and succeed on the highest level. Most leaders dream of the same thing, but most of them think it will never happen to them. And for many that's true—it won't. Why? Because they don't know what it means to be a winning coach.

Banker Walter Wriston, in *Harvard Business Review*, says, "The person who figures out how to harness the collective genius of the people in his or her organization is going to blow the competition away!" That is what a great leader does: He harnesses the collective genius of his team members. He knows how to select, motivate, and empower his people.

In over thirty years of leadership, I have been privileged to lead some wonderful teams of people. Through those years, I have discovered that in order to become a dream team coach, a leader must develop ten qualities.

THE QUALITIES OF A DREAM TEAM COACH

As Charles Frances once said, "You can buy a man's time, you can even buy his physical presence at a given place, but you cannot buy enthusiasm . . . you cannot buy loyalty . . . you cannot buy the devotion of hearts, minds, or souls. You must earn these." The following ten characteristics of a dream team coach are qualities that will earn a team's respect and loyalty, and they will motivate and empower the people to play like a dream team.

1. A Dream Team Coach Chooses Players Well

Throughout the book, I've given a lot of attention to identifying and selecting potential leaders. And you already know how to go about developing people into effective individual players. Choosing the right people is vital. Red Auerbach, longtime Boston Celtics president, said, "How you select people is more important than how you manage them once they're on the job. If you start with the right people, you won't have problems later on. If you hire the wrong people, for whatever reason, you're in serious trouble and all the revolutionary management techniques in the world won't bail you out." Another great sports leader, Lou Holtz, put it this way: "You've got to have great athletes to win. . . . You can't win without good athletes, but you can lose with them. This is where coaching makes the difference." Both men recognized that you have to begin with the right raw materials to create a winning team.

As Bobb Biehl says in *Increasing Your Leadership Confidence*, along with clear direction and sound finances, having the right players determines 60 to 80 percent of the success of any company or organization. If you want to give yourself a chance to win, start by picking winners.

> **Having the right players determines 60 to 80 percent of the success of any organization.**

I can identify what a winner looks like for my organization. I can tell whether a person has the potential to be an all-star contributor. I want the people close to me to:

Know my heart:	This takes time for both of us and desire on their part.
Be loyal to me:	They are an extension of me and my work.
Be trustworthy:	They must not abuse authority, power, or confidences.
Be discerning:	They make decisions for me.
Have a servant's heart:	They carry a heavy load because of my high demands.
Be a good thinker:	Our two heads are better than my one.
Be a finisher:	They take authority and carry out the vision.

Have a heart for God: My heart for God is my driving
force in life.

When a person displays those qualities, I know he or she has the
potential to play on my dream team.

2. A DREAM TEAM COACH CONSTANTLY COMMUNICATES THE GAME PLAN

Every good coach I've ever seen has worked from a game plan.
He's got a plan not only for each individual game, but also for the
development of the whole team over the course of the current and
upcoming seasons. Once the game plan has been drawn up, he then
communicates it to his team on an almost continual basis.

Bear Bryant, the late University of Alabama football coach, effectively communicated his game plan to his players. He recognized there
were specific things his players needed to know. Five points explain
what he believed a coach should do:

Tell them what you expect of them. This tells them how they are
to fit into the game plan so they know what they should try to do.

Give them an opportunity to perform. This gives them a chance
to be a part of the game plan, to carry out the vision.

Let them know how they're getting along. This lets them have an
opportunity to learn, improve, and increase their contribution.

Instruct and empower them when they need it. This gives them
the means to learn, improve, and increase their contribution.

Reward them according to their contribution. This gives them
incentive for their effort.

The process must begin with communicating the game plan. That
is the key to productivity. But it must continue with the exchange of
information. Or as Sydney J. Harris said, information is giving out,
while communication is getting through. When there is interactive

communication between the team leader and his people, it empowers them to succeed.

3. A Dream Team Coach Takes the Time to Huddle

Another important part of the communication process is huddling. When a team huddles, it recalls the game plan and how it is to be implemented. When players don't take time to huddle, the results can be disastrous—or even comical.

The story is told of a gentleman who was walking down a residential street when he noticed a man struggling with a washing machine at the doorway of his house. When he volunteered to help, the homeowner was overjoyed, and the two men together began to work and struggle with the bulky appliance. After several minutes of fruitless effort, the two stopped and just looked at each other. They were on the verge of total exhaustion. Finally, when they caught their breath, the first man said to the homeowner: "We'll never get this washing machine in there!" To which the homeowner replied: "In? I'm trying to move it out!"

I find that things are never too busy or urgent to take the time to huddle. Here are five things that a huddle provides:

Focus. No matter how often or well a coach communicates the game plan, it never hurts to use huddle time to get people to refocus on what's important. In basketball, successful coaches take time-outs to huddle the players, especially when the opposing team is causing them to get out of their game plan. When they huddle, they go over the fundamentals to get back on track.

Even in politics focus is important. In 1992 following what analysts called flat campaigning by all the candidates, Bill Clinton was elected president. One reason was he was able to keep the campaign agenda focused on the areas where the American people most wanted change.

An opportunity to listen. When the team gets together, all the players and coaches have a chance to exchange information. Communication must flow both ways. When the coach is receiving the right information, it helps him send out the right information. New information can also prompt a coach to make adjustments.

An opportunity to make personnel changes. Sometimes the adjustments coaches need to make are changes in personnel or their responsibilities. Often the best way to solve a problem is to allow a different player to tackle it. A good coach can see that and is willing to make a change.

An opportunity to make play changes. Other times, the players are fine. What needs to be changed are the plays being run. Flexibility is a valuable quality in a coach. The best coaches are good at making necessary adjustments.

An opportunity to rest. Sometimes players just need an opportunity to stop, take a breather, and regroup. A well-timed huddle can help the team revitalize so they can carry on and succeed.

4. A DREAM TEAM COACH KNOWS WHAT HIS OR HER PLAYERS PREFER

Bringing out the best in team members requires that their coach know them and what is important to them. Padgett Thompson, a Kansas-based training organization, asked employees to rank their workplace wants in order of importance. They published those findings in *Training and Development Journal.* Of the many items they listed, the three things employees most valued were:

- Appreciation for a job well done

- A feeling that they're "in" on things

- Management understanding of their personal problems

Padgett Thompson then compared these results with the things supervisors *thought* employees would value. By comparison, the supervisors ranked these three items eighth, tenth, and ninth.

The supervisors' lack of knowledge concerning their employees may account for another survey statistic reported by John D. Hatfield and Richard C. Huseman in *Managing the Equity Factor*. It states that 85 percent of the workers across the United States said they could work harder on the job. More than half claimed they could double their effectiveness "if they wanted to."

The truth of the matter is that people don't produce because they aren't motivated or appreciated. Their leaders don't know what they want. People often change jobs for personal reasons, not for professional ones. And their emotions play the greatest part in their motivation. Good coaches know what their people prefer, and they use that knowledge to attain the team's and the individual player's goals.

5. A DREAM TEAM COACH EXCELS IN PROBLEM SOLVING

"A great leader doesn't treat problems as special," said Al Davis, successful owner of the Los Angeles Raiders. "He treats them as normal." Successful coaches never have "perfection" as their goal. If they did, they would fail every time. We live in an imperfect world where problems always occur. Certainly, a leader should strive for excellence, but he should expect problems to occur. And believe it or not, he should welcome them. Problems almost always create opportunities—to learn, grow, and improve.

All leaders can become good problem solvers. To do so, they must do four things: They must anticipate problems *before they occur*. They must maintain a positive attitude *while they occur*. They must use all their

> **Problems almost always create opportunities—to learn, grow, and improve.**

resources to solve them as quickly as possible so they *cease to occur*. And finally, they must learn from them so the same problems *do not occur again*.

Most issues requiring a coach's problem-solving skills fall into one of three categories. They are either player, preparation, or game issues:

Problem-solving issues with players. Issues with players require good communication skills as well as good problem-solving skills. One common problem is that the players don't work together as a team. (See Chapter Seven for ways to resolve this problem.) Another problem may involve players who are facing personal issues that require a coach's assistance and patient understanding. Possibly the most frustrating problem occurs when a player is not reaching his potential. A good coach must work with the player to help him identify his goals and then motivate him so that he begins to grow again.

Problem-solving issues with preparation. Probably the most common problem associated with preparation is the boredom factor. Many of the basics that must be taken care of in the preparation process can be boring. Good coaches provide a climate that minimizes boredom and reminds players of the positive results that preparation brings.

Related to the problem of boredom is morale. When morale is low, so is production. Good coaches keep their players' attitudes positive.

> **Good coaches approach each opponent from a fresh perspective.**

The last problem is a failure to prepare differently for different opponents (or projects). Good coaches approach each opponent from a fresh perspective and with creativity. If each new opponent is regarded as unique, success is more likely to come to the team.

Problem-solving issues with the game. As I discussed before, good coaches always approach the game with a game plan. That is a proactive approach. However, because problems do occur, good coaches also recognize that they may need to make reactionary decisions— decisions that should be made quickly then communicated clearly and immediately.

I once read that General Ulysses S. Grant kept a rather simple-minded soldier close to him at all times. When he prepared to give an order to one of his generals, he first gave the command to the common soldier to be sure he could understand it. In that way, he was sure all of his communication was clear and understandable.

Finally, all coaches recognize that their decisions will be criticized. No matter how the problem is solved, someone will say it was the wrong decision. A coach must learn to follow his convictions despite the roar of the crowds.

As you prepare for problems, keep in mind these words by Tom Landry, former head coach of the Dallas Cowboys. He said, "A successful leader has to be innovative. If you're not one step ahead of the crowd, you'll soon be a step behind everyone else." Approach problem solving creatively. And use all your people as resources. That's one of the reasons you've worked so hard to select and develop them.

6. A DREAM TEAM COACH PROVIDES THE SUPPORT NEEDED FOR SUCCESS

The greatest environment of support is created when coaches decide to be facilitators rather than dictators. The more the players and other coaches are involved, the more successful the team. Total control by the coach, even if he is somehow able to achieve it, is never as effective as a group effort. Look at the difference between how dictators and facilitators operate:

DICTATORS:

1. Hoard decisions.

2. Make decisions alone or restrict them to an elite group.

3. View truth and wisdom as their domain since they are the leaders.

4. Surprise their workers with edicts from above.

5. Guard their own interests.

6. Take for themselves.

FACILITATORS:

1. Push decisions down line.

2. Involve others as much as possible in key decisions and give people space to make those decisions.

3. View truth and wisdom as being accessible to everyone throughout the organization.

4. Let those responsible decide how the jobs will be done.

5. Serve everyone's interest by developing people.

6. Give to the organization.

In addition to providing an atmosphere of support in which everyone's participation is encouraged, great coaches also give their people plenty of affirmation. There isn't a player in the world who doesn't respond to it.

Another way the best coaches support their players is by simplifying the players' lives. Can you think of anyone who responds positively to bureaucratic red tape? I believe that:

Forms, Forms, Forms + Rules, Rules, Rules =
Frustration, Frustration, Frustration

If I can simplify, I do. I want to give my most creative and innovative people an open field to run in, not hoops to jump through.

Finally, one of the best ways to provide lasting support is by creating a winning tradition for the organization. Rookie professional players drafted by teams such as the Boston Celtics or Dallas Cowboys often speak admiringly of the team's tradition of winning. That tradition creates a positive atmosphere. It creates an invaluable momentum.

When a team gets a few wins under its belt, it creates a positive attitude and momentum. When it gets a few seasons of wins under its belt, it has a tradition. Then instead of the coach having to go out and find winners, winners come looking for him.

7. A DREAM TEAM COACH COMMANDS THE RESPECT OF THE PLAYERS

Without respect, a coach will never be able to get his players to do what he asks. In *The Seven Habits of Highly Effective People*, Stephen Covey states it this way:

If I try to use human influence strategies and tactics of how to get other people to do what I want, to work better, to be more motivated, to like me and each other—while my character is fundamentally flawed, marked by duplicity or insincerity—then, in the long run, I cannot be successful. My duplicity will breed distrust, and everything I do—even using so-called good human relations techniques—will be perceived as manipulative.

It simply makes no difference how good the rhetoric is or even how good the intentions are; if there is little or no trust, there is no foundation for permanent success. Only basic goodness gives life to technique.

Respect must be earned over time. There are no shortcuts. It is earned through the consistent embodiment of three attributes:

> **Respect must be earned over time. There are no shortcuts.**

Trustworthiness. People never respect a person they cannot trust. Never. The best coaches know this and work immediately on letting their players know they can be trusted. Mike Krzyzewski, head basketball coach of Duke University, put it this way: "If you set up an atmosphere of communication and trust, it becomes a tradition. Older team members will establish your credibility with newer ones. Even if they don't like everything about you, they'll still say, 'He's trustworthy, committed to us as a team.'"

A caring attitude. In all my years of leading people, I must have said this more than a thousand times: "People don't care how much you know until they know how much you care." It's true. If players sense that you really care about them, that you have their interests at heart, they will listen to you and respect you. As former University of Michigan head football coach Bo Schembechler said, "Deep down, your players must know you care about them. This is the most important thing. I could never get away with what I do if the players felt I didn't care. They know, in the long run, I'm in their corner."

The ability to make hard decisions. Players cannot respect a coach who cannot make the hard decisions necessary for a team to succeed. When a coach is willing to make those decisions, the players know he is acting in the team's best interest. They feel secure, and they in turn are more likely to act in the team's best interest themselves. Tom Landry said, "Perhaps the toughest call for a coach is weighing what is best for an individual against what is best for the team. Keeping a player on the roster just because I liked him personally, or even because of his great contributions to the team in the past, when I felt someone else could do more for the team would be a disservice to the team's goals." He would also lose his players' respect.

8. A Dream Team Coach Does Not Treat Everyone the Same

One of the biggest mistakes a coach can make is to believe he must treat all of his players the same. Coaches are hired to win—not to make everyone happy or give everyone equal time, money, or resources. Every player must be given support and encouragement. But to believe that everyone must receive the same treatment is not only unrealistic but destructive. When all players are treated and compensated the same, poor or mediocre performance is being rewarded the same as outstanding contributions by the best players.

Great coaches give opportunities, resources, and playing time according to players' past performance. The greater the performer, the greater the opportunity. When you have a player like Michael Jordan, former Chicago Bulls great, you want to put the ball in his hands as often as possible.

> Give opportunities, resources, and playing time according to players' past performance.

There will be times you aren't sure about a player's performance level because you haven't had time to observe him. This is especially true when you have a rookie player. When that happens, give him frequent but small opportunities, and try to vary the opportunities as much as possible. If you do, you will soon be able to determine his caliber of play. And that will show you how to respond.

9. A Dream Team Coach Continues to Win

There is only one challenge more difficult than winning that a successful coach faces: continuing to win. As tennis pro, golf pro, and former Olympic champion Althea Gibson said, "In sports, you simply aren't considered a real champion until you have defended your title successfully. Winning it once can be a fluke; winning it twice proves you are the best." Nearly anyone can point to a single victory they've had. But it takes more than one win to make a great coach. It takes continued positive performance.

Putting together successive winning seasons is so difficult in sports that teams bring in consultants such as psychologist Bruce Ogilvie to help them learn how to do it. In the July/August, 1988 issue of *Success* magazine, journalist Dan Gutman writes that Ogilvie suggests the following major points to ensure success:

Work on specific skills. No matter how many successes a team has had, there is room for improvement. There are people on the team who have not yet come close to fulfilling their potential. Work with each team member to foster improvement and growth. Focus each player on a new goal for the season.

Make a change. Every winner's temptation is to continue doing things exactly as before. But that is a flawed approach to success. You and your team will end up standing still, and another team will blow right past you. Use the momentum you've gained from past successes to continue to change and grow.

Reward the unrewarded. Every team has unsung heroes—people who were underappreciated for their contribution to the team's success. Find those people and reward them with praise, money, and further opportunities.

Transfer the burden. As I've said before, success always comes at a price. If your team has succeeded, it is because some members of the team have carried the burden by making sacrifices. They have given up time with their families, worked long hours, put their primary goals after the team's. Some people will have made such extensive sacrifices that they cannot continue to make them. Give them a break and transfer the burden to others who are willing and able.

Above all, don't dwell on yesterday's victory. If your focus is on what's behind you rather than what's ahead, you will crash. It's like the story I heard about salesman during the month of June. In the sales meeting held on July 1, the manger said, "I want to congratulate Kent on a job well done. He has sold more cars in a month than any other salesman." Everyone applauded. "But that was last month. Now let's focus on July." Celebrate victories, enjoy them briefly, and then look forward.

Another way to help players continue to win is to help them avoid burnout. The best way to do that is to see it coming and avoid it. Workplace psychologist Beverly Potter believes burnout can be prevented when it is caught in time. She suggests that a person look for lack of energy, sleeplessness, lack of creativity, inability to make decisions, chronic anger, bitter or sarcastic language, or physical symptoms such as exhaustion, tension headaches, body aches, and nausea.

John Madden, sports analyst and former championship coach of the Oakland Raiders, was a victim of burnout. He was once asked what the first signs of his burnout were. He said, "You won't have the energy because you won't have the interest. Suddenly, you don't care about the draft. You're not interested in minicamp. You don't care who the best college linebacker is. You don't care if they've signed any of your veteran players to contracts. When you don't care, it's time to go . . . you're history . . . you're done." Because he burned out, he was not able to continue coaching. The same can happen to you or your players. To continue winning, you've got to avoid burnout.

10. A Dream Team Coach Understands the Levels of the Players

One of the most common mistakes a coach can make is to misjudge the level of one of his players. If the leader doesn't work with each player according to where he is in his development, the player won't produce, succeed, and develop. According to management consultant Ken Blanchard, all team members fit into one of four categories with regard to the type of leadership they need.

Players who need direction: Players who need direction don't really know what to do or how to do it. At this stage in their development, you need to instruct them every step of the way. Anything these rookie players produce will be essentially what you do through them because they aren't capable of working independently.

Players who need coaching: At some point, a rookie starts being able to do more of the job on his own. He becomes more independent but still relies on you for direction and feedback. The two of you will be working in partnership.

Players who need support: At this level, the player is able to work without your direction. But he will still require your support and encouragement.

Players to whom you delegate: At this stage the player can be given a task, and you can be confident that it will be done. This player only needs you to lead. Provide vision on the front end and accountability on the back end, and the person will multiply your efforts toward success.

DELEGATION: THE DREAM TEAM COACH'S MOST POWERFUL TOOL

A leader may possess all ten of the previously mentioned characteristics, but if he does not learn the art of delegation, then he will never find himself coaching a dream team. Delegation is the most powerful tool leaders have; it increases their individual productivity as well as the productivity of their department or organization. Leaders who can't or won't delegate create a bottleneck to productivity.

The other benefit of delegation is that it increases the initiative of the people within the organization because it gives them a chance to grow and accustom themselves to succeeding.

If delegation is so important to a leader's success, why do some leaders fail to delegate effectively? There are many reasons:

> **Delegation is the most powerful tool leaders have.**

INSECURITY

Some leaders are afraid that if they're not in control of everything, it means they're not doing their job. They fear that others will criticize them for shirking their responsibilities. The bottom line is they are afraid that they will lose their job.

LACK OF CONFIDENCE IN OTHERS

Some leaders believe their employees are not competent enough to do the job, so they never delegate anything. They fail to realize that people grow into delegation by being given a chance to perform, make mistakes, and learn from them. To be successful, all leaders must eventually take the crucial step of allowing others to take part of the load. Leaders will make mistakes in delegation, and the people to whom they delegate will make mistakes. But that is when learning takes place.

LACK OF ABILITY TO TRAIN OTHERS

Successful delegators cannot simply dump tasks on their people without preparing them for the tasks. If they do, their people will fail and resent them. Instead, they must train their people both before delegating and afterward when mistakes have been made. When leaders learn to train others, they are better equipped to delegate.

PERSONAL ENJOYMENT OF THE TASK

It is difficult for people to give up tasks they love to perform. But sometimes giving up an enjoyable task is the best thing leaders can do. The question leaders must ask themselves is whether the task can be done by someone else. If so, it should probably be delegated. The leader should focus on performing tasks no one else can do, not simply on doing tasks he or she enjoys.

HABIT

Similar to enjoyment of a task is habit. Just because people master a task doesn't necessarily mean they should continue doing it. When a task becomes simple and straightforward, the leaders doing it should delegate it and move on to something more complex.

INABILITY TO FIND SOMEONE ELSE TO DO IT

Mark Twain once said, "Never learn to do anything. If you don't learn, you will always find someone else to do it for you." Although he wasn't serious, there is a kernel of truth in his statement. That truth is you must always be looking for people to whom you can give tasks. The times that people will track you down to ask you for something to do will be rare. A leader who can't find people to delegate to may not be looking hard enough.

RELUCTANCE CAUSED BY PAST FAILURES

As I mentioned, when leaders' early efforts to delegate fail, they sometimes become reluctant to delegate. As Ken Allen states in *The Effective Executive*, we should not try to rely solely on ourselves as a result of delegation failure, nor should we blame the people to whom we have given the task. "Rarely is delegation failure the subordinate's fault," he notes. "Maybe you picked the wrong person for the job, didn't train, develop or motivate sufficiently." If you have had trouble with delegation in the past, don't give up. Try to determine why the problem occurred, learn from it, and give delegation another try.

LACK OF TIME

Not having enough time to teach another person to do a job is probably the most common reason people give for not delegating. And not delegating is probably the most common reason people don't have enough time. Inability to delegate due to lack of time is short-term thinking. Time lost in delegating on the front end is recovered at the back end.

For example, let's say a leader takes an hour to perform a certain weekly task. He determines that to teach someone else to do that task, it will take him five hours initially, then an hour a week for the following three weeks. That totals eight hours of his time—*one whole day that he will lose* out of his busy schedule. He could continue to do the task himself for the next two months by devoting the same amount of time.

However, if he thinks long term, he realizes that by the end of the year, the eight-hour investment he makes will give him an additional forty-four hours of time to do other tasks. *That's one whole week of time he has gained!* And there is also the added advantage that the employee he has delegated to is better equipped to take on other tasks for him in the future. To break the vicious lack-of-time cycle, a leader needs the right person to delegate to and a willingness to put in the initial training time.

AN "I DO IT BEST" MIND-SET

Leaders who believe that to have something done right they have to do it themselves will end up accomplishing very little. The greatest problem new leaders have is their reluctance to move from *doing* the job to *managing* the job. Edgar Speer, chairman of U.S. Steel, said, "You don't even try to control how people do their jobs. There's no way to do that, furthermore, no purpose. Everyone does the job a different way, and they all want to show how well they can do it their way. The function of a supervisor is to analyze results rather than try to control how the job is done." If you want to do a few small things right, do them yourself. If you want to do great things and make a big impact, learn to delegate.

If you recognize yourself in any of the descriptions above, you probably aren't doing enough delegating. If you begin to miss deadlines, and crises become increasingly frequent, these may also be indications that you need to delegate tasks. And be on the lookout for employees under you who are ready to conquer new worlds—this is a prime time to delegate jobs to them.

STEPS TOWARD DELEGATION

Easing people into delegation is important. As I mentioned earlier, you can't simply dump tasks on people if you want them to succeed. I delegate according to the following steps:

Ask them to be fact finders only. It gives them a chance to get their feet wet and to become acquainted with the issues and objectives.

Ask them to make suggestions. This gets them thinking, and it gives you a chance to understand their thought processes.

Ask them to implement one of their recommendations, but only after you give your approval. This is a critical time. Set them up for success, not failure. And give lots of encouragement.

Ask them to take action on their own, but to report the results immediately. This will give them confidence, and you will still be in a position to perform damage control if necessary.

Give complete authority. This is the final step—what you've been working toward.

It is the job of a coach to make team members do what they don't want to do so they can become what they've always wanted to be. It can be done with the right tools and the right attitude. The more you work on your skills, the more you work on your own development; and the more you give of yourself to your players, the more successful you can become as a coach. If you truly give it all you've got, you, too, can someday coach a dream team. It will be one of the greatest joys of your life.

Here are two quizzes to help you gauge some of your coaching skills. The first one concerns delegation.

MISCONCEPTIONS ABOUT DELEGATION

QUESTIONS:
Answer each question as either True (T) or False (F).

1. Always delegate to the subordinate who has
   experience with similar tasks.   T   F

2. The person you delegate to should have as much information about the task as possible.   T   F

3. Controls should be built into a delegated task from the beginning.   T   F

4. In delegated tasks, monitoring the method is as important as getting the desired results.   T   F

5. The crucial decisions involved in a delegated task are still considered the territory of the delegator.   T   F

6. Always make the delegated task seem like a challenge even if it's drudgery.   T   F

7. Delegating means assigning work.   T   F

8. Don't offer advice when delegating.   T   F

9. Use the same procedures and systems of accountability with every subordinate when delegating to avoid favoritism.   T   F

10. If a subordinate fails in a delegated task, do not delegate to him or her again.   T   F

ANSWERS:

1. FALSE: If you repeatedly delegate similar tasks to the same people, they won't get additional opportunities to grow. It also shortchanges less experienced subordinates who need a chance to develop.

2. TRUE: The more background information you give the person who is about to do the task, the faster and easier the delegating process works. For more

experienced subordinates, you may be able to provide some information and then give them ideas on how to obtain additional information on their own.

3. TRUE: Controls not only help prevent disaster, they also give you the confidence to delegate.

4. FALSE: This is one of the most common pitfalls of an inexperienced delegator. Results are everything. Demanding that other people use your method can stifle initiative and creativity needed for successful delegation.

5. FALSE: This is another common mistake poor delegators make. With true delegation comes the right and responsibility to make decisions.

6. FALSE: Deceptive characterization of delegated tasks insults subordinates. And it erodes trust.

7. FALSE: True delegation includes handing over the rights and responsibilities to determine what work must be done, how it will be approached, and who will do it.

8. FALSE: Let people handle tasks their own way, but give them as much advice (and vision) as you think they need before they get started. Make yourself available to answer questions, but don't constantly peer over their shoulders or solve their problems for them. Learning to solve problems is part of the development process.

9. FALSE: Tasks are different, and so are people. The difficulty of the task as well as the experience and skill of the person must always be taken into

account. When you delegate, tailor the system of accountability to fit the delegatee.

10. FALSE: Don't give up on a subordinate because of a single failure. It might be due to circumstances beyond the person's control. The failure could even be a result of your method of delegation. Examine what went wrong and why.

SCORING:

Give yourself one point for each correct answer:

9–10	You're a top-notch delegator.
6–8	You know the fundamentals, but keep learning.
5 or less	You've uncovered a serious weakness in your leadership skills.

If you are currently responsible for leading or supervising people, you are responsible for their interaction as a team. This second test will help you determine how well you are doing as a coach:

HOW WELL ARE YOU COACHING YOUR TEAM?

Answer the questions using the following key; then total your score.

1 - Haven't thought about it yet

2 - Just in the early stages

3 - Solidly in progress

4 - Nearly accomplished

5 - Fully accomplished

1. I have chosen my players well. 1 2 3 4 5

2. I have proven to my players I care about them. 1 2 3 4 5

3. I have encouraged them to care about one another. 1 2 3 4 5

4. I know what my players prefer. 1 2 3 4 5

5. I actively encourage team growth. 1 2 3 4 5

6. I have developed a team that "fits." 1 2 3 4 5

7. I support my players. 1 2 3 4 5

8. I have taught them what is important. 1 2 3 4 5

9. I frequently show them the game plan. 1 2 3 4 5

10. I have modeled paying the price to them. 1 2 3 4 5

11. My players are willing to put the team   1 2 3 4 5
before themselves.

12. I have developed a good bench.   1 2 3 4 5

13. I have encouraged each player to find   1 2 3 4 5
and play his role.

14. I have my players' respect.   1 2 3 4 5

15. I reward my players according to their   1 2 3 4 5
performance.

16. I have built a winning tradition.   1 2 3 4 5

17. I expect and prepare for problems.   1 2 3 4 5

18. I know the level of all my players.   1 2 3 4 5

19. I take the time to teach and delegate.   1 2 3 4 5

20. I do only the tasks that cannot be   1 2 3 4 5
delegated.

SCORING:

90–100   You are a great coach with a dream team; you're ready for the championship.

80–89   You are an excellent coach; keep fine tuning your team and your skills.

70–79   You are a solid coach; don't' stop now; keep up the good work, and strive for the excellence that is within your reach.

60–69   Your players are beginning to look like a team; keep learning and building.

Below 60 You have a lot of work before you, but don't despair; use the principles in this chapter to begin team building and improving your coaching skills today.

NINE

THE LEADER'S FINEST HOUR:
REALIZING VALUE TO AND
FROM LEADERS

Alex Haley, the author of *Roots*, used to keep a picture in his office of a turtle sitting atop a fence. He kept it there to remind him of a lesson he had learned years before: "If you see a turtle on a fence post, you know he had some help." Haley remarked, "Anytime I start thinking, 'Wow, isn't this marvelous what I've done!' I look at that picture and remember how this turtle—me—got up on that post."

Both developed leaders and the people who developed them are like that turtle. They've gotten a lot of help. Their view from the fence post is made possible by others. Through the development process, the new leaders and the developers have value added to their lives.

Adding value to a person is much more than personal promotion or organizational improvement. It is true that people who have been developed get promoted. And it is equally true that organizations improve and expand when they have leaders devoted to the development of others. But adding value is much more than that. It is the enrichment of people's quality of life. It is the expansion of their

> People development is life-changing for everyone involved.

life purpose and capabilities. People development is life-changing for everyone involved. In *Bringing Out the Best in People*, Alan McGinnis said, "There is no more noble occupation in the world than to assist another human being." And as I noted in Chapter Four, Emerson said that we always benefit ourselves as well when we assist others.

VALUE ADDED TO NEW LEADERS

Several years ago when I was still leading a church as well as a business organization, I surveyed many of my leaders to illustrate the concept of adding and receiving value. I did that not necessarily because my organization offered the best examples, but because I knew them well. To examine what value I have added to leaders, I asked about ten people to give me some feedback. I requested, "Tell me about the value I add to you and the value I receive from you so that we can teach others what we do."

What follows is a summary of their responses. People said many kind things, but that is not the reason I am sharing their responses. I share them because I want to offer concrete examples showing that the development of people yields tangible results which can be recognized and later passed on to others. (In Chapter Ten I will share how some of these people are carrying on the development process with others around them.) After you spend time developing your people, you will find that they will respond in the same way that mine do.

MODELING

Most of the leaders in my organization identified modeling as something important that I do for them. One person said, "You set the pace of the organization. You never ask for more than you are willing to give yourself. This 'watermark' provides continual motivation for me to give my best." Modeling is an important motivator because it shows people not only what you expect, but what can be accomplished.

One of the most important things that my people said I model is a dedication to continue growing personally. When they see it in me, they recognize its importance. And they soon adopt that belief as their own. Even if they leave me tomorrow, they will continue to grow because they now recognize that belief as their own.

VISION AND DIRECTION

The leader of every successful organization casts vision for his or her people. I have always made sure that the people around me know my vision, because without that focus we cannot accomplish our goals. A staff member observed, "His ability to keep focused on the big picture . . . keeps me from having tunnel vision." Said another, "He provides vision and direction. By keeping in touch with him, I know that I am staying on target with my professional focus." Burt Nanus, in *Visionary Leadership*, wrote, "There is no more powerful engine driving an organization toward excellence and long-range success than an attractive, worthwhile, and achievable vision of the future, widely shared."

Having and sharing a vision does even more than drive an organization. It also gives people vision and direction for their individual lives. As they contribute to the larger goals of the organization, they begin to identify more clearly a vision for themselves. As that vision becomes clearer and that sense of direction stronger, their lives become more meaningful.

ENCOURAGEMENT AND AFFIRMATION

Everyone I surveyed said that they felt encouraged by me. That delights me because I want more than anything else to let my people know that I love them and want the best for them. One person said,

"He gives me personal encouragement and affirmation. He's the best I have ever seen at this in my life. Almost to a fault . . . Sometimes I run into people who are not doing something real well [but] their opinion is that John loves them." Another said, "He cares about me personally, and I believe he has my best interests at heart. He wants me to win. His positive attitude and encouragement let me know that he is happy when I succeed. He cares about what is most important to me—my family."

People in our society are underencouraged. They desire encouragement desperately but get it infrequently. There are two main reasons why the people in my organization feel very encouraged. First, I have spent time getting to know them and developing relationships with them. I know who they are, where they've come from, who their spouse is, who their children are. I know their gifts and their goals. I really know them. Second, I love them, and I express that love to them on a regular basis. I'm not talking about simply praising them for the work they do. I let them know that I care about them and love them as people first. There is no substitute for a relational foundation with people. You must have that to build upon if you are going to develop people. Even if you do nothing more than get to know your people and love and accept them, you will have added value to their lives.

BELIEF IN THEMSELVES

Most of the people I have spent my time developing are not shrinking violets. Even before they met me, they were not timid. Yet even people who already have confidence can be encouraged to believe more strongly in themselves. One staff member wrote, "John will often drop by my office to see how I am doing, to affirm me, to tell me once again how much he appreciates the load I carry. From the beginning, he encouraged me to do anything I dreamed. He encouraged me . . . to take on projects that I've never tackled before, and to always keep growing."

One of the ideas I examine in detail in my book *The Winning Attitude* is that it is impossible for people to perform consistently in a manner inconsistent with the way they see themselves. This is true no matter what positive or negative circumstances people face.

Believe in people, and they will rise to fulfill that belief.

People who believe that they can succeed do so even when repeatedly dealt adversity. Others can be given the best of everything in life and still fail because they see themselves as failures.

When I know the leaders in my organization, believe in them, encourage them, and help them to succeed, it helps to strengthen their belief in themselves. I try to help them win increasingly larger victories. People almost always rise to meet your level of expectations. Believe in them, and they will rise to fulfill that belief.

WILLINGNESS TO TRY NEW THINGS

"He gives me confidence to risk and thereby reach new heights. And all the while he has a sincere positive belief in me," one of my leaders said. One of the most important results of people's belief in themselves is their willingness to try new things. When people do only what is comfortable for them, they get into a rut. They stop growing. But by being willing to take risks, people perform tasks they thought were impossible. They achieve more than they thought they could and become more than they thought they were. The kind of growth that comes with risk adds incredible value to people's lives.

PERSONAL DEVELOPMENT

I have made it a practice to set aside time to develop those around me. One leader said, "You have purposefully mentored and coached me now for more than a decade." I give my leaders time for counsel and advice. I help them wrestle with difficult situations. I also schedule time for equipping them on a regular basis. Several leaders cited the monthly leadership instruction that I give as being valuable. Another reminded me of the experiences I've shared. She said, "He always wants the people around him to be able to experience with him the privileges and opportunities he has been given."

> **Look for opportunities to share yourself with people.**

I try to give my people what I can. Sometimes it is time with them. At other times I am able to give guidance. If I can share a valuable experience, I do. As an example, that same staff member mentioned how with my help she was able to have breakfast in Korea with Dr. Cho, pastor of the largest church in the world. Another one of my staff members had always dreamed of meeting Billy Graham in person. When I had an opportunity to meet with the great evangelist, I shared that experience with that staff member by taking him with me. These two incidents were exciting to my staff members, but they were no more valuable then the more common growing experiences that I try to share with them day to day. I look for opportunities to share myself with my people, and you should too.

COMMITMENT TO PERSONAL GROWTH

By now you know how important personal growth is to a person's success. It is what adds the greatest value to a person's life. Here is what one leader in my organization said about it:

> John is committed to growth, both personally and corporately, no matter what the cost. Because he lives on the edge, always desiring growth and challenge in his life, he gives me energy, motivation, and courage to make the tough decisions and never to become satisfied. John has had to fire people, say no to people, and prioritize his life in order to keep growing. He is willing to pay the price of loneliness as a leader!

As she indicated, I'm not the only one in my organization paying the price of personal growth. All of the top leaders around me are dedicated to it, day in and day out. If I were to leave the organization tomorrow, they would continue to pay the price necessary to keep growing. And as Walter Lippman said, "The final test of a leader is that he leaves behind in other people the convictions and will to carry on."

EMPOWERMENT

I have found that people become empowered when you provide them with three things: opportunity, freedom, and security. I give my leaders opportunities to do new things for the organization, the freedom to accomplish those things using creativity and initiative, and the security of knowing I will back them up, even when everything doesn't go as planned. Said one staff member, "You have assured me that you will do anything in your power to help me, which provides me a sense of security and trust." I love to see the people in my organization succeed, and empowering them makes that possible.

> People become empowered when you provide them with three things: opportunity, freedom, and security.

Empowerment can be a tricky thing to give. You have to balance your own needs with the empowered leader's development while always keeping in mind the best interests of the organization. One of the leaders in my organization identified this as the "rope principle":

> John is constantly giving me enough rope to allow me to get the job done myself, but not so much that I hang myself . . . He also balances the development of the person with the good of the organization using the "rope principle." He will wait a little longer than he prefers to get something accomplished if the staff member will be developed in the process,

but he will never let the rope go so long as to hurt the organization as a whole.

One of the leaders I surveyed identified empowerment as the characteristic that adds the greatest value to leaders. He said:

> Motivation, believing in, mentoring, and all the other traits tap into what is inside the person. Empowerment adds a new dimension to the person that did not and often cannot exist or come into existence on its own . . . There is a great responsibility with the gift of empowerment. With the wrong motives a leader can empower for his/her own good rather than for the good of the people and the organization. John has always put the organization and individual people before himself.

Adding that new dimension to a person in your organization will not only make him a more powerful leader, it will also enable him to receive the value of the next item on the list.

Being a Part of Something Greater Than Themselves

> To live a worthwhile, meaningful life, a person must be a part of something greater than himself.

To live a worthwhile, meaningful life, a person must be a part of something greater than himself. I challenge the people around me to live a life that has not temporal, but eternal, impact. I want each member of my staff to become the person he was created to be—to reach his potential.

One of the most encouraging comments in the survey came from one of the people closest to me at INJOY. He said, "He allows me to accomplish greater things with him than I could alone." That is one of the greatest rewards of adding value to people's lives. It comes back to you multiplied.

VALUE ADDED TO ME BY THE PEOPLE
I HAVE DEVELOPED

If I were only able to add value to my people and receive nothing in return, I would still do it. But that's not how it works. No matter how much I give, I always receive more in return. It's absolutely incredible.

> One of the greatest rewards of adding value to people is that it comes back to you multiplied.

In my years as an organizational leader, I have found that all employees are one of two types: salary takers or salary makers. The takers give as little as possible and take their salary. The makers give everything they've got and make a contribution beyond the salary they earn. I have found that people who are willing to be developed are always salary makers. You can see the difference between the two types of people by the things they say:

SALARY TAKERS	SALARY MAKERS
What will I receive?	What can I give?
What will it take to get by?	I'll do whatever it takes to get it right.
It's not my job.	Whatever the job, I can help you.
Someone else is responsible.	I'm responsible.
How can I look good?	How can the team look good?
Will it pass?	Is it my best?
The paycheck is the reason I work.	The paycheck is a by-product of my work.

| Am I better off because I work here? | Is the team better off because I work here? |
| Pay me now, I'll produce later. | I'll produce now. You can pay me later. |

Here are the specific ways the leaders in my organization add value to me. This list consists of the items of value they identified in response to a memo I sent them. I added "Balance of Gifts." It is an added value important to me that they did not specifically identify.

LOYALTY

Many of the leaders in my organization identified loyalty—to me and to the organization—as a characteristic of the esteem they feel for me. One person joked, "I might not walk off a cliff for him, but I would certainly consider it!" Others mentioned their desire to protect the interests of the organization because they believe in it, or the desire to protect me from minor pressures that I don't need to handle myself. I am grateful for all of these things.

I also recognize the loyalty of my leaders comes from their belief in what the organization is doing and their sense of commitment to the team. The people around me work beautifully together. They always seem ready to jump in and do whatever they can. They put their own personal interests beneath the best interests of the team.

ENCOURAGEMENT

Encouraging others makes them want to encourage you too. One of my leaders wrote, "I make it a point to continually encourage John. I believe we all need encouragement from time to time. He is a great model in this area, and I take great joy in reciprocity."

I am naturally a very positive person, so I don't get down in the dumps. But my schedule is often very demanding, and I do get tired. When that happens, my staff is always there for me. Not only do they encourage me, they also offer to help carry the load in any way they can.

PERSONAL COUNSEL AND SUPPORT

A valuable result of developing leaders is the advice and counsel you can receive from them. I benefit from the knowledge and wisdom of the leaders in my organization. One of them said, "I am able to confront and share with John what I think or feel, even when I know he may disagree. I'm not a yes-person." I enjoy hearing the perspective of another leader. And I respect honesty. In fact, the opinion of a person who doesn't agree with me often teaches me more than the perspective of someone who agrees. Another leader said, "I believe that John knows that I am always prepared to provide input to him in any area he requests and desires. He also hopefully knows that he can count on me for 100 percent support." I appreciate the support and advice I get from my people. It adds incredibly to my life.

FOLLOW-THROUGH

I have a great group of people around me that I call "door closers." I call them that because I can hand off a task or project to them and know that they will follow through with it to the very end and close the door behind them. They implement ideas, complete projects, handle details, and perform problem solving for me. They also create and implement their own ideas within the context of the vision I cast. They are constantly furthering the goals of the organization. As one of them said, "I free you up for more important work. I carry part of the load."

The work these leaders do is very important to me and the organization. It must be done, and it is something they can do effectively. Each time I am faced with a new task, project, or activity, I always ask myself, "Is there someone else in the organization who can do this effectively?" If there is, I delegate it. I allow someone else to do the follow-through. That, in turn, leads to the next valuable thing that the people around me give to me.

TIME

I have many highly skilled, effective leaders working in my organization. Partly due to the time I have spent developing them, there are few things that they can't do for me and the organization. That allows me more time to do the things that only I can do or that others cannot do as well. As one person in my organization said, "I free him up to do what he does best: teach, lead, preach, motivate, etc." Time is an incredible gift to receive. The people around me free me from being a slave to the urgent so that I can accomplish the important.

BALANCE OF GIFTS

Like all people, I have strengths and weaknesses. Some of my areas of weakness I have been able to improve through personal growth and development. There are other areas where I have much room for improvement, especially in areas that go against my temperament. The people around me add value to me by balancing out my deficiencies with their gifts.

I was born with a sanguine choleric temperament—emphasis on choleric.[1] I enjoy making things happen. And I'm always moving forward. Stopping to reflect on what I've done in the past is not one of my strengths. For example, when I was a pastor at Skyline Wesleyan Church there were times when I would teach principles in a sermon that I later could teach to others outside the church or include in one of the lessons that I sent out to leaders each month through INJOY. But once I finished the last Sunday service, I wouldn't think about it again. That was a weakness.

Fortunately, the people I've developed help me to round out those areas of weakness. In the case of my sermons, for over ten years I had an assistant who would ask me questions each Monday to make me reflect on what I'd taught. Then she made notes on my comments and filed them away for my future use in other lessons.

ATTRACTION OF OTHERS

For an organization to continue building and growing, it must continually attract new people of high quality. In Chapter Three I shared with you that it is important to have leaders identify and recruit potential leaders. As important as that is, I can't give it as much time as I'd like. But the leaders in my organization do. They are constantly raising up new leaders. Unlike many people who head organizations, I have been fortunate never to find myself in a place where I had positions of leadership to be filled and no people to fill them.

PEOPLE DEVELOPMENT

Every leader I surveyed listed the development of other people as one of their top priorities and as a way they add value to me. They know that the development of leaders adds more value than anything else they do. Of people development, one leader wrote, "This is my passion. To select, equip, and develop people to love God, and to love and lead people." Another leader said, "I give depth to his leadership organization through discipling others and passing on to others what he has done for me, i.e., providing an environment for growth." And their development of people is focused not just on others around them, but also on themselves. They continue to be committed to their own personal growth. As one leader commented,

"I work on maintaining personal integrity and the development of my character for the sake of the organization and its influence." And what he does in his own development continues to make a positive impact on everyone in his sphere of influence, including me.

INCREASED INFLUENCE

Truly the bottom line on developing the leaders around you is that it increases your influence. In *Developing the Leader Within You*, I give what I consider to the be the greatest definition of leadership: *Leadership is influence*. One of the leaders I surveyed said, "I represent you to the masses that you cannot touch on a regular basis due to sheer time and numbers." For example, back at Skyline, the church I led, attendance on a busy Sunday was close to 4,000 people. If I wanted to touch each of those people personally by meeting with them for just thirty minutes, in addition to all of my other responsibilities, I would have had to meet with more than ten people every day for about six hours, seven days a week, for fifty-two weeks without missing a single person or taking a single day off. At the end of a year, I would have met with everyone who had attended Skyline on *one* Sunday. No one could keep up that kind of pace.

But even though I couldn't personally meet with every one of those people, I could still influence them—through my team of leaders. Each of them reached out and touched hundreds of lives. And each of them developed a team of leaders who, in turn, reached out and touched others' lives. As I continued to grow personally and develop others, my influence continued to grow. By the end of my life, if God grants me the productive life I anticipate, I will have positively influenced over ten million people—not just by myself alone, but through the leaders I have developed around me. As one of the top leaders in INJOY said, "I afford him the opportunity to increase his influence way beyond what he could do by himself single-handedly."

When you develop leaders rather than followers, they will do the same for you. And they will carry on the tradition just as some of my leaders have. The final chapter of this book describes how four of the leaders I developed have become first-rate developers of leaders in their own right.

TEN

THE LEADER'S LASTING CONTRIBUTION: REPRODUCING GENERATIONS OF LEADERS

It is time for a new generation of leadership," John F. Kennedy said in a television address during his 1960 campaign for the White House. Perhaps no president realized the need for successive generations of leaders more than Kennedy, the first commander-in-chief born in the twentieth century. He emerged as the nation's leader on the brink of a decade filled with radical changes.

As I explain in *Developing the Leader Within You*, most people believe that each new generation of leaders is born rather than developed. They think that new leaders come out of the womb as leaders and simply wait until they are old enough to take their rightful places in society. As a result, many leaders are willing simply to produce followers, expecting new leaders to show up on the scene when their time comes. Those types of leaders have no idea how much they are limiting their own potential and the potential of the people around them.

As I have said before, a leader who produces followers limits his success to what his direct, personal influence touches. His success ends when he can no longer lead. On the other hand, a leader who produces other leaders multiplies his influence, and he and his people have a future. His organization continues to build and grow even if he is personally unable to carry on his leadership role.

As a leader you may have followed all the guidelines in this book. You've created the right climate and identified potential leaders. You've nurtured, equipped, and developed them. You've built a great team and learned to coach them. At this point, you may think your job is done. It's not. There is one more crucial element, and it is the true test of success for a leader who develops other leaders. The leaders you've developed must carry on the tradition of development and produce a third generation of leaders. If they don't the building process stops with them. True success comes only when every generation continues to develop the next generation, teaching them the value and the method of developing the next group of leaders.

> A leader who produces other leaders multiplies his influence.

> True success comes only when every generation continues to develop the next generation.

I have spent the greater part of my life developing leaders who are in turn producing another generation of leaders. And by the way, the new generation of leaders they are developing includes many people chronologically older than they. In fact, up until a few years ago, the majority of people I spent my time developing were older than I am. I was called to begin dedicating myself to the process of developing leaders around me when I was still in my twenties.

TRAITS OF A POTENTIAL LEADER

Many leaders make the mistake of believing that they can only develop people like themselves—in personality, temperament, natural abilities, and socioeconomic background. But that is not true. Leaders can develop many kinds of people. When I was a pastor at Skyline there were four people I considered to be my greatest successes in leadership development, and what was required for their development was very different in each case. Yet they were developed, and they added incredible value to my life—at that time, more than anyone else outside of my family. Each person not only lightened my load and extended my influence, but they were especially successful at carrying on the tradition of developing leaders around them.

Each of the four people presented a different challenge to me as a developer of leaders. They had very different levels of experience. Their temperaments were different from mine and from each others'. Some had well-developed relational skills, while others didn't. But despite their differences, they all were capable of becoming leaders and of developing other leaders. I have found that there are three things that are required for a person to become a leader:

DESIRE

The ability to become a leader begins with desire. It is the only thing that the developer cannot supply. The amount of desire will largely determine the potential leader's progress. Great desire can overcome a multitude of natural deficiencies in a leader.

RELATIONAL SKILLS

In all my life, I have never met a great leader who did not possess good relational skills. They are the most important abilities in leadership. Without them, a person cannot lead effectively. Many people believe that relational skills are determined at birth and cannot be learned. But that's not true. People's

> **Relational skills are the most important abilities in leadership.**

temperaments incline them to relate to others in a particular way, but they do not dictate their relational abilities. Even the most introspective, melancholic person can learn to develop good relational skills. For nearly everyone, relational skills can be learned and improved.

PRACTICAL LEADERSHIP SKILLS

These are the "how tos" of leadership that a person acquires through your modeling, equipping, and developing. These, too, are learned.

When I came into contact with each of the four leaders I will introduce to you, they all had different skills, but they had in common great desire.

A FOLLOWER BECOMES A LEADER

Barbara Brumagin, who was my personal assistant for eleven years, came to me as a highly competent secretary. She worked hard, and she had a wonderful servant's heart, but she did not lead others. It wasn't a natural part of her personality, nor was she well equipped to lead. She had always been a follower, but I could see that she had great potential. And even more important, she had great desire.

When I first came to Skyline Church, I began looking for an assistant, and Barbara was recommended to me by one of the pastors on staff. When we met to discuss the position and I began asking her questions, she was uncommunicative almost to the point of being rude. I quickly changed tacks and began doing the talking: showing her my goals and vision for the church, myself, and her. After listening for a few minutes, she began communicating with me. I immediately saw that she would be perfect for the position, and I hired her. I found out later that she had come to the interview against her will because she had envisioned being a secretary in a church as boring and devoid of growth opportunities. She was more interested in learning and growing, and grow she did. Barbara was like a sponge.

With Barbara's development, I went slowly. It took her about two years before she felt really confident in her position and began showing signs of leadership. I modeled leadership, exposed her to teaching, and worked interactively with her. I was always careful to spend time explaining not only what things I wanted her to do but also why I wanted her to do those things. She once told me that she felt like she was getting personally developed every day. After we had worked together for a few years, she knew me so well that she could answer any question for me or make nearly any decision in the same way I would. In fact, she and I once took a personality test. I answered each question, and then she took the same test and answered the questions as *she thought I would*. When we compared answers, she had only missed two questions. She was quick to point out that she had missed one of those because I had answered it wrong—and she was right!

You may have people you are preparing to develop who are non-leaders like Barbara was. If you do, there are four things to keep in mind as you develop them:

MAINTAIN A POSITIVE ENVIRONMENT

People who do not already possess leadership skills must have an environment that is positive and conducive to their growth. Without that environment, they will be afraid of growth. With it, they will be willing to learn and try new things. Provide the environment; then keep them close to you so that they can begin learning how you think.

EXPRESS HIGH BELIEF IN THEM

People who are not naturally inclined toward leadership and who have no leadership experience often get discouraged easily. Because they have not been leaders before, they will make mistakes. They may make a lot of them, especially in the beginning. Their development is likely to be a long process. By expressing a high belief in them, you encourage them to persevere, even when things get tough.

EMPOWER THEM

In the beginning, followers are reluctant to assume leadership roles, so they must be empowered by their leaders. Start by walking alongside of them and giving them authority in your name. As time goes by, others will begin to reframe their view of the new leaders, and the new leaders' view of themselves will also change. Eventually, people will begin recognizing them for their own authority.

PLAY TO THEIR STRENGTHS

It is critical that you begin the development process by playing to their strengths. Because they have experienced few successes in leadership before, they need a few wins under their belts. It really accelerates the development process, and the new leader begins building momentum.

When you begin developing a follower into a leader, the time and energy required will slow down your progress. You may be tempted to stop developing the person, but don't. It could be a terrible mistake. In the case of Barbara, developing her took a little bit of time in the beginning, but not only did she more than make up for it by giving me eleven wonderful years of service, she is now passing on what she has learned to others.

A MANAGER BECOMES A LEADER

When I first met Dan Reiland and his wife Patti at a leadership conference I was holding in Indiana, he was still a seminary student. Dan had been a member of Skyline, felt the call to ministry, and gone to seminary before I became Skyline's senior pastor. He then returned as an intern during my first year at the church.

Dan's development was very interesting. Dan's smart, he's a good scholar, and he was a good student in seminary. He had often been put in charge of the activities he was involved in, and he had even been the president of his class. But despite his good qualities, he wasn't a leader. He was really more of a manager.

Managers think differently from leaders. Managers tend to focus on tasks and systems. They have narrow vision, and they sometimes tend to be dogmatic. And most of all, their focus is not relational. Dan tended to focus on tasks and the work at hand. He was a hard worker, but he put tasks ahead of people. I remember one day several of us were talking in an office hallway, and Dan walked right through us without saying a word. It was at that point that I knew he and I needed to have a serious conversation, or he wasn't going to make it on my team.

I was able to sit down with Dan and confront him about his relational skills, because he knew that I believed in him and genuinely cared about him. Ironically, I found out that Dan really loved people, and in his heart, he wanted to relate to them. But his internal desire wasn't made clear by his actions. People working with him had no idea how much they mattered to him. It was then that I began spending extra time with him developing his skills to relate to others as a leader does. I taught him to walk slowly through a crowd, interacting with people rather than going past them in order to accomplish tasks. Now, as I mentioned in Chapter Three, he became the executive pastor of Skyline and was invaluable to me. His ability to relate to others has become one of his strongest qualities, and he considers it foundational to his ability to lead.

> **How big
> we think
> determines
> the size of our
> accomplishments.**

If you have potential leaders who think like managers, your goals are to help them develop better relational skills and change their pattern of thinking. While you have to *slow down* to teach a follower how to lead, you may have to come to a *complete stop* in order to help a manager become a leader. The reason is that you will sometimes need to stop what you're doing, walk the person through your thought process, and then explain why you're doing what you're doing. You must constantly show them the big picture until they begin to see it for themselves.

I have found that all true leaders share some common characteristics in their thinking.

LEADERS THINK BIG

They always look at the big picture, and they know that their success is only as great as their goals. As David Schwartz said, "Where success is concerned, people are not measured in inches, or pounds, or college degrees, or family background; they are measured by the size of their thinking. How big we think determines the size of our accomplishments." If you consistently show the people you are developing the big picture and keep stressing possibilities rather than problems, they will start thinking big.

LEADERS THINK IN TERMS OF OTHER PEOPLE

Leaders don't focus on themselves and their own individual success. They think about the success of the organization and other people. They have an other-people mind-set. To develop others, you must teach them to think in terms of how they can promote others, develop others, take along others.

LEADERS THINK CONTINUALLY

People who are not leaders are content to sit back and allow others to do the thinking. Leaders are constantly entertaining new ideas, considering new resources, thinking about improving, contemplating finances, managing their time. Thinking continually enables leaders to keep stretching themselves and growing their organizations. As you develop leaders, model this kind of thinking, and promote it by asking questions.

LEADERS THINK BOTTOM LINE

While others get bogged down in the details, leaders look for the bottom line. If you often ask the people you are developing to give you the bottom line, they will soon begin determining what it is before you ask for it. Eventually they will begin thinking in those terms un-prompted.

LEADERS THINK WITHOUT LINES

People who are not leaders automatically gravitate toward lines—limitations set by others. Maybe people are taught this in kindergarten when they are instructed to stay within the lines while coloring. But leaders are more creative than that. They look for options and opportunities. They try to take things in a new direction, or beyond the limit. Progress and innovation are made by people who think without lines.

Progress and innovation are made by people who think without lines.

LEADERS THINK IN TERMS OF INTANGIBLES

Leaders are abstract thinkers. They think in terms of intangibles like timing, morale, attitude, momentum, and atmosphere. They read between the lines. They anticipate the unexpected.

LEADERS THINK QUICKLY

Leaders size up a situation quickly and then seize it immediately. Two reasons leaders are able to do this are that they think in terms of the big picture, and they do their homework so that they have information to use to help them make decisions quickly.

As Dan developed as a leader, he took on a tremendous amount of the load for me. He ran Skyline for me, directly led thirteen pastors, and oversaw a staff of more than forty. But Dan did more than that. Where he most excels is in the development of other men. Since 1987, Dan has selected a handful of men each year to personally develop. Already he has worked with and developed more than one hundred of them.

Dan's development of leaders is systematic and strategic. He constantly looks for potential leaders to develop, and he sees himself as a lightning rod, able to capture and focus the energy required to make men grow. For his part, he says he is effective because he always keeps in mind the *vision* of developing leaders, he maintains people development as a *lifestyle*, and he renews his *commitment* to it regularly. The key to the whole process, though, is relationships. He says that the men he develops grow as leaders due to their relationships with one another, the equipping that they receive, and the synergy of their interaction with him and one another. What sustains the whole process, though, is the relational part of it—the area in which he himself has grown the most.

A LEADER CHANGES LEADERSHIP STYLE

When I hired Sheryl Fleisher on my Skyline staff, I knew she was a strong leader. She had vision, was able to make decisions, thought big, and had a bottom-line mentality. But she also tended to be autocratic and a bit dogmatic. She was a leader, but she did not lead relationally. She described herself as having been "mission-minded" rather than "people-minded."

The turning point in Sheryl's development came when she handled a difficult situation with a person less effectively than she could have. She describes the way she did things as "politically naïve and relationally stupid." Soon after it happened, I sat down with her and told her that I supported her and believed in her but that she would have to grow and change her leadership style if she wanted to make it on the team. Not only did she grow as a leader, she became one of the team's best leaders.

With Sheryl, my goal was not to change her personality. It was to change her mode of operation, her style of leadership. She relied on structure and position to establish her leadership. I wanted her to become a relational/empowering leader. There were times that I had to stop what I was doing and do some backtracking to retrain her, but it was definitely worth the effort. Any time you want to change a leader's style, you must do the following:

MODEL A BETTER LEADERSHIP STYLE

The very first thing you must do is show them your better leadership style. If they don't see that there is a better way to lead, they will never change.

IDENTIFY WHERE THEY ERR

Observe them to determine where they make their mistakes. You won't be able to help them change if you don't know what must be changed.

GET THEIR PERMISSION TO HELP THEM CHANGE

If they are not committed to the process of change and to allowing you to help them, all your effort will be wasted. People will give you their permission when they hurt enough to need change, learn enough to want change, or receive enough to make them able to change.

Show Them How to Get from Here to There

Even when they have the knowledge that they need to change and the desire to make a change, they may not be capable of making a change. Show them the way, step by step.

Give Immediate Feedback

Because you will be helping them break bad habits, you must respond to their actions immediately. Learning something for the first time is always easier than unlearning something that was learned wrong. I learned that lesson when I had to unlearn my golf swing. When you retrain people to lead relationally, give them immediate feedback for both the good things and the bad.

As Sheryl grew and began to lead from the heart, she became a wonderful developer of leaders. She identifies people development as her passion in life. When she became the pastor of personal growth ministries at Skyline, she, like Dan, was always searching for people to develop. She listed the following qualities in the women she was to develop:

F *aithful*	They must be consistent in their actions, reliable, and committed.
A *vailable*	They must be accessible to her personally and willing to grow.
I *nitiating*	They must be inquisitive and hungry to grow.
T *eachable*	They must be receptive to her style of mentoring and teaching.
H *onest*	They must be transparent and honestly willing to develop others.

Sheryl and I once sat down to talk about the way she develops people. I think she lost track of how many people she worked with, but she is very aware of the positive effect her mentoring had on Skyline. She told me that her joy is to recognize where people are, meet them there, love and accept them, and then mentor them. Her goal is to get them to develop into the people they were created by God to be. And she wants to get them to carry on the tradition of leadership development. She succeeds too. She mentioned that one of the women she developed pointed out *six generations of leaders* in one room who had been mentored starting with Sheryl. That's quite an accomplishment. Today Sheryl continues to make an impact as a staff member of Willow Creek Community Church.

A GOOD LEADER BECOMES A GREAT LEADER

Dick Peterson was already a first-class leader before he met me. When I came to Skyline, he was a manager in what was America's premier corporation at the time—IBM. In fact, Dick was one of the top three managers in the country in IBM's administrative area. Had he stayed with IBM, his next step would have been to regional management, then on to a vice presidency. And I'm sure he would have made it. As a leader, he was probably in the top 5 percent in the country.

When I had been at Skyline for about a year, I asked him to become a member of the church board. I wanted him on the team. I knew he would be a great contributor to the church and me, and I believed he would also benefit from the experience. You see, I give more thought, time, and attention to the development of the people on my board than to anyone else, with the exception of my family. Board members are the top leaders and influencers I have contact with.

I spent three years developing Dick while he was on the board. I built a good personal relationship with him, I spent time equipping him, and I constantly challenged him to grow. Once when I was preparing to fly to Dallas to talk to some people about ways to begin equipping leaders on a larger scale, I took Dick with me. He was a part of the discussion that gave birth to INJOY. As a leader, he jumped right in and helped get it off the ground. He started as a volunteer. He later resigned at IBM to run INJOY full time for more than a decade.

One of the beauties of developing a person who is already a strong leader is that it gives you momentum. Where a leader must *slow down* to develop followers, *stop* to develop managers, and *backtrack* to change the style of misguided leaders, he can actually *speed up* as he strengthens good leaders. They practically teach themselves. They pick things up just by being around you, often with little to no effort on your part.

If you are fortunate enough to have strong leaders in your influence, begin developing them by doing the following:

PUT THEM ON A PERSONAL PLAN FOR GROWTH

Most good leaders are growing, but they frequently do not have a personal plan for growth. After you have gotten to know them—their strengths, weakness, desires, goals, etc.—sit down with them and prepare a personal growth plan tailored to them. Then follow up periodically to encourage them, check their progress, and help them make adjustments.

CREATE OPPORTUNITIES TO STRETCH THEM

It is while doing activities that we thought were beyond our capabilities that our greatest growth occurs. It actually accelerates our development. It also gives us additional opportunities to apply the principles we are learning. As you further develop leaders, plan to put them in situations that will stretch them.

LEARN FROM THEM

Whenever I spend time developing someone who is already a good leader, I learn too. You will also learn much from leaders as long as you maintain a teachable attitude. Plan shared projects with them. It's a great way to learn and to get tremendous things accomplished at the same time.

Dick's development has transformed him. He was already a strong leader, but now he is a strong builder of leaders. Developing people is now like breathing to him. Without it, he wouldn't be who he is. That is the key to developing the leaders around you. As a leader, you must make the development of others a lifestyle. When you live it, your success in life is multiplied exponentially. Your influence is expanded incredibly beyond your personal reach. A positive future is assured for you. Leaders who do not develop people will one day find themselves hitting a wall in their success. No matter how efficient and strategic they are, eventually they run out of time.

I found that to be true in my life. I cannot personally create more material than I am currently creating. I cannot mentor more people than I am presently mentoring. I cannot travel and do more conferences than I do now. I am a very energetic person, but I have reached my own physical limits. The only way I can now do more is by doing it through other people. Any leader who learns that lesson and makes it a lifestyle will never hit the wall again.

So I ask you, are you developing the leaders around you?

NOTES

CHAPTER ONE

1. Tom Worsham, "Are You a Goose?" *The Arizona Surveyor*, 1992.

CHAPTER TWO

1. Edwin Markham, "Man Making"

CHAPTER THREE

1. John C. Maxwell, *The Winning Attitude: Your Key to Personal Success* (Nashville, Tennessee: Thomas Nelson, 1993).

CHAPTER FOUR

1. David A. Seamands, *Healing Grace* (Wheaton, Illinois: Victor Books, 1988).

2. *Success Unlimited* (Magazine no longer in print).

CHAPTER FIVE

1. Bobb Biehl, *Increasing Your Leadership Confidence* (Sisters, Oregon: Questar, 1989).

CHAPTER NINE

1. Florence Littauer, *Personality Plus* (Grand Rapids, Michigan: Revel, 1994).

ABOUT THE AUTHOR

John C. Maxwell is an internationally recognized leadership expert, speaker, and author who has sold over 16 million books. His organizations have trained more than 2 million leaders worldwide. Dr. Maxwell is the founder of EQUIP and INJOY Stewardship Services. Every year he speaks to Fortune 500 companies, international government leaders, and audiences as diverse as the United States Military Academy at West Point, the National Football League, and ambassadors at the United Nations. A *New York Times*, *Wall Street Journal*, and *Business Week* best-selling author, Maxwell was named the World's Top Leadership Guru by Leadershipgurus.net. He was also one of only 25 authors and artists named to Amazon.com's 10th Anniversary Hall of Fame. Three of his books, *The 21 Irrefutable Laws of Leadership*, *Developing the Leader Within You*, and *The 21 Indispensable Qualities of a Leader* have each sold over a million copies.

BOOKS BY DR. JOHN C. MAXWELL
CAN TEACH YOU HOW TO BE A REAL SUCCESS

RELATIONSHIPS

Encouragement Changes Everything
25 Ways to Win With People
Winning With People
Relationships 101
The Treasure of a Friend
The Power of Partnership in the Church
Becoming a Person of Influence
Be A People Person
The Power of Influence
Ethics 101

ATTITUDE

Success 101
The Difference Maker
The Journey From Success to Significance
Attitude 101
Failing Forward
Your Bridge to a Better Future
Living at the Next Level
The Winning Attitude
Be All You Can Be
The Power of Thinking Big
Think on These Things
The Power of Attitude
Thinking for a Change

EQUIPPING

The Choice Is Yours
Mentoring 101
Talent is Never Enough
Equipping 101
Developing the Leaders Around You
The 17 Essential Qualities of a Team Player
Success One Day at a Time
The 17 Indisputable Laws of Teamwork
Your Road Map for Success
Today Matters
Partners in Prayer

LEADERSHIP

Leadership Promises For Your Work Week
Leadership Gold
Go for Gold
*The 21 Most Powerful Minutes
in a Leader's Day*
Revised & Updated 10th Anniversary
Edition of *The 21 Irrefutable
Laws of Leadership*
The 360 Degree Leader
Leadership Promises for Every Day
Leadership 101
The Right to Lead
The 21 Indispensable Qualities of a Leader
Developing the Leader Within You
The Power of Leadership